T0301101

TÜRKIYE

Also by Julian Sayarer

Life Cycles (2014, 2023)
Messengers (2016)
Interstate (2016)
All at Sea (2017)
Fifty Miles Wide (2020)
Iberia (2021)

Julian Emre Sayarer

TÜRKIYE

Cycling Through a Country's First Century

First published in Great Britain in 2023 by Arcadia Books

An imprint of Quercus Editions Limited
Carmelite House
50 Victoria Embankment
London EC4Y 0DZ

An Hachette UK company

A CIP catalogue record for this book is available from the British Library.

ISBN (HB) 978 1 52942 995 4
ISBN (TPB) 978 1 52942 996 1
ISBN (Ebook) 978 1 52942 997 8

10 9 8 7 6 5 4 3 2 1

Designed and typeset in Warnock Pro by CC Book Production
Printed and bound in Great Britain by Clays Ltd, Elcograf S.p.A.

MIX
Paper | Supporting
responsible forestry
FSC
www.fsc.org
FSC® C104740

Papers used by riverrun are from well-managed forests and other responsible sources.

Contents

Bu kitap 2023'teki büyük depremde hayatını ya da sevdiklerini kaybeden herkese ve bu felaketten daha da güçlenerek çıkacak olan toplum ve ülkeye adandı.

This book is for all who lost their lives or loved ones in the great earthquake of 2023, and the stronger society and country that will be built out of that disaster.

هذا الكتاب لكل من فقد حياته و احبائه في الزلزال المدمر عام ٢٠٢٣ ، و إلى المجتمع و البلد الاقوي الذي سيقوم من اطلال تلك الكارثة.

Ez vê pirtûkê diyarî dikim ji bo wa kesên ku bûne qûrban di erdheja mezin ya sala 2023'an de û jiyana xwe yan jiyana hezkerên xwe ji dest dane û ji bo welat û komelayên ku werna avakirin piştî vê felaketê.

Αυτό το βιβλίο είναι αφιερωμένο σε όσους έχασαν τη ζωή τους ή κάποιο αγαπημένο πρόσωπο στο μεγάλο σεισμό του 2023 και στη δυνατότερη κοινωνία και χώρα που θα χτιστεί μέσα από αυτή τη καταστροφή.

Այս գիրքը նվիրվում է բոլոր նրանց, ովքեր կորցրել են սեփական կյանքը կամ հարազատներին 2023 թվականի մեծ երկրաշարժի ժամանակ, ինչպես նաև այդ աղետի հետևանքով ավելի հզոր երկիր կառուցելու հեռանկարին:

این کتاب تقدیم به همه کسانی است که جان خود یا عزیزانشان را در زلزله بزرگ سال ۲۰۲۳ از دست دادند، و به چشم‌انداز ساختن کشوری قوی‌تر در نتیجه این فاجعه.

A Note on the Turkish Alphabet

The Turkish alphabet, since it was romanised from the Ottoman script in the early Republic, is pronounced phonetically and, with the following exceptions, letters and diphthongs represent the same sounds as they do in English. Within the text, Turkish is written without italics.

c   as the *j* in *joke*

ç   with a cedilla is *ch* as in *champion*

ğ   the soft g, or yumaşak g, is silent. It extends the vowel before it

i   with a dot on top is as the *i* in Istanbul

ı   the *i* without a dot is a harder *uh* sound, as in *cup*

j   is soft, as the *s* in *measure*

ö   with an umlaut is soft, as the *u* in *cure*

ş   with a cedilla is *sh* as in *shout*

ü   with an umlaut is an *oo* sound, as in *cube*

ay   pronounced as *eye*

List of Illustrations

1. Preparing to set out from the childhood home of Mustafa Kemal Atatürk, in Selanik/Thessaloniki city centre.

2. The Greek roadside is adorned with graffiti, most of it from far-right groups. On the walls of a quarry are painted nationalist slogans and messages against Muslims.

3. Nearing the Turkish border, riding through the rich delta region of the Nestos River, named Karasu in Turkish.

4. I crossed the Meriç/Evros River at dusk. After centuries together, it feels strange to have such a small river as such a significant Greek–Turkish border. Many refugees have lost their lives in its waters, facing increasingly brutal pushbacks from the European Union.

5. It is hard to imagine a city that cares for animals quite like Istanbul. On a rainy day, cats harass a street vendor. Someone has given a street dog a blanket, and cardboard for a mat.

6. Crossing the Bosphorus. Beneath the Galata Tower, passengers of one of the many city ferries throw bread and simit to the seagulls, which often know to follow these boats.

7. One of the fleet of drillships purchased by Turkish Petroleum to develop offshore gas in the Black Sea and Mediterranean. The country has long identified a need to cut its costly reliance on energy imports.

8. Posters of Recep Tayyip Erdoğan outside a football stadium in the Istanbul neighbourhood where he grew up. The poster is for 2023 and reads "Turkish Century, Starting".

9. Swimmers relax on a day in late summer as a cargo ship powers north up the Bosphorus.

10. Ortaköy Mosque, with the Bosphorus Bridge behind it, is one of the most iconic sights in Istanbul. The location is a popular one in the many Turkish soap operas exported worldwide.

11. Across the Sea of Marmara, near the city of Bandırma in Balıkesir Province, dusk settles as I look for food and a place to camp. Unlike me, the highways of the country rarely rest.

12. A boatyard with the world's longest suspension bridge, Çanakkale Köprüsü, in the background. It adds an important non-Istanbul connection between Thrace and Anatolia. The central span of the bridge is 2km, or – symbolic to the centenary year – 2023 metres.

13. A father and daughter sit on swings at the Çanakkale beach. Across the water is the Gelibolu Peninsula, or Gallipoli, where in 1915 Atatürk famously led a crucial defeat of the British invasion with its ANZAC forces.

14. Bringing in the olive harvest. This sight, and that of loaded tractors taking their olives to the press, is a common one all down the coast, and at this time of year across the wider Mediterranean, from Tuscany to Palestine.

15. A couple in Izmir do some relaxed night fishing, watching the lights of the metropolis across the waters of the Gulf.

16. I ride through Izmir close to October 29th and Republic Day. Flags of Atatürk and Türkiye hang from every balcony in this staunchly Kemalist city celebrating, in this image, the 99th anniversary of the Republic.

17. Breakfast in a mountain village. Complete with many glasses of çay, and lots of homemade jam, this collection of foods powered most of my journey.

18. The picturesque village of Şirince stands in the hillsides of the Aegean. I went to visit the nearby Maths Village, an idealistic learning project that has established itself as a centre of excellence in mathematics.

19. Four young riders from the local cycling club find my campsite in the grounds of a mosque. They interrupt their ride to play in the mosque and interrogate me about my journey, then ride home.

20. The Gara Guzu craft brewery makes artisan beers from a small premises up in the mountains of Muğla. Its reputation for quality means it now ships everywhere from Japan to the UK, and of course Istanbul.

21. Regular irrigation from melting snow leaves rich fields for farming. A brief stretch of flat as road and bicycle heads back into mountains.

22. Börek – layers of thin pastry filled with potatoes, spinach or minced meat – was also common in my fuel intake. With çay and my notepad, it was often the perfect start to a day, and a gathering of thoughts.

23. November 10 marks the anniversary of Atatürk's death. Here it is commemorated at a monument in Antalya, with many wreaths laid from parties across the political spectrum.

24. Melon harvest lines the highway in autumn, with the crop sold to passing drivers.

25. The city centre in Osmaniye. Even at the time, the dramatic ridge of mountains I had to cycle over that day looked like tectonic plates pushing together and upwards. A few months

later came the earthquake on the East Anatolian Fault, with Osmaniye one of many devastated cities.

26. A woman takes her children down to the water at the Port of Mersin. Long into the night the cranes will continue loading containers onto cargo ships.

27. A driver heads down from the mountains. Beside the the van a new road is being built, one of many in recent years that helped shorten journeys and integrate regions across the country.

28. A truck stop in mountains just above the Syrian border. Truck drivers and wind turbines were some of my most regular companions on the road, with half of Turkish electricity now generated by renewables.

29. A bicycle joins the crowds at Abraham's Cave in Şanlıurfa, where the Prophet Abraham is said to have been born. People of all faiths now visit to pay respects or simply admire the architecture.

30. Boys cycle across the road in Diyarbakır, Türkiye's largest Kurdish-majority city. Across the road is bunting for the HDP, a political party that has been essential to building dialogue between the Turkish state and militant groups.

31. The River Tigris, known in Turkish as Dicle, goes decorated in autumn colours as it flows beyond the Diyarbakır city walls and towards the nearby Iraqi border.

32. Two young men sell the last of their pomegranate harvest, a sight that accompanied me across the country. The road here begins moving into higher mountains, and autumn into winter.

33. Near Bitlis a maverick sheep takes the long way round, joining the many hundreds being led by shepherds between remote villages.

34. Lake Van reflects the sky at the city of Tatvan. A quiet corner of the country, in 2020 the lake saw tragedy when a boat sank carrying 61 Afghan migrants. They were making their way into Türkiye to escape the impact of US sanctions on their lives in Iran, just over the horizon.

35. The second-highest mountain in Türkiye, Süphan, stands over a small house with the words Önce Vatan, "Nation First", written on its side.

36. The snow-capped mountains that mark the Türkish-Iranian border. It made for a beautiful but intensely cold last week of riding up high.

37. Ishak Paşa Sarayı is a seventeenth-century Ottoman palace, in the mountains near Doğubeyazıt. Tea is sold at a café. Just east of here begins the old route of the Silk Road into Asia.

38. In the city of Kars, tables are pushed back as Cossack dancers perform in a local restaurant. The dance is one of many signs in Kars of a city full with centuries of Russian, Turkish and Ukrainian cultures all meeting and mixing.

39. The ruins of Ani beside the Turkish–Armenian border. The call to prayer echoes through the gorge and its buildings built by Armenians, Turks and Greeks. Efforts now intensify to open this border, allowing Turks and Armenians to visit one another's countries more easily.

40. The Doğu Ekspresi, or East Express, is an overnight train that runs through Anatolia, between Kars and Ankara. I loaded my bicycle on board and began the journey back to Istanbul.

Author's Note

This journey was ridden and the book written in an atypical time. A US–Russia proxy war in Ukraine, and associated sanctions on Russia, had sent energy prices rocketing and created a global crisis of inflation and living costs from which Türkiye was far from immune. Recent history had seen Türkiye lead military opposition to Russia in both Syria and Libya; it had for years supported Ukraine out of kinship with a Turkic population of Crimean Tatars, broad commitment to territorial integrity, and memory engrained since Ottoman times of the dangers of Russian expansionism. Nonetheless, with the stakes so high, and the US directing European policy, Türkiye worked to resist a spirit of escalation that risked a headlong rush to war.

Misdiagnosing the inflation crisis as controllable only by interest rate policy, the major Western central banks in Frankfurt, Washington DC and London hiked interest rates, squeezing economies and pushing households and many good businesses to the wall. Already accustomed to interest rates of around 10 per cent, the Turkish Central Bank bucked the global trend of further rises, and as a result saw continued inflation, but also economic growth, while investors kept their capital in companies and the stock market. Still the global constriction of credit hit hard. Instead of increasing interest rates, the government raised the minimum wage, doubling it, and in so doing helping sustain the millions of working poor in the country. There was no single, easy or perfect solution to the inflation those I met were grappling with, and the centenary I cycled the country to mark was also to see a general election that took the proportions of a referendum on a generation of leadership by Recep Tayyip Erdoğan and his AK Party, leaving people acutely conscious of their place in the political spectrum.

Against this already charged backdrop, on 6 February 2023 the East Anatolian Fault snapped, striking south-east Türkiye and north-west Syria with successive earthquakes through cities I had just cycled. Where necessary or possible, in Osmaniye, Gaziantep and Hatay, I have recounted as far as I can know the fates of people and places I encountered, but I met so many strangers, who showed me such warmth along my way, that it is impossible to know or even consider that some may have been taken from us in that disaster. Consolation and comfort have been hard to find as the book moved forward; the heartbreak of the Turkish people is enormous. The one comfort and cause for optimism is that so too, as I hope this book attests, is the size of Turkish hearts.

Prologue

The shape of a bicycle shows from under the large sheet laid over it. Handlebars stick out against the material, a pedal too, and the gentle slope of the wheels. Like a person sleeping beneath, the outline of its body is visible, and I voice in my head an apology for the fact that I am about to wake it and call it so abruptly back to service. In a moment that portends the same process of uncovering that is to follow, I take in my hands two fistfuls of cloth, and pull. I often wonder if our perception has been shaped by film and its technology, or if such moments of gravity might always have appeared in slow motion in our minds, even before cameras showed us how that might look. The sheet lifts momentarily high as I pull it up, and then the fabric gives a low crack as my wrists and arms snap back, and the ballooning shape of the sheet pulls taut before collapsing – until next time – useless at my side. Leaving only my bicycle. In the gloom of the garage, a beam of daylight through the door catches the curve of the wheels' rims, like two slender smiles, as if the bicycle knows what is to come.

I make another silent request, perhaps a prayer, but one way or another directed at some power higher than me. The bicycle has shown me the world, from the lanes of the Midlands to the back streets of London, Palestine, the Uyghur lands, Sonoyta and so much more besides. I ask for it to be my magnifying glass again, the instrument that helps me to see everything more clearly. Show me one more country, one already dear and close to me. In this last thing I feel uncertainty, hoping it can show me somewhere familiar so well as it always did somewhere new.

For all that I know the country I am to visit, setting out is always daunting. That moment where I am still in one life, sedentary, but about to revert to my other life, on the road. To live out of my bags, sleep under the stars at the end of the day, and roll through the world. I know that I love that way of life, but at this stage – every time – it looms over me. Do I still love it? Will I love it again? Is it still the same? Am I still the same? I will put myself in the hands of chance and wait, or, rather, roll. The blessing but also the difficulty of discovery is that you have no idea what is about to happen.

Perhaps there is an aptness to this state of mind, readying as I am to ride across Türkiye, at the end of its first century. *Here*, I stand on a threshold of one life and prepare for another. *There* is defined, at least by the West, as the land of bridges. Türkiye, for some, is the bridge itself: East meets West in a threshold all of its own, different from but similar to the one I stand on here, because, at the end of the day, a threshold is always a threshold. A threshold represents a moment of change and all the emotion, excitement, suspense and doubt that such a place instils in us.

For the record, and to manage expectations, I reject this idea of a country as a bridge, but maybe there is something to be said for starting from a false assumption and working backwards. I reject the bridge because I reject the need for a Turk to stand between a European and an Arab to keep the European civilised, to help a European brain understand an Arab, or the inverse. I reject the racism, or at best exoticism, which underlies Western perceptions of the need for a Turkish bridge between themselves and Arabs but not between them and Armenians or Georgians, despite the geography implying the same requirement. I don't view Türkiye as a bridge for the same reason I don't view life in binaries; for the same reason I am fond of the wheel of a bicycle, or the Dome of the Rock over Jerusalem, because I prefer not to believe in sides, and so I like circles, I like curvature, I like edges – one single side that neither stops nor starts. The bicycle wheel, I like to think, mirrors a truer nature of the world. One where stories do not begin or end, they just have points at which we join or take our leave of them, are sometimes active and sometimes passive, where no energy is ever destroyed but instead acted upon as it takes new forms. I see Türkiye not as a binary bridge but more as the centre of a network, for the same reason Napoleon once said that if the world were a single state then Istanbul would be its capital. It is seldom that a Frenchman is right about something in the Middle East, but here is an instance of it.

Türkiye sits at the world's centre, but not in the sense in which all countries centre themselves: US classrooms have maps with the Americas in the centre, British classrooms Europe, and Japanese Japan. Türkiye is central more through being approximately a median point of most of the earth's populations; equidistant from the Chinese and US east coasts, beside the European land mass, the Arabian peninsula and the vast African continent adjoining Eurasia. Think of the world as a neural map: flows of energy, humans and capital, with a little faith thrown in occasionally, and it is here. This is where all points meet.

Some see it differently. They take an interest in Türkiye and only Türkiye. It is as if they open the filing cabinet and pass Trinidad, Tunisia, Türkiye, Turkmenistan, then track back a little, and resolve to take out the file marked *Türkiye*, while others pick *Tunisia*. I cannot do this anymore. Once I did, but now the filing cabinet drawer springs out, it explodes, and with Türkiye come Iraq, France, Palestine, Syria, Greece, Libya, that Tunisia docket too. There are files strewn everywhere, and only sometimes with coherence. I can give a review of Türkiye, but I cannot remove the context of the world in which it sits, for this is a country, not a performance. The bicycle also rejects these rigid categorisations, just as surely as it will roll through everything.

There is, too, the question of judgment. Many are the times I've spoken with Western journalists who commended Türkiye for things like hosting the world's largest refugee population, or supporting democratic movements in the Arab world, but overall condemned the country's political record. And though certain that I willed far harder than they ever would for the resolution of that which Türkiye gets wrong, I couldn't help but wonder who gave them the authority to hold the report card, and to fill it out with such gravitas. And more than that, I wondered by what entitlement they were able to dissociate as they did from the errors or evils of their own states, so that they could then sit in judgment on all the world's other countries, and ask for answers. Few in Türkiye sit in concerted judgment on the moral failings of the West, despite the chaos it has sown on all the borders we are soon to travel and see for ourselves.

TÜRKIYE

RUSSIA
N
K SEA
GEORGIA
Tbilisi
ARMENIA
Kars
Yerevan
Doğubeyazıt
Ağrı Dağı
(Mt. Ararat)
KIYE
Diyarbakır
4
Lake Van
IRAN
R. Tigris
Şanlıurfa
3
ersin
Gaziantep
Mosul
R. Euphrates
SYRIA
IRAQ
Lefkoşa
Nicosia
LEBANON
Beirut
Damascus
Baghdad
Jerusalem
PALESTINE

Part 1

Selanik to Istanbul

PART ONE

BULGARIA

Black Sea

SELANİK/
THESSALONIKI

Kavala

Tekirdağ

ISTANBUL

GREECE

Aegean Sea

TÜRKİYE

N

0   100 km
0   100 miles

Selanik – 6 October

Where to start a story of modern Türkiye is a hard decision. From many options, none inside the current borders, I stand in the western Ottoman city of Selanik, now known to the world as Thessaloniki.

I might have started in Holborn, London, in a café that is run by Iraqi Kurds and I have visited for over a decade. With these men I have talked sometimes with amazement at the corruption of the leading Iraqi-Kurdish clans, sometimes with fear at the onslaught of Daesh in Sinjar, but always with warmth through many years of turbulent regional politics. One afternoon I waited for my falafel with a Somali man, and of Türkiye he said in an accent that showed him as much Londoner as Somali, "Not gonna lie, your country is doing good things for my country."

The Turkish state builds infrastructure in Somalia, including training its military. In a country trying to end the fracture of its civil war, this can play a vital part in consolidating factions or militias into a single army. Because democratic and political arrangements often flow from military ones, building a military has through history been a feature of building a nation or state. In return, and in addition to a military presence there on the Horn of Africa, Türkiye hopes to build a space launch station in Somalia, because – looking in another direction, neither east nor west but up – Somalia is closer to the equator, where the earth's surface spins faster and so things can be launched more easily into space.

I could have started in Manhattan, after a taxi ride from JFK Airport with a driver from Adana, southern Anatolia, who told me how he'd made it to New York back in the eighties, hopping aboard a container ship bound across the Atlantic from the port of Hamburg. Since then I've found at one of the JFK terminals a large piece of stone set with Iznik tiles, gifted by the Turkish Republic to the people of the US, so they may have some beauty to look at as they await their flight out.

Or I could have started at the fair Croatian city of Šibenik, on the Adriatic coast I once cycled down, the summer after leaving university, en route to Istanbul. Having arrived in Istanbul, I went one afternoon to visit Rustem Paşa Mosque, a small, serene mosque near the old Egyptian Bazaar that is more modest but somehow more exquisite than the famed mosques of Sultanahmet. I researched who this Rustem Paşa was, learning of a fine Ottoman general who came, by chance, from Šibenik, a mark of how far the Ottoman and Muslim worlds were integrated into Europe before successive genocides and massacres – from Spain to Bulgaria to Srebrenica, and which Europeans seem unable to admit to or grasp their nations are built on – transformed Europe from a continent of diversity into an austere project of Christendom. Now that this work is done, now that the vast majority of its native Muslim, Turkic, Jewish and Arab populations have each in their turn been removed from Europe, Europeans have grown to think of themselves as secular and peace-loving, blissfully untroubled by the irony of having reached this conclusion only after expelling everyone else and fighting two world wars between themselves for good measure.

I could have begun on the Kazakh steppe, where once I rose drowsily from sleep on the cushions of a farmer's front room, into which I had been invited to rest from the hot afternoon sun. I opened my eyes and saw on the television what seemed like the familiar sight of Ortaköy Mosque, beside the Bosphorus. And I asked, because the Turkish and Kazakh languages overlap, if this was indeed Istanbul that they were watching in their soap opera, one of the many that Turkish studios came to export far and wide. And it was.

Or perhaps Bizerte, North Tunisia, where the French committed a final massacre in 1961 as they left Africa. On visiting Bizerte, I learned it was also one of the home ports of an Ottoman corsair by the name of Oruç Reis, or sometimes Barbarossa – Red Beard. Born in the fifteenth century on Lesvos, Reis was famed for sailing the Muslims and Jews of Iberia to the safety of North Africa during the Spanish Inquisition, and Oruç Reis was the name given to a Turkish drill ship that, at the time of my visit to Bizerte, was involved in gas explorations off the northern and Turkish part of Cyprus.

I could have started at any of these places, which convey something of the great and diverse reach of Turkish, Turkic and Ottoman history, links stretching far beyond the country we are about to travel.

But in the end I begin in this backstreet of Selanik, at a modest house with a single pomegranate tree in its courtyard garden. It has sturdy stone walls painted white and wooden shutters on its windows, and it sits under perfect blue Mediterranean skies, with a plaque written in Turkish, Greek and French on the garden wall. For here, in Selanik, is the house where Mustafa Kemal, or Atatürk, was born. And so, perhaps ironically, here in modern-day Greece starts a story of the Turkish Republic. Occasionally for their amusement, someone will try to provoke my reluctant nationalism by saying that this, surely, means Atatürk was Greek. The answer to which, if someone chooses to be so provocative, is rather that Selanik is in Türkiye.

Of Türkiye some things are well known and others not. At the risk of boring people who already know this, because I don't wish to leave behind those who do not, I should start by saying that, when he lived here, Atatürk was not known as such, but by the name Mustafa Kemal. Only in the years after 1923 and independence, when the Turkish government introduced surnames to the Republic, did he take the name Atatürk. It was one of many breaks, such as the move from the Ottoman script to the Latin alphabet, from ways perceived to be Eastern, and families gave up names that denoted Ottoman rank, place, or any but Turkic origins. Atatürk, appropriately then, is derived from *ata*, meaning "father" and *Türk*, so that Mustafa Kemal became literally in his new surname "Father of the Turks".

In the newness of this name-taking, Turks – having chosen them – sport a great many varied and wonderful surnames. I once taught a Gökay, meaning "sky moon". Sönmez is a popular one, meaning "cannot end" or "cannot age". I once knew a Gezegen, meaning "planet", and an Akbulut or "white cloud". Ilkay means "first moon". Ayçiçek, which means "moonflower", is actually, astronomically contrary to most of the world, the Turkish for a sunflower. There are many *ay*, with *ay* meaning "moon". There are also many *mez* suffixes, which means "cannot", so that we often have Korkmaz (cannot fear), Dönmez (cannot turn, presumably back) and the Sönmez, already mentioned. I know an Öztürk (pure Türk) and a Şentürk (happy Türk), earnest surnames often taken by minorities in the new Turkish Republic to assert their place in and loyalty to it, after the Ottoman collapse exacerbated the ethnic divides that the Western powers, needling and nefarious, had never failed to stoke.

In fairness, first names are no less wonderful. We have Yunus, or "dolphin"; my friend Harika means "wonder". Her mother once suggested a child's name of Hediye, meaning "gift". I know Yeşil, meaning "green". I was always fond of Yağmur, with its silent G, that oft-bemoaned but vital bringer of all life: rain. And I also loved Eylül, the name of the month of September, which marks the change of season to beautiful autumn. Bahar, meaning "spring", is a name no less pleasing. I know a Destan ("myth"), and a Demir ("iron"). Deniz, the name of my nephew, is a common one; it means "sea". A friend's girlfriend, Diren, means "resist".

From this we learn a crucial lesson: Turks are poets, natural poets, even in their names. Their hearts are steeped in a romantic spirit that is found almost everywhere. In the country is the most beautiful and unashamed sense of passion and wonder at what it is to live in this magnificent world, under and inside that vast galaxy whose stars and planets in turn go referenced in so many names. Turks do not suffer that affliction of inhibition, that timidity before the universe, that is the defining characteristic of so much of modern Western society, tamed by money as it has been, a malady policed further in the Anglosphere by the conservatism of first a Victorian and now neo-Victorian prudishness so stiff it can only abate with the aid of alcohol or the glimpses of honesty provided by sarcasm.

Don't misunderstand me, though: I love the Turkish spirit, it warms my soul, but sometimes, too, you see through it. You notice that the talk is not being walked, that it comes to people far easier than the act. There are downsides to such lofty sentiments being ever present, just as the average person in the US can talk so readily of freedom but is content to live their whole life through with their head inside a cage. I confess to a fondness for the way, though often they barely know how to say a single word, Brits once in a while muster the conviction to utter something of consequence and, when they do, you can know they really mean it. Politically speaking, and especially in this part of the world, this of course does not preclude the possibility that the British may simply be lying.

In all these names though, so attuned to the wonder of nature, there is a sort of pagan spirit similar to that of the Native American, and indeed, there is a kinship there. For Turks, proud as they are of the heritage of the Turkic peoples of Central Asia, of Mongolia, Siberia and the Steppe, will often profess a solidarity with Native Americans. The country's more unpleasant nationalists take as the national animal, if any, the wolf, that fierce but fine creature which we would do well to reclaim from this political appropriation. The wolf, with its connotations of wandering, searching, has something of the native and nomadic spirit in it, a thing unusual to find at the heart of a nation state identity, which is often built on the extinguishing of that very thing. Whenever the US returns to its insincere politicisation of the brutalities that Ottomans visited upon Armenians (those visited by Russians and Armenians against their neighbours, as violence at the end of World War I built towards its awful crescendo, tend not to be worthy of attention), saying it will call it a genocide, Türkiye in recent times suggested that it would then recognise as genocide the US extermination of the Native Americans all the way from Texas to Maine and back to Oregon, a crime that in its totality, methods and unalloyed one-sidedness is arguably more worthy of the label.

Forgive me what may seem like a digression. We must cover a lot and time is short, but each digression will add a new layer of understanding, joining yours with mine, so that before long we will simply be riding together. Perhaps, in a way of seeing where the world is interconnected, there is no such thing as a digression anyway. A nation state is only the fiction that holds the people in it, while it is the meaning of the names of those people, the person-alities they assume and the lives they lead, that truly represent it.

24 Apostolou Pavlou Street, Selanik – 8 October

The rules of diplomacy dictate that this house, as a consular entity, is Turkish territory. As such, however much the Greek and Turkish states may spar, here the Greek state, with an armoured police bus, stands guard to protect the Turkish state from the excesses of the Greek street and those nationalists who previously targeted the premises. Nearby, the rules of tourism prevail, so that adjacent cafés have their menus in Turkish and sell Turkish oddments, from biscuits to Atatürk coffee cups.

There is one exception; a chalkboard menu that offers Turkish coffee as Greek coffee; perhaps a point of diplomatic contention with the stakes too high. On the terrace outside the café, the Greek and Turkish languages rub shoulders in the conversation on the air, just as once – beautifully – they would have throughout the city of Selanik. Inside the garden of the house are a few men and – perhaps – more women, since women in Türkiye often have a particularly strong sense of gratitude to Atatürk for rescinding some of the religious conservatism of the Ottomans, reforms that acknowledged the voting rights of Turkish women long before the French or Swiss had managed such things. Walking through the old house with women and girls in dresses and shorts are women in hijab and abaya. These shared visits to Atatürk also point maybe to another divide coming down in the Republic, for under the early Republicans who first built modern Türkiye, women were to be set free – unless they were visibly Muslim. The followers of Mustafa Kemal, in the tradition still known as Kemalism, undid some of the restrictions on Turkish women, while creating new ones, perhaps most notoriously the prohibition of the headscarf in universities and public institutions. These new restrictions were sins that Western history books tended for a long time to view as forgivable, or as no sin at all.

There are more visitors here than when last I came, in a cool spring a few years ago, and I wonder if this is because of growing nationalism, a rebirth of Turkish-Greek curiosity, or simply the weather: the sun is shining warm and bright. Inside the garden and house, men, women and children, Turks of all faiths and political persuasion, unite by taking selfies. Indoors the visitors pose with a few mannequins: Mustafa Kemal sits motionless, presiding over their audience with him. In a cabinet is a plain silver basin with Mustafa's name on it in Ottoman script. A golden tray is decorated with a black cherry tree and blossom. I do not covet objects, but here are two items that tempt me towards materialism.

The cliché of Türkiye as a place of crossroads or more tension than any other is one I am reluctant to add to, but in Atatürk's earliest years, on this street, historical forces are already exerting their pull on him. His father wishes his gifted son to be educated in the new schools and under the reformed curriculum of the late Ottoman period. His mother favours traditional learning, and wins the parental battle but not the war when a young Mustafa quits the religious school and enlists in the one of his choosing. When Mustafa is still just a boy, his father dies, leaving his son that grief which is the ultimate tension for a young heart and mind to meet, even if it also instils the priceless lesson that nothing is permanent: change happens. The family move into a smaller house adjacent to this one, renting out the larger property, and entering a life of financial precarity in the place from which all revolution stems: the lower reaches of the middle class.

Having lost her husband, Mustafa's mother is loath to let her son begin a military career. Once more, however, he insists. Mustafa finds meaning in his officer's uniform, kinship in his fellow cadets and a growing spirit of patriotism. He still pushes the limits, however, befriending writers and poets in this city of intellectuals amid a rich, cosmopolitan mix of Greeks, Turks, Jews, Muslims, Arabs and Christians. All are as one. In him is an accomplished military commander in the making, but also a warrior poet. His military instructors warn against an excess of poetry, though they too are ignored by Mustafa. The spectre of the order, however, may explain his ability to at times engage the authoritarian mindset more common in history than poetry.

In his late teens, he leaves the great city of Selanik for military college in Istanbul, a few hundred kilometres away. Together these cities form the twin heart chambers of the Ottoman north Aegean and the Sea of Marmara. Back and forth they beat, a flow of cosmopolitan culture and ideas, pamphlets and dissent, as the teetering Empire moves towards a constitutional monarchy, then threatens to relapse into a sultanate. The European powers stand over it all, watching, waiting for it to fall, waiting for the pickings, concerned at the prospect of an ageing Empire reinvigorated by democracy, fearful that these ideas could spread south to Cairo, that Egypt may be caught up in the revolutionary current similar to the one Türkiye is so spectacularly about to unstopper.

Greek and Turkish identities within Selanik experience a friction they have never known before. Five centuries earlier, in 1430, the city of Selanik was brought into the Empire, and since then it has been a home to all peoples, from Anatolia to Iberia. It was to Selanik that so many Sephardic Jews made their way after the Christian fundamentalists of Spain, as is their way, drove them out with the Muslims in 1492. In 1913, with the help of the British, Selanik is split from this history and brought into the idea of Greece. Its loss, like that of Tripoli and Benghazi as Italians invade Libya, in the face of a colonial aggression soon spanning all fronts, foreshadows an Ottoman weakness that wrenches at Mustafa's heart. Finally, in 1914, the Ottomans attack Russia and in so doing enter World War I alongside Germany and the Central Powers. It is the most disastrous of decisions and the first step in a defeat that will bring down the Empire, marking the greatest tragedy in modern history. Russians, British, Italians and French pull together at the seams of Ottoman lands and communities, stoking antagonisms wherever they can, and backing any separatists they can find with a constant supply of lawyers, guns and money. The British and Russians work together, backing Greeks in the west and Armenians in the east. The British want the Ottomans weak enough to rule over, but not so weak as to disintegrate and take with them the more convenient administration of the territory. In some ways, this will be the model of the republic that follows, particularly after Türkiye joins NATO: neither so strong as to have ideas, nor so weak as to cause concern. Turkish autonomy is deemed problematic – but problematic for whom is a separate question.

Kept at the house are letters from Atatürk that testify to who he was, and convey something of the man who loved not only the Türkiye he helped to build, but also the Empire that preceded it. Though in so many ways – empire to nation state, faith to nationalism – the two were in opposition to one another, connecting threads exist and can be seen in Atatürk's devotion to both. His correspondence tells of his longing for the lost Balkan lands he had known as home. Atatürk was stationed as a young military officer in the Ottoman army in Damascus, Syria, where he was remembered for both his scrupulous attention to duties and also his fondness for drinking. Balkan, Arab, Anatolian: it is apparent that every inch of the Empire's territory has made him who he is, proud citizen of a single country that is as much Damascus as Istanbul, as much Selanik as Beirut.

In those letters is the urgency of a young Atatürk as he speeds to Tripoli, then Tobruk and Benghazi, upon the Italian invasion of Libya in 1911. He writes of the necessity of haste, of action, of service:

Thinking of the degree of sacrifice we owe to this country, the service conducted so far seems worthless. Our conscience warns us that our mission will not be considered over until the warm and familiar horizons of this country are completely cleansed and our ships return to the Tobruk, Derne, Benghazi and Tripoli harbours. The country shall find safety and the nation shall find happiness. Because there are many sons of this nation who are willing to sacrifice their own safety and happiness for the general safety and happiness of the nation.

There is a yearning for, an empathy with, what is now Greece, what is now Syria, what is now Libya. Mustafa Kemal speaks of service for *the country*, when in Syria, while heading to Libya, and speaking as a Turk. A spirit in Anatolia can still long for the Balkans even while journeying to the Maghreb. It is all one, there are no borders, and the country of which he speaks is the Ottoman Empire. It was not perfect this empire, it could no doubt be improved upon, but in it – unlike its peers, and every empire since and before – was more concern for uniting than dominating. From a present day so beset by nationalism, besmirched with Nazi ideas of blood and soil, I see sadness more than failure, and even some merit, in a political unit that fell in part because it could not see nationalism, believing that people should be seen and grouped by spirituality instead, and that those religions could coexist. We will take no lessons from those colonial powers who during this same century were hunting buffalo to extinction, paying bounties for scalps, and giving Native Americans blankets laced with smallpox. Who in India were teaching Hindus and Muslims lessons in a very European brutality and division.

The Ottomans rose and then fell as a project rooted in spirit over borders. A Jewish friend from Palestine, whose family were settlers in the early twentieth century, once told me of her grandfather, conscripted alongside Palestinians into the Ottoman army to repel the British invasion during World War I. It was another world, and in it so many false distinctions since fabricated were inconceivable. Considering how the states separated from it or manufactured out of it were then picked off one by one by Western armies and Western bankers, it is hard not to see that in such unity lay greater strength than that which replaced it. There is more, so much more to say, but it must wait for the road. Places up ahead will return us to this subject.

Before setting out, I sit a while beneath an old pomegranate tree, a tree that is as fine a symbol as any of what this country means to me. Its regal fruits are still green, but the points of their crowns have formed, and their leathery skins are beginning to blush red. The tree was planted by Ali Reza Efendi, Atatürk's father, and the young Mustafa played as a child in the same shade where I now wait to begin. The trunk of the tree is old and thick, wizened and knotted with age. I sit and I think, considering the magnitude of everything. The War of Independence, the new Republic, the Centenary, the great victories. I am soon to set out, across this Türkiye, on its one hundredth birthday, and beneath the pomegranate tree I wonder: what does victory look like today?

Beginnings

A man walks over as I photograph the house, asking in a mixture of English and Turkish if I would like him to take my photo. I hand over my camera and he steps away in order to fit the whole building into the camera frame. I pose with my bicycle. He takes us portrait. He takes us landscape. I thank him as he hands back the camera. He has straight black hair and a sparse beard. He smiles.

"You live here?" I ask.

"Yes, I married a Greek woman." He gestures to the bicycle. "Where are you riding?"

"First to Istanbul," I reply.

His eyes light up. "I rode to Georgia, across Türkiye. Two years ago. Then I came back and finished here."

I smile. "How is it here?"

"It's fine," he replies, "the same. Selanik is a lot like Izmir."

"Where's your memleket?" I ask, this word for the place that you are from, the earth that made your family, and which is essential to Turkish identity.

"Diyarbakır," he answers, and I smile at the idea of that place, far from here, but on my route, in the east of Anatolia.

"I'm going there."

"Really?" he laughs.

I nod and smile, not wanting to take it further, I don't want him to have to say more, define who he is by place, or find the right word for it. But maybe he is happy to talk. Lightly I ask, as if it were as incidental as the question should be, "You are Turkish-Kurdish then?"

He smiles, but rolls his eyes as if physically, just as the nearby hills are about to tire me, he is wearied by what that question encompasses. He gives a small shrug.

"I don't speak Kurdish. It's all the same. Turkish, Kurdish, Greek. To me it is the same thing."

I retreat from my enquiry, ashamed to have asked, to have had my reservations but to have put the question to him anyway. We return to Turkish. I ask him his name and we both brighten, as if it is remiss that we neglected this.

"Yiğit," he answers, and I smile, because it is a name that is dear to me, one that before long we will meet again along our road.

"Yours?" He puts out his hand.

"Emre."

We clasp hands, and smile at one another in our different kinds of kin, not least of all the bicycle I pull upright. Yiğit, waving, is my last sight as I take hold of the handlebars, mount, and finally begin my journey.

The road out of Selanik goes up and up, looping round like the curve of a large question mark, the city the dot at the base of it, asking if I'm sure about what I'm doing. Is this a good idea? Is this a bad idea? I've cycled these roads out of Selanik before, across Thrace and into Türkiye, to Istanbul. Even across Türkiye and down the Aegean coast. But each time I knew I'd never reach further into the country, and I always felt a guilt that I'd seen so many places but such a small strip of this one I felt I knew quite well. Only miles bring entitlement, and here until now I have covered so few.

Maybe it is a good idea simply because it is a big idea, and big ideas are necessary to see the world clearly, but when enacted have a tendency to instil doubt. It is a journey of some four thousand kilometres, the length of Europe again. It is mountainous. There will be wolves. As always, it is the road and the bicycle that ease me into it, that pull me from the plan and restore me to the moment. At the top of the switchback road out of Selanik, the incline flattens and lifts onto the crown of the hillsides. My arms and legs no longer require all my energy; some can return to my brain. I notice the familiar smell of pine. The green needles carpet the forest. A fire engine is pulled in, with two fire fighters in heavy, heatproof overalls sitting off duty on a bench, smoking cigarettes. The first of the ride's stray dogs is startled by me, and so in turn startles me, jumping to its feet and barking loudly, its slathering, fleshy jowls swinging with each movement of its head, a jolt back into the world and out of my thoughts.

The month is October, early in it, and as I ride by, smelling then seeing my first fig tree, the dry and puckered fruit that remain remind me that, for fresh figs, September would have been the better month. This is perhaps the first error of my ride, though if it proves to be the greatest, then all has gone well. Blackberries atone. Small apples have fallen from their slender branches overhead, baking on the hot road with a smell of compote. A few olive trees have escaped their groves and now grow close to the road, producing green oil as my wheels roll over them at this, the start of harvest and pressing season. Soft and dirty-white, a small flock of sheep moves towards me, traversing rock and ridge as effortlessly as clouds above skim the hills. They are hardy animals, not the creatures of British pasture, and they know this land. Some of the sheep are large and stout, others are lean, athletic, long-limbed and alert as they look calmly around. Behind them, a shepherd appears, carrying a sturdy long staff, a thing as proud and pronounced as the broom of a moustache that is parallel to it, hanging nicotine-stained over his top lip. He wears a bulky waistcoat, its pockets full with the needs of his life, trade and animals up in the hills. He gives me a small nod, and then, with his flock, he is gone.

Finding my rhythm, riding east, I consider that fatal weakness of 1920 and the Treaty of Sèvres, when Türkiye lost these lands. It was not that they and those in it were ours, but that we were also theirs. Türkiye in 1923, at the Treaty of Lausanne, was an entity strong enough to dictate events again. The term Sèvres Syndrome still surfaces from time to time to describe Türkiye's institutional memory of the trauma caused by its fragility back then: the inability to resist either the West or the Russians moving to strike. I have heard Westerners argue this Turkish anxiety about territorial integrity is insincere, and it is in turn revealing that they believe so, suggesting that they maybe perceive a country more secure than that country sometimes feels. Let me say simply that a country is only safe from such concerns when there is no need to regularly mention the names of the treaties that founded it. Better still, when their names have been forgotten. The state just is, and always was.

In achieving that fate, in growing to dictate events rather than having them dictated unto you, moving from Sèvres to Lausanne to whatever now awaits, it is a vital strength to recognise your own weaknesses. Atatürk fixated on the failings of the late Ottomans, they consumed him, and from that Türkiye was rebuilt until it could once more assert itself upon history. To confront your flaws and weaknesses is strength. To hide from your flaws, or silence those who speak of them, is no strength at all. Where you do not acknowledge weaknesses, they proliferate, and from there they corrode even what is good. A country must be strong enough to discuss its weaknesses, and speech must be free because that is the only way hard truths can be told, and stated in the most effective way.

For Atatürk, it is apparent that his articulation of weaknesses is exclusively at the service of the Ottoman Empire and Turkish Republic. Atatürk wants the betterment of the country, but he does not see himself as better than the country. He is respectful of Western ways – overly respectful at times – but also a proud Turk, cognisant that the West is no true friend. He, like many, writes in pamphlets his thoughts of what needed to be done to rescue and repair the country. I ask myself: could he do so today? Would people listen if he did?

It is of note, however, that, as everything falls apart, as there grows that abyss of war into which the power of words is at times foolishly

44

cast and lost, Atatürk does not seek to write but to fight. He takes flight and joins the forces at Tripoli. History is readied with words, but it is made by acts. This vital lesson he knows.

Of Greece

To understand modern Türkiye, we must also try as we ride to understand modern Greece. For in the efforts to reimagine Greece as a purely European entity – a fake concept given or taken away depending on mood or need – you see the weakening of the Ottoman space. The Greeks were an engine in Ottoman commerce, cultural life, community, and I only stop short in extolling this role so as not to feed the supremacist Greek current that likes to forget this was achieved alongside, and together with, Turks, Arabs, Kurds, Africans, Assyrians, Armenians and all the rest. Giving the Greeks a European identity to replace their Ottoman one represents a fundamental Western success in the dismantling of the Empire. The downside for the Greeks is that this trade is destined to leave them and their political culture bemused, mystified, because it is now predicated on a denial of their history, of who they truly are, an identity for which they now go searching through falsehoods to find.

So where to begin the history of modern Greece? 1827. Battle of Navarino. Off the coast of the Peloponnese. There the British, Russian and French fleets aid the Greeks by smashing a significant portion of the Ottoman navy, a course of events that the Tunisian and Egyptian vessels sailing alongside are powerless to alter. 1829. Thanks to Navarino, Greece is made an independent state, but it will be independent inside the orbit of the powers that made it. 1920. Treaty of Sèvres, signed after World War I. A loser's peace is forced on the Ottomans. Greece is given swathes of western Türkiye, including Izmir and influence across the Istanbul region, which is designated an international zone resembling something like a free port administered by and for the European powers. 1923. Treaty of Lausanne. All these gains prove fleeting when the Turkish War of Independence rolls through, culminating – despite the best efforts of those same powers – in Turkish victory. Greece admits to war crimes in Asia Minor, a fact recorded in the treaty if not in history. With the exception of some islands near the Turkish coast, seized by the Italians and later handed to Greece by Mussolini's fascist government, the war ends in the frontiers that Türkiye and Greece share to this day. But all this is mere detail.

1943. World War II is drawing to a close. Greece has been occupied brutally by the Nazis. Mussolini holds the islands. A civil war begins, between socialists and patriots on the one hand and a fascist government, plumped with Nazism, on the other. The British and the US intervene. They support the socialists and patriots . . . only kidding, of course they don't. You know who these guys back! Bitter fighting ensues. Come 1949, Greece is exhausted. With Western help, the fascists are victorious and the stage is set for the foundation of modern Greece. Still, even in the home of democracy, after this rampage of fascism and civil war, it is hard to create actual democracy. Riven by the divisions of conflict, with leftists, artists, intellectuals all exiled or imprisoned, in 1967 Greece sees the installation of a military junta by coup d'état. Brutality escalates, torture is rampant. The US, as with its shah in Iran, as everywhere, has primed the Greek secret services in the art of repression, anti-communism, revolution-proofing. Greece is purged. The junta retain control until in 1974 they go too far and organise a coup on Cyprus too, their aim being to annex the newly independent island. For this they will use a brutal Hellenist militia, known as EOKA, which seeks to drive Turkish Cypriots out of their homes and off the island. Türkiye intervenes, moves to protect Turkish Cypriots in the north, so Greek annexation fails but the island is left divided. Back in Athens, this debacle sparks new levels of fury against the junta, already loathed across the country. From the National Technical University, in the proud neighbourhood of Exarcheia, a revolution rolls out. The dictatorship falls. The people have had enough, but on the way to this victory, much has been lost.

So commences the Third Hellenic Republic in which I now cycle. Democracy begins to take hold. 1981: Greece joins the European Union. It is an irony of history that the Turkish intervention to protect Cyprus, a decision so maligned in history, creates with the fall of the junta the conditions according to which the EU will let Greece in, but comprises one of the factors keeping Türkiye out. The existential anchor of Greece is now nothing more noble or exotic than that which underpins the EU: regulatory alignment with the European Coal and Steel Community of 1951. The trajectory that Greece is now on finds its spirit and meaning only in the industrial pact designed for the effective management of coal and steel after World War II. Philoxenia is out, blast furnaces are in. Greece is nothing but capitalism, smoothed. In 2001, Greece adopts the euro, a single currency, but only nominally single. Greece still borrows money at Greek rates, not German rates. It cedes authority for its monetary policy – and thus its national budget – to the European Central Bank. The price of everything triples overnight. A one-drachma coffee becomes a one-euro coffee, despite one euro equating to three drachma. Wages remain at the drachma rate. The Greek currency becomes unnaturally strong, its exports unnaturally uncompetitive.

Even as the economy worsens, Greece remains proportionately the biggest EU spender on arms and weapons. Animus with Türkiye is essential to this robbery, and many line their pockets by stoking it. Deutsche Bank prospers in the financing, BNP Paribas and the French still more. Because corruption thrives on big-ticket arms purchases, because a gangster's cut of a haunch of cured meat yields less than the same cut on a fighter jet or ten, a parasitic elite enjoys the spoils, paid for by the poor Greek population. The arms race, in which Greece cannot in any case compete, and which is far less profitable than partnership, comes at significant cost to Greek–Turkish relations.

Finally though, the game is up. 2015. Money talks and Greece must answer: bankrupt. The people are not to blame, they never are. The people want out, back to drachma, autonomy. They vote for it in a referendum. No. *Oxi!* But the government fails to deliver, they are now too entwined with the euro, with European coal and steel. A bailout occurs, the people will pay, the foreign banks will get their money. French banks, overexposed, get a fine share of repayment on debts that by rights ought to have bankrupted them. The distribution of bailout costs across the EU means others pay more than they were on the hook for: German taxpayers are annoyed, thinking they've paid Greek pensions, though in reality the poor suckers have merely covered the bonus pool in La Défense. Greece is now truly European, but is a whipping boy, a runt. Public services are stripped, EU passports are sold. Some Greeks feel proud to be admitted, but the Western financiers make no secret of their contempt for these lazy Mediterraneans.

From our vantage point, across the Aegean, it isn't hard to see that the Greeks are only Europe's Turks. East is a relative concept. Greece to us is family, it runs deep. To the Western mind, it is no more than the G in the P-I-G of PIGS: Portugal-Italy-Greece-Spain. Bruised and humiliated, Greece has nonetheless been pulled westward, granted entry, but to a club that thinks little of it.

This shift though is only one of business, of money. It is neither flesh nor blood, and so we must hope it is not irreversible. The event that catalyses everything is the Syrian civil war. 2016. Fighting escalates. With air space open, the Syrian middle class who could afford to do so have long since flown out. Those who could not afford to be picky have endured all they can but have now made overland journeys out, through Türkiye, and across in some cases those narrow straits or rivers into Greece. On Lesvos, I speak to a Greek woman. "One morning there were three Syrians on the beach, by the boats. I went home to get them warm clothes, some food. The next day there were one hundred. The next a thousand."

This was how it went. Tens and then hundreds of thousands

arrive. Thousands die in unsafe crafts; the straits and rivers become graves thanks to a European refusal to offer safe passage to those who have fled wars and tyrants the West created in the first place. The Hellenic coastguard rescues many thousands, but in the end Greek opinion turns. A left-leaning SYRIZA government, a government that understands what it means to be Greek, that understands where Greece sits in the world, can point to Greece on a map, is voted out. Border cooperation, police cooperation between Greece and Türkiye, collapses. The Greeks pull the plug. An unashamedly right-wing government is voted in. Pushbacks begin. On land and at sea. War-traumatised refugees have teargas shot at them, rubber bullets, real ones, too. Refugees in rudderless boats are pushed out into open water. Only the swimmers survive. Make it back to Türkiye if you can. Video images: machine guns fired by the coastguard into the water surrounding dinghies filled with fleeing humans. Greece is broke, Greece is poor, Greece has had its dignity stripped, and in such times – weak as humans are – to be given the power, if never the right, to take the dignity of another is a comfort for some.

As the inhumanity in Greece begins to rise, however, the role of the EU is of paramount importance. There is no chiding. Greece is obeying ECB strictures these days, has learned how to wear the straitjacket. Greece is the good kid. Inhumanity is something the ECB can give Greeks for free. Ursula von der Leyen shows up from Lower Saxony, brings an entourage. One of those white women who talks feminism as brown women drown, and even that with the neoliberal misandry that says nothing on this earth is worse or more innately guilty than a brown-skinned Muslim man. (Be proud my brothers, we know truth, and history will vindicate all you have endured.) Von der Leyen, she asserts the Greek right to defend itself. To defend itself against refugees, against war victims, against orphans and the forsaken. To defend itself?

However uncomfortable a truth, it is important to understand that the ideological root of Europe is, whatever the more recent efforts in soft power, imperialism. From the Spanish conquistadors to Franco, to the Belgians in the Congo, the French in Vichy and beyond, the settlers the Dutch dispatched to the Americas. Everywhere is imperialism, updated only with a guilty philosemitism that gives Israelis a free and brutal rein in Palestine to atone for the European guilt that Hitler went too far in doing to white people what was meant only for black and brown.

The European Union offers Greece its blessing to go to mortal lengths to protect its Lebensraum. This, however arbitrary its borders, is done in the belief that the European Union must maintain its purity of blood and soil. It is done by expunging a Greek history alongside the merchants of Istanbul, of Aleppo, of Damascus. The only glimmer of hope that Europe can one day rise above this xenophobia comes from Angela Merkel, a lone German chancellor, the daughter of a clergyman, who has in her spirituality enough to insist a million Syrians are humans to whom a rich country can afford to give refuge.

Greece, however, is no rich country. It takes years and an election to undo their instincts, but the Greek state learns how to let refugees drown. They join the club. The work of the CIA, of the British, priming the country for two centuries and more – backing the fascists of a civil war, the junta that follows – is complete. The Greeks reject the cosmopolitanism of both Ottomanism and Ancient Greece. Greece undergoes a European loyalty test, undertaken in the Mafia styles of Sicily but with the fascist organisation and vindicating narrative of the Third Reich, Vichy, Il Duce. Reaching hands sink into the Aegean, and with that grasp breaks a millennia-long Mediterranean bond.

The Greeks would now sooner let people die than live with Arabs – those who translated and preserved their great texts, who saved Aristotle and Plato when Europe succumbed to its intermittent barbarism and found no use for them. The Greeks, who coined so many of the words that gave form to the churn of politics so that we could better understand our *oligarchy*, our *dilemmas*, our raging *kakistocracy*. Who also came up with the words that explain the better natures of our hearts. Who described *philoxenia*, that love of humanity. Who even as Orthodox Christians still shared in a Mediterranean-mediated humanity that made them one with the Muslim Ummah, the wider Islamic family. In that kinship, Greeks had often suffered and long understood the brutalities of European Christendom and recognised – when all is said and done – that it knew best of all how to persecute. "Better the Turkish turban than the Pope's tiara", as the old saying went, but with this maxim discarded, Greeks have at last been domesticated, brought under the wing of the West.

To achieve this, however, the Greeks have not only killed Arabs but also themselves. Greece grows ever more politically confused, like a woman who has lost her true family and isn't welcome in her new one, but is suffering memory loss, and so does not realise that these are not in fact her true relatives. Greece has become a client state. Little more than the Acropolis stuck atop not a rocky escarpment but an approved set of books, and a graveyard. The Greeks – a people that knew resistance – have been sold and cowed. These are the same Greeks who fired an anti-tank missile into the US Embassy in Athens in 1996. Who went back for more with a rocket-propelled grenade in 2007, who let the US know that they could not be castrated or spayed, that they were a proud people who knew only too well what the US helped do to them during their civil war, and that Greece belongs not to Washington DC but to the Mediterranean.

Greece becomes plasticated, becomes only a Parthenon fridge magnet sold in Plaka. As with anything that comes into contact with the US power system, Greece becomes fake. Capital and bombs. Coal and steel. Greece is given a historical wash; it can keep its ancient identity, its "Birthplace of Democracy" accolade, but these are no longer lived ideals, they have become no more than wipe-down surfaces. The Greeks will go with these leitmotifs of the ancients as the Israelis do their leitmotifs of Judaism. Greece, coincidentally, begins to downgrade its historic support of Palestine; it enhances its support of the Israelis. These two entities, with help from the statelet in south Cyprus, are pulled closer in an effort to bring the Mediterranean under the US wing.

This may sound bleak but I am not hopeless. Somewhere, somewhere, we know Greece remains indelibly that land and tongue that gave form to philoxenia. Philoxenia is betrayed. Philoxenia is banished, left to wander sadly in the beautiful hills above Florina. But Greece remains, in that Lesvos woman who, finding refugees, goes to bring food. Greece remains, in that same woman who then sets up a kitchen and a restaurant so that refugees should eat not from plastic trays upon their knees but from a ceramic plate. Greece remains.

One life illustrates the story better than all the rest, for Greece remains in the heart of Kyriakos Papadopoulous, that coastguard lieutenant who braved all storms and who – hand clasped to forearm – pulled so many thousands from the sea. And yet, and yet . . . his heart, it gave out. Aged just forty-four. From such death, from so much trauma. From being asked to witness an inhumanity, a neglect of other humans, which in itself is so very un-Greek. But dear Kyriakos; Kyriakos *canım*. Now there was a brother. By Zeus, but there was an Ottoman heart. There was a Greek.

But enough of this for now, it is too sad and we have distance to cover. Our Istanbul and their Constantinople. One and the same. My grandfather's village, beside Prespa. Turks, Greeks, Arabs, Ottomans. One and the same. Our minds and hearts, always open to our sisters and our brothers, the Greeks, who will one day come home to us.

Kavala to Xanthi – 11 October

On the Strymonian Gulf, on a quiet beach, I watch a large moon rise and wonder where I will be next time it is this full. Its corridor of light shines yellow-white down the rippling black sea. In Turkish this corridor of moonlight reflected on water has a word: yakamoz. It is a word much-loved in Turkish society, and often I think of the head start in creativity, or romance, that comes from belonging to a culture that somehow knew it must have words for the most beautiful of life's sights. That to savour these sights is what makes and keeps us human, and so they must be adequately described. These are my thoughts as sleep takes hold. The sun will wake me with its first wan light, the moon will be pale. In the sky, the blue of night gives way to the red dawn, foreshadowing too the trade in the colours of the flags coming up ahead.

From Kavala the change begins to take hold, I feel borders begin. This is no longer the road between the fair city of Selanik and the fair city of Kavala. Here is the start of the way out, here is where Greece begins to lose interest and Türkiye is yet to begin. The last time I rode this stretch was 2012, and I notice a change in the graffiti on the roadside. Then, much acrimony was directed towards Germany, perceived boss of the European Central Bank, responsible at the time for the disciplining, or humbling, or breaking of Greece, depending on how you saw it. Back then, the graffiti said *Merkel is a bitch!* and stickers showed her face on Hitler's body. Germans were Nazis.

Nazism continues to be a feature of the Greek roadside this autumn, though it seems to have been adopted more favourably:

a Nazism in blue and white. Having lost in the fight against global finance, in their graffiti at least, Greeks seem to have taken to a nationalist fight instead.

A billboard showing Cyprus, with blood dripping from the north of its map, is at least what I would expect in a typically shrill Greek howl against Türkiye. Why anyone in the outskirts of Kavala has given time and money to it is a greater mystery, but the image is at least less sinister than those painted on the underpasses. There I ride by a catalogue of swastikas and Nazism, consciously conjoined with the global, or at least European, far right. Someone has troubled to write the distant grievance *Kosovo is Serbia* on a concrete wall. A stone quarry has been hewn from the mountain over the roadside, its sheer white edifice printed with a flailing Greek flag, but also daubed in red paint *Islamist Πείνα* (Peína), which I later learn means *Islamist Hunger*. I think how misguided this is, given the unlikelihood of being allowed to go hungry in Muslim countries. *Soros* is daubed alongside it, *Patria* in Cyrillic for domestic consumption. I think of Lakis Santas and Manolis Glezos, those old Greek patriots under Nazi occupation, who on a night in 1941 scaled the stone wall of the Acropolis to take down the swastika flag, refusing to let it fly over Athens. And now Greeks scale quarry walls to paint it up themselves, with no Nazi even having to ask. Dear Manolis; how his ghost must hurt.

In response, the Greek left has not been entirely idle: *ACAB* has been added to the quarry wall also. The anarchist *A* inside its circle has been daubed close, perhaps overlapping slightly the name of Soros. Showing that the Greek spirit persists, near an olive farm baked in sun is a clear graffiti sentence for the Greek prime minister, who would once have been called far right but now is par for the European course: *Hang Mitsotakis from the trees of Evia.*

There is still resistance to fascism in Greece, but it feels outnumbered. Now and then there come entire stretches of matt grey paint, with the solvent of the graffiti still visible underneath, evidence of authorities trying to clear up, to navigate or negotiate the mess.

Perhaps it was to remove the most egregious graffiti, or perhaps only to remove as much graffiti as possible, but the palimpsest provides an honest chronicle of the state. In the Greek graffiti is the political spectrum: an ascendant fascism, a beleaguered anti-fascism, and some desperate and scarcely legitimate political centre in matt paint that couldn't be rolled on fast or thick enough to cover the chaos spreading from its own mismanagement.

It was not always this way. Even in modern times, in the 1980s, after Türkiye in its Cyprus intervention helped the Greeks bring down their junta, Prime Minister Andreas Papandreou, of the socialist PASOK, outlined a three-way foreign policy for Greece. The proposal was to make good on its geography and culture, establishing Greece as a relevant power in Europe, Balkans, Mediterranean, and to distance itself from the United States. Papandreou, along with anyone paying the slightest attention, had seen how the US military and its agents had swarmed through Greece and helped stitch together the junta, one small prong in their European-wide anti-socialist mission, headquartered in Rome and known as Operation Gladio. The Papandreou vision was not warmly disposed towards Türkiye, but in it at least was some ambition, some regional awareness. Greece had its Palestine policy, its Libya policy. A desire to make use of its cultural ties, through Orthodox Christianity, to the Coptic Church of Egypt, to the Orthodox Christians of Jerusalem and all Palestine. Greece was to support Palestinian liberation, Arab nationalism. In all this, Greece made good its own cultural connections east and west, and in this Greek ambition to be a country worthy of its own history, the so-called "bridge" of Türkiye gained a second lane. That bridge became twice the width. Two countries could at least share this absurd responsibility, where now we are only one. For centuries this country belonged to something far greater, and now it plays second fiddle to each local or Atlanticist tyrant that comes knocking.

Of course, deep in the country, there is ambition to undo such a breaking-in. A friend who lived as a young man in both Türkiye and Greece once told me that he had met so many Greeks who pledged a willingness, even an enthusiasm, to die in the retaking of Constantinople, that there would be none left alive to do the taking. A suggestion, then, for those Greeks with an eye set on Istanbul: make it yours again, become one with us and part of something greater with your neighbour, rather than something lesser with those far away.

Riding by Balkan villages, I consider how mixed these lands would once have been, with Greeks and Turks living together five centuries and more. Further on our road, in the province of Antalya and the village of Kayaköy, houses still stand empty from the population exchange, where the Turks of Greece were sent to Türkiye and the Greeks of Türkiye the other way, but the Turks of the village refused to take the homes of their friends – colleagues, lovers, neighbours – they had never wanted to see leave.

If the arrangement – as in any period of history – was not always perfect, it was at least a coexistence. The Turks and Muslims of Greece have been all but removed, but still it is not enough for the fascist mind. The very idea of this presence, now or ever before, must be attacked. It is by this pathogen that fascism becomes totalitarian: that memory can never be removed enough because the problem is located not in the other human but in the fascist mindset. Centuries of ethnic cleansing and historical revisionism remade Muslims, Arabs and Turks – the latter often Christians and Jews – as outsiders in Europe, a continent in which once we lived together.

I recall a conversation over drinks with a friend one evening in Istanbul. We talked of the Balkans, and she said her grandfather had once upon a time been Bulgarian. "The Balkan Turks do not talk about what happened to them," she remarked sadly. "I remember he told me stories of childhood, of how the Danube would freeze in winter, and how he learned to ice skate on the frozen river. Stories like that. But that was all."

Türkiye does not overindulge these stories, although they abound in society, chronicling traumas, in the truest sense of the word, from events visited upon relatives of very recent history and even those still alive. As a result, Turks do not readily self-identify as victims. This can be a healthy trait, because if you internalise too deep that you are a victim, you risk becoming one, and then can be nothing else. Silence can harm no less though. For if you have suffered, real and deep, and you do not talk of this, then you continue to suffer. And in the hardness you demand of yourself, you can make others suffer too, or fail to see that you are capable of inflicting suffering on others.

The shift from Ottoman script to Roman compounded this collective loss. Although the Republic brought with it a rapid growth in literacy, official documents, personal diaries and letters could within a generation no longer be read by much of the population, leaving their contents to fade from memory.

Although the new Turkish state rarely spoke of what happened in the Balkans, it is not because the hurt was not felt. Atatürk was after all a child of the Balkans and in him is a clear longing, dislocation and sense of loss. The words of a song for Macedonia that he loved:

> My lover's heart aches.
> I can't amuse myself, I can't be comforted,
> I can't stay in these places.
> The plains of Vardar; the plains of Vardar,
> I'm broke, I can't return home.

It always amuses me to think that Atatürk was said to have sung this when in *good* spirits – perhaps an insight into how the Turkish soul is at home in melancholy. It takes from it a poetry that in the end is hardly melancholy at all.

Not that it is important anymore, but because the road elicits such thoughts, I think of who to blame for all that loss. The Russian tsars were instrumental, but in the removal of the Turks from the Balkans, few names stand out more than the British politician William Gladstone. His notions of a "moral", crusading Christendom provided the same foreign policy touchstone that a century and a half later led Tony Blair to torch his own political legacy with the Iraq War.

Following violence from Ottoman irregular forces in response to unrest in Bulgaria, correspondents were duly dispatched and the necessary media furore ensued. Gladstone – out of office, looking for a cause – demanded in 1877 that the Ottomans be removed "bag and baggage" from the Balkans. Aware that after centuries of living side by side with Bulgars, Turks comfortably comprised half the Balkan population, Gladstone's rival of the day, Conservative Party leader Benjamin Disraeli, was more reserved, conscious that this was tantamount to a call for ethnic cleansing. Among the instinctively racist British political class, however, Disraeli's more accurate and measured reading of the situation was ascribed to his being a Jew, for the Jews – accurately, in fact – were regarded as having greater kinship with Muslims and Turks. Stoked by the moral panic in London and Moscow, Russia sent troops to the Balkans in support of Bulgar militias that massacred at will. A convoy of refugees made its way towards Istanbul, and the Balkans were emptied of their Turkish population.

For all the tragedy, it is in that initial reaction of Disraeli that I find hope. It belongs to a time before the fake history and theology used to promote Zionist policy in Palestine infected the West with the revisionist proposition that Muslims and Jews – both of whom have always had more to fear from Christians than one another – belong in enmity and not kin. It is my faith that those centuries of history will outlast the blink of an eye of Zionism, just as Europe – from Srebrenica to Cordoba to Komotini – will slowly awaken to the question: what happened to its Muslims?

Xanthi to Komotini – 13 October

The rubber of the tyre spreads a little as I push down on the bars. At a petrol station I stop, a large fluffy dog bounds out and jumps up at me, starts licking my arm and then mounts my leg. The owner of the garage pulls it back in, laughs, gestures that of course I should borrow his air line. He's handsome, with swept-back greying hair and a strong jaw. A sort of seventies rockstar is preserved in his style, as if those were the records he grew up on, but he had to content himself with running this tyre stop instead of playing stadiums. On the wall over his shoulder are many photos of him: with friends, with football teams, by himself. On the opposite wall are football shirts and scarfs, scarfs from all over Europe. I see a couple of Turkish scarfs and smile. Point out Trabzon. He tells me his family is from Trabzon. He is Pontic. Those Greeks who were population-exchanged out of the Black Sea region of Anatolia. I tell him my grandfather was a Turk from near Florina, population-exchanged to Izmir. We shrug and smile, as if to say that was unfortunate, but just the way it went.

He counts to three in Turkish: bir, iki, üç. He recites other Turkish football teams. I ask if I can take his photo, and he motions to say we'll take a photo together or not at all: like we're friends, like he will not be made into just my cultural artefact. We take it, there we are. He points, gesturing that he'll add us to his wall. We smile at one another: humans, families, all of us nothing but twigs floating on the river of history. Here we float beside one another a while. Sometimes we are washed into an eddy, a few gather together, a structure forms, perhaps a bird's nest, a great rainfall comes, the river rises, and again we are washed away, we are gone.

*

In the final hundred Greek kilometres, I think constantly of the population exchange that took my own grandfather across the Dardanelles to Türkiye, and introduced such hardship and trauma into his young life. My great-grandfather, his father, died a year after making the journey, leaving Grandpa Mustafa barely ten years old and the man of the house. There is something cold, a capitalism, to those human transfers of 1922 and 1923. On account of the order-liness of the exchange, the Greek president, Eleftherios Venizelos, nominated Atatürk for the Nobel Peace Prize. There is an eeriness here too, as if the mutual love and shared culture of Greeks and Turks were to be sunk into a final heartrending transaction, whereby they would not be together again. Was the harmony of the exchange underwritten by the very love that meant it need not have been so? Peace is almost always preferable to conflict, life preferable to death, but sometimes as I ride, a part of me asks if some violence would have been more natural, more human, than this autopsy conducted by new state powers upon their old communities. Another part of me, wiser, counsels against this hot-headedness, reminds me that history is long, and the smoothness of the transaction is what will allow it to one day reverse, or be made immaterial.

Outside a restaurant, a delivery driver looks enquiringly at a sky filling with clouds, and as if sombrely thinking the same thing I am: will I get wet this evening? His beard is thick, skin darker than olive. He takes out a phone, as if to verify his misgiving, and as I have not the first clue of the words in Greek, I ask in Turkish if the rain is coming.

"Yağmur geliyor mu?"

He looks round, a little surprised; says not, that it will be fine. He asks if I'm Turkish, and I tell him my mix: my father from Izmir. I ask where his memleket is. Again the Turkish word for home, the place you come from, almost as important as a person's name. He looks at me sternly. No, put out. As if he finds the question familiar, fatiguing. Like asking "But where are you *from*?" of a black person on a London street. As if with enough emphasis on that last word they will crack beneath the question and finally answer "Nigeria".

He points down at the earth. "Burası" he says, planting it like a stake in the ground. Here. "Burası, Yunaninstan." Greece. I realise that this sort of answer is the inverse of what I'm used to in Istanbul, where people may be second or third generation in the city and still answer Sivas; Rize; Adana – the terrain of their family in Anatolia, as if nobody can truly be *from* a city. As if to answer so would be an insincere story of origin, a place without place, of insufficient authenticity. His assertion that he is from Komotini itself is, I suspect, a tired response to constantly having his belonging as a Turk here in Greece delegitimised. He is also a Greek, and Greece is his home.

"How is life here, for Turks?" I can't help but ask.

His expression is nonplussed. "It is fine. For me it is fine."

I ask about politics: "Mitsotakis?"

"Olsun, olsun," he replies. "Let it be." He says it with a wave of the hand and a sidewards nod of the head, as if to silence my questions, as if they go beyond the pay grade of his work as a delivery driver.

Next morning, back out in the countryside, I stop in the shop of a small town. I buy some biscuits; some for coffee now and spares for energy later. The shopkeeper speaks Turkish from the moment of my merhaba. He is an old man, of the age where he takes the path of least resistance to everything including language, communicating in his own tongue unless he needs to go beyond it. He walks around his shop with a shuffle, a short moustache and – like Atatürk of Selanik – that slightly higher-pitched accent of the Turks of western Thrace. I ask about life here, and he replies unthinking.

"Kötü," he says. Bad. But he says it with a brightness, for he is also of the age where complaining becomes perhaps a form of pleasure in itself, or at least relief, and if you have time to complain, and an audience to listen, can things really be so bad?

"Neden?" I ask why.

He lifts up two empty hands by way of an answer, says simply, "Para yok."

There's no money.

Children

With sundown coming, I see the familiar companion of my shadow down the road before me. I see ploughed fields, crops, rich lakes shimmering in blue, the rippling surface cut through with veins of still water. Here was the Ottoman west, and once more, it is not that all this was ours, it is also that we were theirs. You were ours, we were yours. The words form clearly in my mind. In these lands, when they went, the Ottoman state – quite apart from the suffering – lost most of its European population, some of the most fertile and productive land in all the Empire, and a corresponding collapse in its tax base and state revenue. And yet it barely features in Turkish history. After a century of Ottoman struggles, Atatürk and the early Republicans felt a need to look forward rather than back.

From somewhere, alongside this, I remember Atatürk's great fondness for children. As always with Atatürk, there was an energy to put his ideas into practice. He had the best part of a dozen adopted children, some taken from financial precarity, and he funded the educations of many more. Moved as he was by the obstacles that Ottoman society had placed in the way of women, most of his adopted children were girls. The closest to him was perhaps his daughter Ülkü, while the most famous was Sabiha Gökçen, who went on to be Türkiye's first female pilot, and after whom the second airport in Istanbul is named. In its early years, the Republic inaugurated Çocuk Bayramı, Children's Day, on 23 April, and Atatürk held close to his heart the importance of child development in building an individual, society and country. Writing on the subject, he said:

Many families have a deep-rooted bad habit of not letting their children speak and not listening to them when they do. Poor children are silenced every time they interrupt an adult conversation, which is an extremely wrong, even harmful attitude. On the contrary, children should be encouraged to speak freely and express their thoughts and feelings openly, thereby giving them the opportunity to correct their mistakes and preventing them from becoming hypocritical and dishonest adults. We should support our children to express their thoughts freely and without reservations, stand up for their beliefs and respect sincere opinions of others in return.

Shining through this is an implicit faith in the future which shares, perhaps, a subtle commonality with the absence from Turkish history of what happened in the Balkans. Türkiye was not to be inaugurated in ways that enshrined devastation in its history, so that devastation could always be visited anew upon the country being built. Good things would come, better things would come. Healing would come. I recall the words of Frederick Douglass, the supreme nineteenth-century leader of a slave rebellion against the United States:

"It is easier to raise strong children than to repair broken men."

Checkpoints – 14 October

All is quiet as I ride through the night, making up ground after too lazy a day. The moon is up, is full, or almost full, and its light reflects white on the plastic wall of a small prefab cabin at the road-side. A floodlight glows, its light also white, but somehow hard and cold, with none of the shadows the night and moon so gently cut. Cops, or a version of cops, mill about. They are dressed in black. Guns and handcuffs on hips. They wear large, padded waistcoats covered in pockets: batons, pepper spray, flashlights. Each of them dressed up like a walking prison. No numbers for these guys, not even a badge to identify which strain of state-corporate policing. Just black from head to toe. Their uniform is neither military nor civil, these guys represent nothing but force. Privately hired force. Force without accountability. They bid me stop, call me in. One steps towards me. Unshaven. Hard, cold eyes. Straightforward eyes. You know it: a pro thug.

He speaks Greek, and on account of who he is, I invoke bloody-minded Anglo.

"What?" I ask, snap a little at him and his uniform. Like he should speak properly.

"Where are you from?" The words land right away as I come to a halt.

"Türkiye," I answer. True, but provocative.

"Passport," he escalates back at me.

There is no border here. He has no right. But the most cherished right of state gangsters like this is always to make your life difficult. That is their job, so that becomes their right. I go for my passport.

Appease a little. "Turkish-British," I clarify. Annoyed at myself for doing so as I hand it over. He looks at it. Turns up his nose at the faded insignia. He dislikes me. Probably less than I dislike him, but that's a low bar. He opens it to the page, looks at my photo.

"What's your name?" he asks.

"You're looking at my name," I laugh.

"What's your name?" he snarls.

"Julian Sayarer," I snarl.

"You're alone here?"

"Yes," I scoff into the empty night.

"No family, no friends?"

Jeez, no need to rub it in.

"No," I answer with a smile.

A bus pulls in, pauses our interrogation. A large white coach, intercity. They wave it over. With a hiss of hydraulics and rubber seal going unkissed, a door in the middle of the vehicle presses out and opens. More of the black-clad officers scuttle up to it, tiny beetles climb the steps. Others wait beside me. My guy looks at me firmly, he is the chief beetle it seems. Pro thug, like I say. He sort of sniffs at me, can tell I'm too much privilege, entitlement. At the end of the day I'm a UK passport, however objectionable I am or he finds me. Making my life inconvenient is, after a certain point, more trouble than it's worth. The chief beetle climbs into the bus. I see him walk down the aisle, stooped in the low yellow light of the gangway. Then I hear a sound, an awful sound, a ratchet tightening: again, again. Like my cycling shoes in their lock but harder, firmer, more sinister. Metal. Handcuffs. Then the voice of my guy. "One. Two. Three. Off." I watch dumbfounded at this random roadside.

Shapes move down the bus and then out. Three young men, shackled at the wrist. Young faces. Teenage faces. But really, child faces. Are led off the bus. Maybe Syrian? Maybe Afghan? Who cares? All the passengers are looking at them. As they're escorted off in cuffs. This is their life. These their formative years. They are led in shackles into a cabin. They're gone.

Komotini to Kipoi – 15 October

"Where you ride?" he asks down the length of his bulbous nose and over the top of his spectacles. A wide moustache, large belly. A far younger man sits opposite but something in them is similar and says father and son.

"To Türkiye," I reply to an impressed face, a twitch of interest in the moustache.

"Where you start?"

"From Selanik."

A second twitch of the moustache. Cars and lorries plough loudly by the layby. Sometimes a scooter with a higher pitch. There is a food wagon, built from a van with its cargo portion converted to a kitchen. A hotplate sizzles with a new order of souvlaki. The men at the table seem to want to talk, like they've had enough of one another, but aren't sure what to ask. I help them out, see what they have to say.

"So much history here. I guess here is quite Turkish and Greek."

"Yes," the younger man answers, cradling an e-cigarette. "Three cities. Xanthi, Komotini, Alexandroupoli." He swirls his cigarette. "A big mix Greek-Turkish."

I don't know what to say, so repeat, "So much history," like throwing bread into water to see if the fish will come to the surface. The moustache on the older man twitches, wants to talk, twitches again. He places his palms down. I'm about to get a bite.

"But history only begins with what is written down."

An interesting contention. Orality versus Literacy wasn't what I expected but I'm here for it.

"I don't think so," I say, "we are only talking now, but it is happening."

"But with talking, people can say anything." He points a large finger at the tabletop. "When it is written down, we know it is real."

"But people can write anything down, it doesn't make it true. And people can tell the truth and it never be written."

I smile at the thought that he has no idea I am about to write him down. That I'm entirely right, I will write whatever I want, and he will be read by others on my terms.

"If it is not written," he insists, "it is only mythology."

"But you are Greek," I laugh, as does the younger man, "mythology is important to you!"

"History begins when it is written down! If mythology is important, then Türkiye does not exist!"

Jeez. I've caught a Greek all right. This one bigger than I'd bargained for. I'm saved by the souvlaki placed down in front of me. I give a frown and an awkward laugh. I suspect he is referring to the Turkish Republic, placed into writing in only 1923, full of the creations required of all new nations, the ones that plaster over the cracks of all old nations. I suspect in his mind this is juxtaposed with some eternal existence of the Greeks. I spare him Ottoman history and that his contention is anyway upside-down because, as I have just said, orality exists. The conversation is as important as the document. Turkish history is as ancient as Greek because a human is a human, even if nobody inscribes them in rock, parchment or paper. I spare him an interrogation about the idea of modern Greece and where it leaves the histories of Macedonians, Turks, Albanians. Instead I smile and turn to my souvlaki. I bid him good afternoon and begin to write down our words, to make him history.

The road becomes further overgrown. Concrete crumbles and black-yellow railings rust where they guard the edge of the road over a drop, a brook, a river, a hydropower dam. Whether the railings still have strength enough to keep a vehicle on the road, I am not sure, but in the absence of this function they make a sturdy trellis for the brambles, thick with blackberries. Over the top of these are entire bushels of hops, their pale green flowers bursting plump inside their casing, giving me the sweet, bitter notes of their fragrance as the soft bud folds lightly under the pressure of my finger and thumb. This beauty, a chaos held within the perfect proportions of nature, of human efforts succumbing to a greater, gentle force, is perhaps my favourite aesthetic of this world – a reminder of what was and what will be again, of the futility of building anything in opposition to rather than in harmony with such forces. The abundance of this aesthetic in Greece is the silver lining, or perhaps the bramble lining, of its economic decline.

On the opposite side of the road, a car, a tiny hatchback, is pulled over. Lying on my side of it is the shape of a man. As I get nearer, I notice the car's brightly coloured paint job, its swirling psychedelics, a mirror ball on the dashboard and a pink pom-pom hanging from the rear-view mirror. A sheath of glitter covers the steering wheel. I see a truck swerve to avoid the randomly parked vehicle. Sure enough, on my side, on the hard shoulder, a man is reclining, propped on an elbow. Deeply contemplative. He wears a beat-up leather waistcoat, another broom of a moustache, and I see his head is lowered. He looks solemnly at a tiny ball of feathers with thin feet, the small bird I think he has just hit, that has bounced off his windscreen. He just lies there, leaning on one elbow, in silent vigil for the dead bird as I ride by him and his parked disco car.

In Türkiye there is an expression: delikanlı. It means, "with crazy blood", because for all that Turks and Ottomans have often been marked by outsiders as austere or grim, the country sings with flamboyance and eccentrics. The Ottomans used to be led into battle by a special regiment, The Deliler, The Crazies, who wore special costumes of bright colours, feathers and flashing accessories so as to disorient the enemy. I ride on, looking one final time over my shoulder, at the man reclined on one elbow. And I think there may be a little delikanlı in him too.

The likeness between Greece and Türkiye only grows. A pack of dogs, owned by nobody but the whole community, lie and snooze and play together in the shade of a village square. One evening I buy a glass of wine and plate of baked aubergine. I finish both faster than I mean to, and for no reason other than just because, the owner returns a moment later with a second glass of wine and a plate of sliced melon. Here is a logic, higher than currency or capitalism, and I marvel anew that two places so akin were ever separated. The roadside graffiti also signals not only a coming change of language, but confusion at the separation. Written with yellow spray paint inside a bus stop are the Turkish words *kafam karışık*: my head's a mess. Nearing the frontier I cross an ageing bridge, and marked on it in faded numbers are the weight limits if you are driving a truck, or a tank. Quietly as I cycle, I wish for this borderland to have no concern or use for tanks ever again. I make a small oath of it, and commit it to the autumn air.

Border – 16 October

At the border crossing I wait, eating an overdue meal. Greek TV plays in the corner: tourists rescued from a cave, an old woman mugged in Larissa. Then the main feature: footage of Turkish fighter jets. Worse still, the whole room is watching the stream of junk TV. The picture changes, shows Erdoğan, but his face superimposed onto a body naked except for swimming trunks in a paddling pool. Jeez . . . and this is the news. I remember the cartoon by the so-called satirists at the Parisian comic, *Charlie Hebdo*. Erdoğan: in his underwear and looking up a woman's skirt. Likewise, *Hebdo*'s depiction of Mohammed: naked but for a star over his raised ass, balls-showing.

The determination to sexualise and degrade reveals more about the so-called satirist than their subject, but it is hard to know what to think about someone so determined to insult you. So weirdly determined to sexualise you. There is not much satire but irony aplenty here, after all those centuries when Europeans, led most enthusiastically of all by the French in their Grand Tour, made their way to the Ottomans for a sexual freedom and even excess they could not find back home. Istanbul leaves them spellbound. Flaubert boasts of his handjob from a boy in a North African bathhouse. A century on, after the Ottomans are gone, testimonies abound of Foucault's acts against young boys in Tunisia. The colonial states, meanwhile, export their prudishness. Moroccan laws against adultery are still based on French colonial law. Homophobic legislation from Hamas in Gaza is based on British Mandate law. The communities that suffer them are required to perform a double liberation, against both the foreign colonist and the local prejudice.

Having at last undergone some sexual liberation of their own, Europeans return to insult the places where they became less prudish. I think of Voltaire, in his letter to Catherine the Great of Russia, congratulating her on the massacre in the Balkans: "I wish I had at least been able to help you kill a few Turks . . . It does not suffice to humiliate them; they should be destroyed."

Voltaire at least does us the favour of revealing the extent of French racism towards Turks, of which with time – inşallah – they may be cured. But he is also mistaken. Humiliation is in fact the final death, which is why Islamophobes seek it with such determination.

There is more to all of this, of that I am sure. But not now . . . We'll return to it. I look away from the news and out of the window. Border crossing points. Truck drivers; truck drivers and mothers with impatient toddlers. Most trucks are Turkish, some Greek. One that is pulled in has Iranian plates, an Iranian trailer. I am not sure I have ever seen an Iranian lorry in Europe before, so here at least integration is at work. This gives me heart, because inside this truck is a driver, but so too the company who pays his wage, secretaries filing paperwork, a cargo, a receiver for the consignment, and the petrol station attendants he will meet on his way. All of which means that, on some level and against all the air war of the media, Iran and Europe have moved closer.

Music plays over a radio, something half-familiar to my ears. Is it? Yes, it is. It takes me back, bars of the most saccharine pop though it may be. Perhaps that's the point of saccharine pop: that's what it's for, to live in your brain.

> *Your life ain't gonna be nothing like my life,*
> *You're gonna have a good life,*
> *I'm gonna do just what it takes.*

The song transports me, back to the last time I recall hearing it. The island of Samos, Greece. Why is it playing again now, beside the Meriç River, that other refugee frontier, that European rampart and graveyard? Someone sent it to this radio, I'm sure, another of those endless coincidences that seem eventually to point to something more than just chance.

> *Your life ain't gonna be nothing like my life,*
> *You're gonna have a good life,*
> *I'm gonna do just what it takes.*

It was one of those songs that I suppose lands in a summer, hits, and then hangs around a few years. In 2018 I was on Samos, just across from the Turkish coast, a few years after so many refugees first moved out of Syria, Yemen and Libya. By then the shock of the initial numbers had become managed, albeit in the least human and most industrial way: in camps. The main camp in Samos was fenced in, prison-like, and residents were obliged by curfew to go back inside each night. One dusk, just like this one next to the Meriç, I waited outside a shop, and those tacky but upbeat bars of the song came to me as I watched a woman, I'd guess from Syria, with a young child in a sling upon her back. Carefully she looked over fruit, and the lyrics, as they always do, went straight into my ears, narrating perfectly the scene I saw: "Your life ain't gonna be nothing like my life . . ."

I heard the words a first time, plainly enough, as the relationship between her and me. But then, as I watched the care with which she picked the best grapes and placed them in a cloth bag, as she tested the nectarines for ripeness, they seemed to be sung more as the promise from a parent to her child, sleeping in a sling and with her head rested on her mother's back.

"Your life ain't gonna be nothing like my life, I'm gonna do just what it takes."

If truth be told, the refugees of Samos, and those I spent months with in Athens, often had more life left in them than the Europeans who were trying to help amidst, or rather *against*, the immorality of their own state failure. That Dutch pensioner, leaning heavily on his hoe as he tended to the garden and allotment patch at a volunteer camp. He said this was all he could do now, and unlike so many in Europe, at least he'd had the decency to feel guilt, whatever good that did anyone. The German-Egyptian guy I spoke to in Athens, where he was helping to organise volunteer shifts at the abandoned-then-squatted hotel of City Plaza, where hundreds of refugees were then living. I remember as we spoke, and his eyes glazed, thinking just how tired I was of living in a time where so many of the best people with the best intentions looked all the time as though they might at any moment begin to cry.

The music goes on, I gather up my things and return to the bike, roll on down towards the frontier, passing the line of trucks. Ahead I see the crossing point, the physical frontier that for a cartographer marks Greece and Türkiye, though here on the ground is a midpoint of an indeterminate, bureaucratic no man's land, even if soldiers with large rifles are on hand to assert the cartography should the bureaucratic arrangement ever be called into question. Everything feels more militarised, fenced-off than when last I came this way. On the bridge ahead is the same Turkish booth beside the Greek booth. Red trades blue. Two soldiers at each. Large flags and each nation so side-by-side symmetrical that if for a second you rinsed your brain of political understanding, it would look like a show of solidarity.

At the Greek booth a radio is playing, though the music is so Turkish it could be from a bar in Istanbul, and perhaps does come from a Turkish station. A tsampouna blows. At some point, all the world is united by the idea of taking a sheep's stomach, piercing a hole in it, and blowing a bagpipe note through a hollow stick. To draw taut a length of animal hair and slide the line of a bow across it. And to sing.

On the air is a note of smoke. Somewhere close, something burns. I am forced by instinct to stop and take a photo, even as I try to record it all in my mind. The Greek soldiers wave and smile. I take another of the setting. Then I take a load more: a few of myself, like a smiling idiot tourist, in case they make me delete my pictures and want to watch me do so. From ahead I hear through a radio, then louder in a shouted confirmation, "No photos!" The order seems to be from the Turkish side, but the Greeks appear to have taken a liking to me and my bicycle, reject this imposition on them from the other side, as if while I am on their side they are fine with me taking photos. A short, stocky soldier with a kind face, as kind as a face can be when it holds a rifle, comes up to me seriously. "You want to take photo?" Like he has a gun and is ready to vouch for me. I opt to avert an incident, am heading that way and Türkiye can easily make me delete whatever Greece allows me to take. Keep it calm. I stop with the soldiers a moment, let the moment diffuse into the dusk.

"You from here?" I ask.

"Thessaloniki," replies one. The other shakes his head and says only, "National service."

Both look incredibly young, or maybe I just feel older. One is smooth-cheeked and clean-shaven. The other has no sign of a beard. Most of all their eyes are innocent. Conscript eyes. National service eyes.

"You here all night?"

"Until 2 a.m., then break, then 4 a.m."

"It gets cold?"

"Yes, above the river."

"Many people cross here?" I ask.

One shakes his head. "Not here. The immigrants don't cross here because we can see them." He gestures with his hand. "They go north, or south. Other places."

"Your journey OK?" the other asks me.

I smile, and nod, and thank them. These soldiers. So kindly. What did they do? Did they do the unspeakable things? Was it them, or simply others like them? Or others unlike them? Ready to leave, I return foot to pedal with a click.

"You like fishing?" asks one, quickly, gesturing over the bridge at the river to explain, in case he has the word wrong.

"It's OK," I reply, confused. "I used to. A little."

He points to my shoe, the strap on its ratchet.

"Shimano," he says, "they make fishing equipment."

I laugh; it now makes sense. "Yes." I gesture at the rear cassette of the bicycle, the derailleur, then make a turning motion and sound with my hand and one finger. "The same mechanism. Spinning."

A final time we smile, for a simpler world, I suppose. We nod goodnight as I push off. A smell of burning in the air, of burning and the water, cold under the bridge. Burning. Dusk and burning and water. And there it is, shining silver on the last light, a mist of smoke, a bankside of tree cover, an orange firmament and purple sky. All right there, the Meriç river: the Evros river.

Rolling east I look down on it, proclaimed by the Greek government as a "banned and obscure military zone". Here is the frontier of the European Union, one of the Balkans' deepest rivers, and in it now, forgive me but I must, the last resting place of so many who tried to cross to safety as a result of the Syrian, Libyan, Iraqi wars, or since US sanctions hammered down on Iran and Afghanistan. It is strange to contrast the curt "no photos" of the Turkish border with the bonhomie of the Greeks, although it is the Greeks who let innocent humans drown here, who have been known to strip men naked and send them back for Turks to take in. I do not like to take such simplistic sides, but sometimes the truth is a simple thing and numbers do not lie. Perhaps this civility is just the nature of Europe. Europe goes about its evil politely, it always smiles, it always draws up a contract.

There are nuances to the water graves of Europe. The freshwater of Evros means the bodies quickly decompose beyond recognition. The sea of the Mediterranean takes lives in greater number, but salt at least preserves features so that identification is possible and a family may achieve closure. Perhaps you did not expect nor want this in a book about Türkiye? But darling, canım, nor did I, and yet now it is here. This tragedy came to us all, and some simply exist further from it, and better able to ignore their own hand in it.

I didn't want to write about this border. The border at Meriç is so puny, so artificial. That time and integration will erase its significance, I am confident. I did not want to add to its history. Thrace is Thrace, Indivisible, and history will restore as much. But for all the border's artificiality, there is now too much suffering in this river not to mention. Too many Syrian, Iraqi, Iranian and Afghan lives have been lost, along with many others, to the myth of a pure Europe and the power of the United States to destroy countries as and when it pleases.

Either side of me are thick rushes in a muddy riverbank. The river is dark, it feels heavy, slow-moving. Here is a river, here is a border. On the Turkish side of the bridge, a balustrade in red and white. On the Greek side, blue and white. Here is a river, here is a border. This is the edge of Greece and Türkiye, but so too the edge of Türkiye and the European Union. Its opposite border, the English Channel, the British elect to keep as fatal as this one. Looking down at the flowing waters, I think of another river, unnamed. A river in the words of former French prime minister Jean-Pierre Raffarin, speaking of Turkish accession to the EU: "We will not let the river of Islam into the riverbed of secularism."

I wonder if this, this Meriç, was the river that he meant. And I wonder if he ever realised how unsecular a thing that was to say.

Looking back at Greece, I see high fences and bundles of razor wire. Additional to my past visits, I recognise the landscape more recently from news broadcasts. It was here that refugees tried to cross, and Western media said that Türkiye was *threatening* Europe with refugees. To be more precise, they said *Erdoğan* was threatening Europe with refugees, because if you want to vilify a country, it always helps to subsume the entirety of it into one person.

It was telling that Arab, Pashtu or whatever helpless victim of war constituted a threat to Europe, or the meaning of it. It was a lapse in language that revealed the *threat* was in fact contained inside European racism, which the arrival of refugees into Europe would activate as surely as a bullet loads a gun. Better still was the idea that Türkiye had put refugees in harm's way, that Türkiye was guilty of leaving refugees to face the tear gas, baton strikes and razor wire fences of Greek guards. The idea that Greece might have had some agency in this matter occurred only to the more enlightened: an awkward confession that Europe trusted itself to behave in no way but this, and that it also regarded it as its right to do so. That this condition of xenophobia might not describe all Europeans is certain, but more certain still is that the minority to whom the label does not apply lost their continent to those to whom it does.

In the European hysteria at the prospect of refugees arriving, leaving them no choice but xenophobia, also revealed was the familiar Western need to put itself at the centre. For Europeans, the Turkish need to remove some of its millions of refugees was not driven by material conditions inside Türkiye. It was not about housing scarcity, job scarcity, stretching social fabric or the material difficulties of hosting the largest refugee population in the world; no, it was all a plot to intimidate the West. Turkish material reality did not exist, because in the Western mind the outside world does not exist: it is restricted to television, to newsprint. These are the most sacred borders that nothing must cross.

And inside Türkiye? What was the Turkish perspective on all this? The country was told it would receive money from EU budgets in refugee support, barely half of which materialised. It was told it would receive help in resettling migrants, all but none of which materialised. It was told that EU visa liberalisation for Turks would be implemented. I leave you to conclude how that went.

On 19 June 2016, World Refugee Day, with the country already hosting millions of refugees, the Ministry of Foreign Affairs issued the statement that: "Türkiye indiscriminately keeps its doors open to people who escape from oppression and persecution, in line with its historical traditions, and enables them to live freely, far from fear and anxiety."

The Turkish policy, which would have been commendable even as only an opinion, was enacted as state policy.

But enough of this for now. Even if this issue has – unbidden – come to make itself at home along the route we'll take, here I leave it behind and I roll east. A new country. *The* country, the country that remains of the empire which came before it. I see the small glow of burning flames in the chaff of a cornfield. Two long, black parallel strikes count off the first and then second century in scorched corn stubble. Ahead are the towering domed arches of the border crossing. The name Türkiye glows red against the haze of a white light, so bright, and in which everything begins.

Ipsala to Silivri – 18 October

Across the border it changes. Everything suddenly seems bigger, vast, as if the land from here must reach all the way to the Caspian and so great quantities of it are needed. The crumpled hills of western Thrace flatten into rolling plains as grain country begins. Everything stands exposed, affording nowhere to hide as the wind blows through.

Leaving the Meriç behind, I think of the other great bodies of water that came before it. Water and rivers have been integral to the Ottomans and Turks, and to how their relationship with the West was understood. Once the Danube, between Romania and Bulgaria, was seen as the border of the Ottoman lands. To Europe it was a strange, unnerving frontier feared by monarchs because the cosmopolitanism of a multi-faith empire – Muslim, Christian, Jewish – was felt to represent an implicit challenge to the Christian concept of a divine right of kings on which their own power turned.

In the days when water was still easier to navigate than land, the Ottoman Empire comprised three great rivers: the Nile, which helped the Empire make its way into Africa; the Euphrates; and the Tigris. The last two defined the Mesopotamian region and helped supply and navigate down into the Arabian peninsula. As the Empire weakened in the nineteenth century, growing ever more indebted to European banks, creditors set up shop in the Istanbul neighbourhood of Tünel, known also as Pera. Their offices were above one bank of the Haliç, that body of water in central Istanbul known to Europeans as the Golden Horn, with the sultan's palace of Topkapı and the great mosques of Sultanahmet on the opposite bank. So it was that it was the Haliç – today spanned by the Galata Bridge – served as the body of water that in the imagination separated East from West.

In the 1870s, when refugees from the Balkans arrived in Istanbul and the sultan ordered them housed in any empty building available, the far side of the Bosphorus, still traversable only by boat, was not a simple place to reach. As their numbers swelled, amenities were overwhelmed and a typhus epidemic threatened, refugees were dispatched to the Anatolian side to help empty the city. The district of Kadıköy was a place useful at that time for its remoteness rather than its closeness. Advances in suspension bridge and tunnel engineering in the twentieth century made the city of Istanbul definitively into one, criss-crossed by buses and trains and cars as well as boats. Even as it grew less relevant as a divide, the Bosphorus became the iconic body of water that represented not only Istanbul but for some the essence of Türkiye: the meeting of East and West. I consider the Meriç, flowing southwards, and cannot help but think, with no disrespect, how small it is beside all those great bodies of water that went before it. Danube, Nile, Tigris, Euphrates, Bosphorus.

At the first Turkish village, Ipsala, I smile at the sight of old men biding their time outside a café in the main square, just as I left them biding their time outside a café in the main square of the last Greek village, Kipoi. I have left the European Union, but nothing has changed. To the west of where I now stand is a bloc containing the industrial powerhouses of Alsace, Turin and the Ruhr. It is a bloc charged with the legacies of imperialism, economic might and a military grandeur that once enslaved the world, then destroyed everything once that expansion had reached its limits. But as I move through Thrace, I have simply ridden from one village beside the Meriç river towards another village beside the Meriç river. The first village is defined and vested with the powers of the bloc, and the second falls outside them. A few kilometres separate one Thracian river village from the next Thracian river village, though the logic of bloc and border implies that Kipoi shares more with Offenburg 2,000 kilometres away than Ipsala at twenty kilometres, despite it having spent millennia as Ipsala's neighbour, sharing, trading, living. The European Union, I think to myself, could converge for a millennium, but Kipoi will still have more in common with Ipsala.

As I ride I cannot help but consider my closeness to Istanbul. I struggle against that classic weakness of the touring cyclist, and endeavour not to wish away kilometres. I try to resist the desire to feel the welcome of the city already. The wind pushes back, and my muscles and the impatience of my mind remember these long straight roads up and then down broad, indifferent hills. Around me, I see the wind being both resisted and put to work. Long fences with plastic screens surround fields to prevent the topsoil being blown away from an earth made dusty by drought. Lines of trees have been planted, mostly conifer and at varying stages of growth, to make this fence more permanent and natural. Wind turbines spin, and these too are new since I last came this way. Now they drive industry, standing in formation along ridges, and towering over small factories. The blades rotate in the gale, and the electricity powers a conveyor belt beside the hoppers of a grain refinery. I watch the energy of a windmill transferred from the turning of its rotors and down into the turning circular blade of a sawmill. Outside stand lines of lumber the colour of teak, stacked and then plucked into the air by the claw of a crane.

I ride at a time of a global energy crisis, every bit of me delighted these businesses heeded the future and now have free energy. Just across the border is a signpost pointing to one of the first Turkish villages: Beğendik. I smile at the name's meaning, so simple and pretty: "We Liked It". The road presses forwards with the moan of traffic, gravitating like the rest of the country into the pull of Istanbul. To my right appears the port city of Tekirdağ. And I do not remember so many dock cranes and stevedores, and I do not remember so many boats loaded with cargo at anchor in the gulf. To my left a large new hospital building shines in the sun. The Adalet ve Kalkınma Partisi (Justice and Development Party), better known as the AKP, which Recep Tayyip Erdoğan helped found, has for twenty years made it its business to build new hospitals, public transport and airports all through Türkiye, a perk of having a large construction sector that needs to be kept ticking over. No doubt there have been kickbacks from these relations, but it all served to develop and integrate Türkiye, giving regions far from the Thracian city of Tekirdağ the sense that they too are part of the country. Above the hospital against a cloudy sky more turbines spin, and then a large dental hospital comes into view beside the regular one, all of it powered by the wind pushing at me. I see refineries in the distance as the highway rushes east. At a truck stop a retired cargo plane has been parked on a concrete stretch and turned into a restaurant. A shepherd tends his newly shorn flock of sheep that clamber over and into the forecourt of a petrol station, making me smile at this eternal stream of old meeting new.

On a far hill is the large, sooty footprint of a cement factory and its kilns. Nearer the road, identikit holiday villas smother the coast, for a construction sector left idling doesn't only stamp out hospitals, and these concrete boxes now spill through the country in places that were once pristine. In the near distance, still some fifty kilometres from Istanbul, I see the first high-rises, towering apartment blocks of glass, so that as dusk draws near, the road begins to resemble Shanghai or Singapore as much as it does the Istanbul approach I pedalled ten years ago. Soon I will see the extension tunnels being bored on a metro line that in those days had only ten stations. It dawns on me that the old century is indeed gone, and this is not the country I used to know. Things have changed, and all I can think of is the name of the village, Beğendik. Indeed, we liked it. Indeed, beğendik.

Silivri – 19 October

The seaside city of Silivri comes as pleasant in reality as the name rings unpleasant in Turkish politics. Not wanting to dawdle, I roll briefly beneath the walls of Silivri Prison, synonymous with those imprisoned in Türkiye on charges that are widely decried as political. The tragedy is all the greater because I have no doubt, knowing some of those imprisoned as I do, that they, like all of us, want absolutely nothing but the betterment of the country.

People who should not be are still inside these walls. My friend Yiğit lived inside them a while, and though he is now free I still think often of his time there. I thought of him as I met the other Yiğit in Selanik, outside Atatürk's house, and my overemotional mind took it as a sign of what this journey meant. I think of him each time I defend Turkish policy, because my defence does not alter that I loathe what it did to Yiğit and others who had done no wrong. In truth, I see no contradiction here. A large part of why I will determinedly credit that which the Turkish state does right is because I would like also for it to listen when I say that which it does wrong. Due criticism is nothing without due credit: another rule that soon allows you to distinguish the criticism of the patriot from the propagandist.

Just as with the Meriç river, I considered not riding by this place or writing of it. I considered it because Recep Tayyip Erdoğan once recited an Islamic poem at a protest and was locked up for being thought too religious. I considered it because I have family and friends who were once jailed because a US-aligned Turkish military forever interfering in politics thought they were too socialist.

I cannot bring myself to discuss a matter so grave with those for whom political imprisonment is a concern only if they dislike who is doing the imprisonment. That being so, I also cannot tolerate the idea of imprisonment as a mere rite of passage in Turkish politics. And because we won't undo this injustice unless we talk about it, I must talk about it.

How those of you outside of Türkiye help in all this, I am less sure. The immoralities of the world are sadly more intricate than the plain fact that there are cell doors within Silivri that should be unlocked. Just as there are doors that must be unlocked inside Edirne prison to the west, and so too, further west again, in the doors of all those US prisons in a country where one per cent of the population lives inside a jail cell. Closer to my other home are the doors of Belmarsh Prison, in the city where I was born.

I know the charge that waits for me, for seeing Silivri and asking too of Belmarsh, London, where Julian Assange is left to have his brain broken for the non-crime of journalism, for publishing the footage of US helicopter pilots congratulating one another on the bodies of the dozen Iraqi men they have just shot dead in Baghdad. I know the charge, but I believe that I am innocent of it. They call this, I think, "whataboutery", but I mention Silivri and Belmarsh side-by-side only because I want these words to be more than words you simply read. I want these words to leave this page and live with you a little, to live in the place that you call home, in the country that is yours.

The word "whataboutery" is a fiction. It is a made-up word intended to ridicule those who make the logical demand for a consistent application of principles; who reject the formulation that the West is free to do what they condemn in others, be it invasion or incarceration. I am half-British and half-Turkish. Both the *what* and the *about* exist in my brain. I can almost see *what* on one side of the Bosphorus and *about* on the other, where according to the morality of Western foreign policy some abuses are to be condemned, while others are to be excused or tidied or explained away. To see Silivri and not think also of Belmarsh strikes me as strange; they are one and the same thing, different wings in the prison of state power. I am not saying *whatabout* to justify a door staying locked; rather, I am demanding that both doors be unlocked.

States find it remarkably easy to condemn individuals, be they dissidents or merely the first hint of real opposition. They condemn them for insufficient love of country, they allege that they are in fact terrorists, or terrorist sympathisers. Once this is done enough, once that prognosis is broadcast repeatedly, the population is easily convinced that the person is indeed a threat to society and their wellbeing, and they welcome that person's banishment from public life. You may think that you would stand loyally beside the incarcerated, that you would proclaim them a hero and not a terrorist or some other slur. I hope that you are right.

This is one part of the perception. The second is thus, but no less nuanced. Those inside Silivri knew that their commitment to principles carried risks, and yet they voiced and acted out their principles all the same. Western audiences look at Silivri and see people who are more oppressed. But what if they actually see people with greater courage? The Western audience sees its own liberty as evidence of their freedom, but what if, perhaps, it is evidence of their obedience?

In these words, too – an *audience, seeing* – I always think of the great art critic, John Berger, writing of the male gaze in art: "Men act, women appear. Women watch themselves being looked at."

The same has perhaps until only very recently been true of countries. The West acts and dictates events for others to react to. Those others are watched in their reactions. Many, particularly in the elite, learn to watch themselves through Western eyes. Because restrictions of currency and passport keep most Turks inside Türkiye, or struggling to keep afloat if ever they leave, or puffed up with pride if they succeed, inside Türkiye the nature of the whole world's problems can quite easily come to seem like Turkish problems.

Western populations meanwhile are schooled to think themselves either beyond criticism, or that their states are so settled that criticism is useless, while other countries are viewed as sufficiently imperfect or incomplete that they can still be changed. The power of Western states is some three centuries deep, but in the event that a deep information strike is made, the state knows exactly how to strike back, to ensure that the strike is contained and others learn their lesson.

In this sad roll call are names both famous and unknown. Edward Snowden reveals war crimes: exiled. Julian Assange publishes war crimes: incarcerated. Aaron Swartz, that beautiful boy, who uploaded to the internet academic papers that should anyway have been free to read, is hounded by a so-called Department of Justice (sic). Swartz is threatened with a half-century in jail for copyright infringement, and hangs himself at the prospect. Aged twenty-six. His friend Lauri Love, an autistic programmer from Britain, hacks a US government website to install a banner demanding justice. The US demands another century of jail time, this time from Love, demands the British government extradite. They ruin the lives of Love and his family who contest this vile punishment. Finally, thankfully but as always, Love wins.

To Turks it should be clear that the cell doors of Silivri and Edirne and all the rest must be unlocked, quite simply because Türkiye is better than this. With those bodies free, as the minds inside them already are, then the country will prosper all the more. Of how the Westerner should relate to this, as I say, I am less sure. Of the many thoughts that crowd my mind, perhaps one is useful.

For many decades, a group known as the Cumartesi Anneleri, the Saturday Mothers, have gathered near Galatasaray in Istanbul to demand justice and to know what happened to their children – socialists, Muslims, political organisers, mere bystanders – who were disappeared by a past Turkish state that had the blessing of its military. Decades later and still the Saturday Mothers gather, still they face police, because nothing will silence them and their determination for justice. Do not worry, Turks know of their cell doors, and I feel quite sure that nothing will stop the demands for them to be unlocked. Of the West, where people are so averse to making a scene or being laughed at for their beliefs, and as a result grow averse to holding beliefs at all . . . I am less sure.

When I see Silivri and ask also of Belmarsh, I am not saying *whatabout*. I am simply inviting you, with all my heart, to see what it means to be a citizen of the world.

Part 2

Istanbul to Antalya

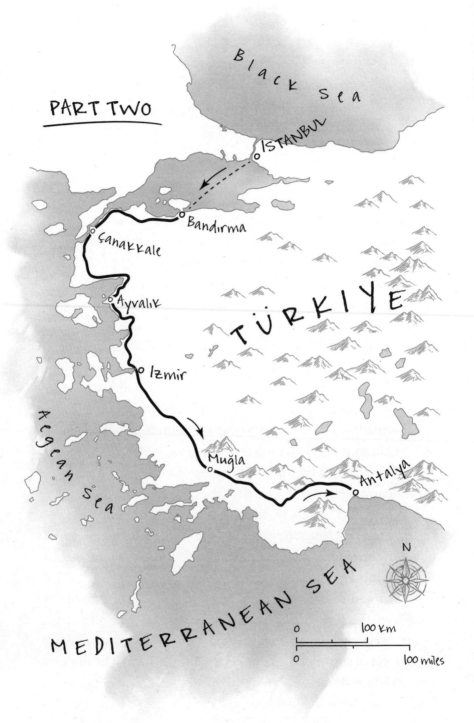

PART TWO

Black Sea

ISTANBUL

Bandırma

Çanakkale

Ayvalık

Izmir

TÜRKIYE

Aegean Sea

Muğla

Antalya

MEDITERRANEAN SEA

N

0   100 km
0   100 miles

Istanbul

The greatness of Istanbul, uncontested throughout Türkiye, is maybe unusual of big cities in the twenty-first century in that – for all its prosperity and acclaim – the rest of the country does not hate it. All across the country and political spectrum, people adore or at least admire Istanbul, even if they do not wish to live there. People love it, politicians covet it. They want it for themselves and to claim it as theirs because it belongs so entirely to all of this country. To some, it *is* this country, even if with a population of 20 million it is too large to be called a microcosm. People see it in their soap operas and, from Thrace to Anatolia, everyone has at least a cousin working here. The conservatives of Fatih and cocktail-sipping poseurs of Cihangir are united in appreciation of its beauty. Nobody speaks of the "Istanbul metropolitan elite" the way Britons do of Londoners, as US citizens do of New Yorkers or San Franciscans, as the French do of their arrogant Parisians. This is perhaps because Turks have a more honest understanding of what the city is: it is migration, from everywhere. It is not always success. It is often grinding work. You do not necessarily escape poverty or find riches in it, but it is yours, a part of the landscape of your own dreams and, even if those are not met, it is still the landscape of your country.

Under and through the illuminated stone walls of the old city arches I pedal. Boys run by in play, and street dogs pad after them. In one backstreet the air smells momentarily of detergent, of warm bleach and of steam lifting in bright light. In industrial laundries, a million white ghosts of Istanbul's linen are washed and now hang, while steam from the building pushes out of a pipe and into the sky. At other hangars and hatches I look in and see large looms, with reels of cotton and lines of thread like spiderwebs. I see the socks and vests of an entire city, nation and continent produced here in the garment district of Europe. Even at dusk and nightfall, the city works.

On this visit I see the city for the first time through the prism of the centenary. I think of what is; I think of what might have been. I go to the diaries of the radical publisher of the late Ottoman period, Sabiha Sertel, and her memoir. She writes at a time of a ruined Istanbul, before the War of Independence has restored that autonomy which is the prerequisite of dignity. She talks of a broken city, where the wealthy war profiteers who grew rich as the country was wrecked by World War I come face to face with the impoverished children of an Ottoman Empire that has fallen, and a Republic yet to be built.

> The Minister of the Navy signed an armistice treaty. Thanks to the treaty, the imperialist states have established themselves in key positions throughout the capital.
>
> Colonial soldiers from Senegal, India and Java patrol the streets in their diverse uniforms. Scottish regiments march around as if on an opera stage, playing their bagpipes and drums, their colourful, chequered kilts hanging to their knees. Along the Bosphorus, the occupiers' flags wave from the fortresses of Rumeli and Anatolia; the Turkish flag has been banished to the back row.
>
> In this time of mourning, only the Greeks still smile. They saunter about, playing the hurdy-gurdy. They sing, drink and carouse day and night, scorning their Turkish compatriots, who have been humbled by war. They tear women's çarşafs [headscarves] and attack young girls. No government imposes order, no police reins them in.
>
> The country has descended into the deepest gloom. Gone

*is the carefree Istanbul of before the war; streets seem nar-
rower, people seem smaller, faces are pale. The collapse of
the Empire weighs on everyone's shoulders. Civil servants
with stern demeanours, hodjas with their robes and sarıks
[turbans], workers, guildsmen – all pass over the bridge with
their heads hung low. For the first time in their history, the
Turkish people are experiencing the pain of losing their independence, and it cuts them to the bone.*

*Foreign officers survey people's homes. If they like a house,
they kick out the owners and move in themselves. Foreign
censors control the press, and only the papers that support
the British are published without interference. Capitalists of
minority origin cover the display windows in Beyoğlu with
adverts that read "Don't buy Turkish products". They openly
act as agents of foreign capital. The Turkish currency has lost
all its value; money changers stand on street corners, eager to
exchange it for foreign officers' dollars, pounds and drachmas.
The stores of Beyoğlu sport the flags of the occupying states,
and Greek-owned stores are guarded by Greek infantrymen
in pleated skirts, red fezzes and long, blue tassels. This is
Istanbul under Occupation. This is Istanbul, whose people are
bereft of identity and hope. It is a city lost amidst the ruins
of a shattered empire.*

How to write it now? How to write it today? Like any place of
such iconic proportions, Istanbul demands to be written about, or
at least you think it does, only to find yourself doing so and then
coming up short. The scale of the place leaves you small beside
it. You think you can capture it, like some almighty butterfly, but
instead wind up with a broken net and two magnificent wings
beating free from you.

I could write the smell of mackerel grilling on the decks of the
boats moored in the Haliç, their chefs in an Ottoman waistcoat and
hats embroidered with gold thread. I could write the ezan of Aya

Sofya and the Blue Mosque, as if these two beautiful buildings were calling out, were speaking back and forth to one another across the empty space of the old hippodrome.

I could write the call of the old man with a cart of hot simit to sell, those plaits of dough baked in a crust of sesame seeds. I could write the call of the man with the cart who collects a city's scrap metal, from photo frames to coat hangers and mangled cutlery. I could write the call of the man in a blazer who from his cart beside the bars of Beyoğlu sells popcorn, kernels rattling and popping in a tin drum atop a bed of glowing embers. On his face with its short moustache is the solemn expression of the working man who, for all the grit and humility of his years on these streets, has no doubt remained poor.

Istanbul is all of this. It is the sheet of cardboard laid out in the underpass and by the shopfronts in winter, so the street dogs sleep with a layer between them and the cold, cold ground. It is the trolleys loaded with the cucumbers, acur, that appear at harvest time and are sold on the streets in a writhing pile of green. It is the moment as you cross the Bosphorus by ferry, especially in spring and autumn as they come into the Bosphorus to calve, when dolphins break the surface of the water and swim beside the boat in what will always be the most joyful moment of public transport, as all the passengers' heads turn to follow the pointed arm of the child who first sees the fin and cries out excitedly, "Yunus!" It is this moment especially that makes me laugh inside, knowing that here is the most beautiful city in the world.

It is those boys pulling trolleys twice their height, filled with paper and card and plastic for recycling. It is the better jobs we will one day create for them. It is the plasters and bruised sinus cavities from the recent nose jobs and plastic surgery for which people come. It is the ageing, portly men from around the world, Arab to Latino and beyond, and the large pincushion of tiny red dots where they have had their hair follicles charged, so that for a few days in Istanbul they look strange, but for a lifetime afterwards it will be to them the place where they had hair transplanted and youth restored. It is the kids jumping in the Bosphorus upstream, then swimming out a few strokes and letting the current drag them down the strait to the next set of steps. It is the passenger who gets on at the middle of a packed, rush-hour bus, and whose travel card makes its way hand-to-hand through a score of strangers to be tapped for payment at the front of the bus, then travels back to its owner. It is the sound of the blind man walking with his cane – "Çakmak var, mendil var" – saying he has lighters and packets of tissues for sale, and the tap of the cane feeling out the kerb as he steps back up to the pavement. It is the speed at which the boys outside even the most self-absorbed and gentrified cafés jump to their feet and place a hand on each of his shoulders to guide him around the tangle of chairs and tables his cane is about to snag.

It is, perhaps most of all, an abundance of feeling. It is Melville, it is Milton and "greedily they engorgd without restraint". It is passions that in this century we are taught not to speak of nor to believe in. But still, you have to try. Outside the bar and bookshop near Galatasaray, a night more than a decade ago, where Ecem, with her raven hair, dark red lipstick, a long black coat and a beauty impossible to believe, walked up the day Hobsbawm died and said, "Well . . . the last column of Marxism has fallen." Only memories are immortal.

This is my city, but it is big enough to be your city too. This city has been so much to so many. It is the feeling I have on the ferry across the Bosphorus, at night and later into winter than I'd like, that I must nevertheless sit outside as the boat crosses the strait, even though it is cold, because I must be closer to it. I must be able to feel it properly.

But this is only the city itself, existing irrespective of you or me. There is also in these cities of such size and spectacle, which draw us ever back to them, something of ourselves that we leave there. How to write it though? So many years of visiting or living here, but this time passing through so briefly, conscious how quickly winter would be bearing down on me. How was everyone, *where* was everyone, as for a few days I put my bicycle to rest?

Some had left, had hightailed out as the world economy deteriorated into its latest twenty-year crisis, or the itch of living elsewhere had grown stronger. Gizem was a lawyer friend, a Bulgar-Turk whose family had left Bulgaria in the mass fear of ethnic violence against Turks that followed the collapse of the USSR. If that had been a sorry childhood dislocation, it at least left her with an EU passport she had finally used. Istanbul was her home, but these days she was making her way in Berlin. Nesrin meanwhile had been obliged to dispatch her Turkish passport all the way to Austin, Texas in order to set up a US tax number that would allow her to pay into the US system, a precursor to a future move she grew increasingly indifferent to. Four months later they sent the passport back from Texas, and curtly said the papers weren't in order. The papers *were* in order.

Turkish-Americans seemed generally to be plentiful and in good spirits. I found more than normal in the bars of Cihangir, a handful armed with foreign educations and determined to put that to work in Türkiye. They were clear-eyed at the challenges but enjoying life, and had spent time close enough to US domestic failure that they were under no illusions at the myth, still at large in many poorer countries, that the United States offered quality of life, freedom or democracy.

As always, people had brought others with them. I met an anti-vaccine Canadian, from the oil wastelands of Alberta, who had wanted to escape the pandemic controls back in Canada. Türkiye had been the first place open to him, but on arrival he discovered he actually quite liked it. I didn't think so much of the rationale that first brought him, but it was novel to find a Westerner moving to Türkiye because it offered greater liberty and had a common-sense government. Soon after arrival, he had met a woman from Istanbul. They were now officially married, the wedding was to take place the following week, and he was in no hurry to see the empty prairies and oil-stained derricks of Alberta ever again. I smiled at the story, for long ago I had realised that nothing I could ever write would represent a service to integration even half as great as the certainty that Westerners would keep on arriving in Türkiye and falling in love.

Others too were building new lives, though without so much privilege in their foundation. Omar, the chemist from Syria, who a decade prior had made his way to Istanbul and started an art space, had now settled and built it into a quite celebrated gallery. I still remember the day he learned his Damascus suburb had been bombed, and headed out to buy a drainage pipe, carpet and plywood to make a cat shelter for the café courtyard, as if he were determined to build life, to expand the world's capacity for a place called home, even if it was for a creature other than himself. Like others among the Syrian painters, sculptors and musicians who had formed a community there, he now had a girlfriend, and the gallery itself was on the culture circuit, hosting events in the Istanbul Biennale. As well as Syrians there were the exiles of the Egyptian revolution, and as successive US administrations set about "Maximum Pressure" sanctions intended to impoverish and distress the Iranian population to the extent that they would try to overthrow their government, many of Iran's bourgeoisie were also giving up their homes and turning to Istanbul. The more privileged among them scraped together the funds to buy a flat and the Turkish residency permit that came with it.

In all of this, it felt as though Istanbul was playing host to the remnant of the Arab uprisings, and if I felt ever more strongly that Türkiye could not be chided by the West, it was because in Türkiye now, building against the odds, were the youths and dreams and remnants of those movements, the revolutions that the West had already shot down once by supporting tyrants and putschists.

Some who hadn't stayed around demonstrated all too sadly the sanctuary of the country and of Istanbul. A friend of the gallery, a talented painter, had returned home to Idlib, the rebel-held province of north-western Syria still protected by the Turkish military. Life in Türkiye had become ever more precarious, and with neither funds nor support from the international community and Turkish opposition parties, it grew harder for the government to maintain any welcome. He'd returned to Idlib to see how it was and, in an erratic moment, had then taken a gun out to the countryside and killed himself. The gallery sold its collection of his canvases and sketches, raising a few hundred euros to send to his family in Idlib, a gift of sorts from the life he'd been so close to forming in Istanbul.

Against the tragedy and hardship, Palestinians as always seemed somehow able to show resilience. One friend had once come to Istanbul to escape the Israeli apartheid and its constant abuses. Gradually, she came to realise that for all its difficulties Palestine was home, the only place that she could be, and so after years of observing the Istanbul bar and café scene, she returned to open her own café in a small town just outside the fair Palestinian port city of Haifa.

For my part, I didn't know where I fitted. English was the lingua franca of Arabs, Iranians, Turks, Syrians and assorted internationals, but they saw the world differently from me. In Türkiye they enjoyed safety from the worst excesses of Western foreign policy, but growing up inside the West, I felt I recognised more clearly than they did the duplicitous harm our actions had created in their own countries. I loved their zeal for life and justice, their bohemian spirit, but the United States war machine and its sanctions mostly escaped their critique. Even if I maybe had a point, I struggled to communicate it, and so in the end I tried less. Their lives had already been so churned-up by events outside their control, and it was easy to see how US power might have represented a distant, unstoppable force. They had lived, witnessed and fled from things I could not imagine, and so who was I to judge?

Istanbul, with its Bosphorus ever flowing, fostered a kind and calming mix of acceptance and resistance. As always, I watched the scenes that defined the city and so the world, confident that even as the asteroid speeds towards earth to dispatch us into eternal night, somewhere in a backstreet of Tarlabaşı, downhill of Istiklal, a grandmother is stuffing mussels with rice cooked in black pepper. Her grandson has no permit to do so but is selling them from a wooden tray outside the metro, waiting to retreat out of sight at the phone call that says the cops are coming, and until then he is squeezing lemon over mussels as hungry punters fill their mouths. This. Into eternity, just this.

Gezi

But where to go and what to do in the city, when time is short and, despite having just arrived, I know I must soon leave? What should I show you in a city that contains so much, what would help you understand it? If before I spoke of adding layers of understanding, so that after we would simply be riding together, then forgive me, for Istanbul is a place of many layers.

Perhaps we should begin in the Zeytinburnu neighbourhood now with its many Afghans? The Aksaray neighbourhood with its long-distance bus station, where Uyghur and Kyrgyz have for many years opened their restaurants, shops and small cargo companies? The Greeks who still count this their home, the Sudanese of Darfur who made it theirs, or the farming cooperatives that feed a city from up near the third bridge at the Black Sea mouth? Maybe the new pier at Kabataş, the hub of a ferry network that also links Istanbul to the greater metropolitan area and Bursa to the south? The tunnel-boring machines that move day and night through the earth to connect the new airport to another new metro line, rescuing the arriving and departing tourists from the strangely meandering routes and suspicious meter readings of Istanbul taxi drivers? There is little in Türkiye for which I will not offer some defence, but, alas, all over the world, a taxi driver is a taxi driver.

If there is to be just one place though, this year in particular, it must be this one. Up the hill I go. I walk towards Gezi, because while 2023 marks a century of the Republic, it also marks a decade of Gezi, and both are beautiful and important events in the creation of Türkiye. It is a park I have passed repeatedly both before and since it became a political landmark in Turkish history. It is where I used to go running when I first moved to Istanbul. It is where I discovered it was also a cruising spot for gay men, when a man I thought was innocently helping me practise my Turkish turned out to be interested in more than just helping me practise my Turkish.

Gezi Park in central Istanbul was, it transpired in 2013, to be turned into a shopping mall, built in the key of an Ottoman barracks. Trees would have been felled, and although wider Istanbul has large forests and green stretches, particularly on the banks of the Bosphorus, lined as it is by almighty trees, many of the city's central districts are heavy with concrete apartment buildings and narrow streets. While in Ottoman times these streets would have held life and earth and plants and people, they have since been concreted and filled with cars. Near Gezi this is particularly so, and to lose that park to a shopping centre would have been an environmental crime against Istanbul, an affront to the life of the city.

Back in May 2013, in defence of the trees above, tents went up overnight as people camped in the park to stop the demolition. The call went out. More people came. The park filled. Two years earlier, Occupy Wall Street had birthed Occupy London, which set up a camp beside St Paul's Cathedral in lieu of its original target, the London Stock Exchange. The Arab uprisings against their dictatorships were alive and showing the world the meaning of courage, and everyone, everywhere, was saying the same thing: "Enough! Basta! Yeter!"

This global language of resistance settled quickly on a name for its task in Istanbul: Occupy Gezi. The tent encampment swelled, and while it started with a tree, soon it came to encompass many discontents. Environmental issues throughout Türkiye, women's rights, queer rights, socialism. A country for all its people. Crowds assembled to push back against police violence, excessive conservatism, political interference in people's lives and tastes. But counter-dissent began. People alleged that this was not about trees, that this was a "mob". "Çapulcu!" admonished Erdoğan. A rabble.

The rabble had strength though, momentum was with it. The word "çapulcu" was repossessed, and the çapulcu danced in the streets wearing their new name as a badge of honour.

It is true that by its peak it was not only about trees, but nor should it have been. Anyone who requests purity from a political movement is only masking their wish that it should fail, because nothing of political note was ever achieved without the making of common cause between different political groups, and only in pulling down our smaller divides do we topple the mighty ones. Leftists and Kurds and the pious, tired of the military and of Kemalist conservatism, together once voted in a new party called the AKP, just as the War of Independence required an alliance of every political leaning and ethnicity in all Thrace and Anatolia.

Such was the quest at Gezi: a just Türkiye for one and all. A tent city sprang up. Workers, businessmen, grandparents, students and football fans joined together with those who had gone first to defend the trees. A friend's friend, a woman in a red dress, was sprayed in the face with tear gas by some police thug, making Gezi solid gold media currency and, in turn, a global event. The movement spread, protest proliferated across Türkiye. Trade unions called a general strike. Actions on the ground took shape. There were reading libraries, yoga workshops, impromptu classes in socialist teaching. Mothers and grandmothers – hijabi women and Kemalists – joined hands in solidarity. Protest, as it does so often, built unity, while the police responded with confusion, and then brutality. Volleys of tear gas were fired. The onions that start so many of our meals were repurposed: placed inside plastic bags and passed between people, their vapours inducing tears to wash out of the eyes the pepper from the gas. A man knocked to the ground by the strike of a water cannon died of head injuries. Berkin Elvan, a young man from Okmeydanı, died when another police thug fired a tear canister at him rather than into the air.

In response, though, the people were not passive. Workers commandeered a digger from a building site and drove it through police barriers, reclaiming streets that protesters then held as part of a growing village. Elsewhere, repelled by crowds, police ran from their positions. Protesters ran for cover from a barrage of tear gas, happily bemused to find open to them the doors of an upmarket hotel. Overnight, protesters picked the lock of a TOMA, an armoured police vehicle. They drove it from its position, covered it in triumphant graffiti, then put it up for sale on ebay, marked "hardly used". From windows and balconies in support, the sound of pots and pans rang out.

A decade on, it is hard to make sense of what that moment truly was. While the protests went on to encompass many things, they were initially in defence of these trees, which above me wave in the wind. A gentle roar of leaves responds to my question of whether those protests were a success. If this question is purely binary – yes or no – then there is your answer. Or, put differently, there is the start of your answer.

Gezi Park was a victory because the rain still runs off the silver-green leaves of its trees when the thermal currents above the Marmara and Black Seas clash and storms beset Istanbul. It was a victory because at the time – unthinkable now – Gezi was a park surrounded on all sides by roads with the nastiest and most clogged of traffic. Today the cars are gone, hidden in underground tunnels, so that where once was traffic, people now stroll and gather, AKP voters swing prayer beads, and the municipality holds iftar meals to break fast during Ramadan. There is more space than before for that vital and most blessed of entities: the public, all of us.

Since then, Istanbul has seen more park space created or upgraded, more public spaces built, more trees planted and, gradually, pavements widened to combat the urban cancer of the car. In this respect, Gezi was one of those victories that is total but slightly unsatisfying, because although your opponent takes your point, they struggle to acknowledge that they have done so, or that your protest became their impetus. The legacy of Gezi is one that benefits not just Istanbul and Türkiye, but a global movement working slowly to liberate cities from cars and consumerism, so that instead we can simply be.

Gezi was a victory because it showed a limit: the limit to which a government in league with a rapacious private sector can push before there is a push back. Gezi was not a revolution, but it hinted that such was possible. The people are not silent. The government paid attention to this, though some demonstrators did not. I have heard friends a little younger than me, students at the time, say they are simply glad they saw it. Others wished that they could have lived in it forever, so sweet was that air: the dream – one that I have never known in Britain – that their country was theirs. Still others wished they'd never known it, for because of that dream, what followed was too sore a loss.

Of these responses, far and away the best is the first. Gezi is a park full of trees, yes, but since then it has become a stepping stone in the long, proud Turkish river of revolution. Gezi means that the country need today look back only ten years for a reminder that the state must listen to them. A reason for the decline that the Western democracies face is they have no recent stepping stones. 1963, the Civil Rights movement, is the closest for United States. Paris '68 for the French. The fall of the Berlin Wall in 1989 for Germany. And for the UK? How long it is since the British knew what it was not to be meek in the face of their regime, since they became a people who crave revolution so deeply they can no longer tell the real thing from its counterfeits.

All this is only one side, however, and one perhaps already familiar. I cheered it on but Gezi was not beyond critique. There was, as with any grassroots movement that gains success and global prominence, a lack of clear aims beyond the trees it was eventually successful in defending. An answer to the question "What do you people want?" was not immediately forthcoming. A forgivable weakness, but a weakness all the same.

Gezi, too, shifted. The spontaneous rush did become organised, idealist. It assumed the aesthetics of Paris '68 and was all the worse for it. The initial imperative shifted to the organised utopian dream. Utopian Dream™. Gezi became a cash-free village: no money was to change hands, there was to be no commerce, no capitalism. The street vendors of Istanbul, who sell corn, simit, chestnuts, were shooed away by those conducting their brave political experiment. Pizzas were delivered instead, doubtless paid for with plastic through a platform domiciled in the United States. Parents picked up the bills. The vendors and their carts were cast out of utopia, a cardinal sin because the first, immutable task of a revolution, anywhere on earth, is to unite working class and middle class. The first task of the powerful, equally, is to break this bond. You do not do it for them. You do not send away the vendors with their carts. Every conversation that takes place across this class dynamic is a revolution in itself, and the legacy of Gezi is durable in part because there were many such conversations.

Gezi was not for everyone. If it was meant for everyone, it didn't always know how to show it. The flags and nationalism of Gezi did not always know how to make Kurdish communities welcome. Much of its energy was as patriarchal as that one it went chest to chest with. Accounts told of observant Muslims, some wearing hijab, being buffeted in their vehicle by crowds of protesters, of feeling that the country they'd finally received a stake in, thanks to the AKP, was about to be snatched back. There can be no denying that a large part of the Turkish middle class, considering itself secular, often defined itself more by the second-tiering of Muslims, and Muslim women most of all. If the AKP grew belligerent and overly conservative, then that was perhaps because it had faced no less. The so-called secularists had set the tone, suggesting that young women going to university in hijab were a threat to liberalism, when clearly their freedom to do so was liberalism itself. It has taken the AKP in Türkiye, and arguably a generation of young Muslims worldwide, to make way for this understanding, by stubbornly clearing the climate of Islamophobia that upheld such discrimination. If the AKP rule itself went into overreach, then even in that may be a tough lesson for the Republican People's Party, known as the CHP, and its Kemalist top brass: that Türkiye is a country of the religious too, that nothing built on their denials is secular or sustainable, and never again should such illiberalism be attempted. It took the CHP many decades to learn this lesson against their illiberalism; the test of the AKP will be if they can learn theirs faster.

Questions reveal more than answers. Ten years on and there is cause for nothing but pride at the revolutionary youth of Gezi. Their demands manifest the importance of youth as described by Atatürk, but this emphasis on the importance of youth, of gençlik, is clearly understood among every political persuasion of Türkiye. In return it is the duty of youth to believe in their right to change everything, to change it all, to make history their own. This instinct is not one that a government can turn on and off at will, but it is – however hard to harness – an instinct that states must covet, for when the youth no longer believe that a country is theirs, when their political system disenfranchises them and their spirit is cowed into believing they have no stake in it, then, well, I am afraid your country is already dead.

Against such large ideas of history and revolution, a story painfully ordinary can often be just as helpful. Not so long ago I rented a flat, downhill of Gezi on the edge of Cihangir. One afternoon I spoke to the landlord, who owned the entire building, while he went about repairs in the flat above. He spoke English, this fashionable guy with a Western style: a small ear-piercing, a thin tattoo encircling his arm. He was a nice man and so I listened, neither sympathetic nor totally unsympathetic, as he lamented the fall in value of the building he had bought ten years earlier. Counting on his fingers, he rolled off the calamities that had befallen Türkiye in that time, each driving down the value of his property. On his thumb: "In 2016 we had this coup attempt." On his index finger: "Before that we had the airport attacks, by Daesh. People stopped coming." On his next finger: "I don't know if you saw this Gezi, like a riot, at the park." He pointed.

Inside I smiled, looking at this man so Western in his fashion, in his worldview and travel, but who when describing this event that I saw as important protest, and others as glorious revolution, referred to it as only a riot. Not because he had even one socially or religiously conservative bone in his body, but because the landlord will follow any religion or none: his favourite and only holy book are the deeds.

And if all this is how Gezi can be seen internally, then what of the rest of the world? How to read it from the outside? Gezi as a protest was a success: its demand for a new Türkiye swept the country. Government lost legitimacy. Police lost control. It was a democratic event and it retains that cherished label of "peaceful protest", but it would be a tall order to claim it was always peaceful. People fought back against the police, they erected barricades. When in 2011 police shot dead an unarmed black man in Tottenham and all London took to the streets in indignation, there was no doubt in the corridors of power, as with the landlord, what that "peaceful protest" was to be called: a riot.

It is impossible, too, to separate the fact that detentions following Gezi started happening only after Türkiye was hit by a coup attempt that blew up an entire wing of parliament, and saw men crushed under tanks driven by rogue army traitors. Detentions started happening after in Syria, unchecked, the US sent arms to separatist militants on Turkish borders. This is not a context in which Western states experience their "peaceful protest", and in that context, I would not like to see what a Western state would do.

If this is the context in which it is incumbent upon the outsider to read the events of Gezi, then now, ten years on, it is incumbent also upon Türkiye to separate Gezi from events that had nothing to do with it. There is so much more that I could say, but it is already beyond time that I left Istanbul. Away from this park and city so well documented, an entire country warrants every bit as much attention.

Sea of Marmara – 24 October

We slide out of port, out past the queue of boats waiting their turn in the Bosphorus. Grain ships and gas tankers and ocean liners stacked high with container units all sit at anchor. Sleepily I watch the city slip away until there is only open water punctuated by one or two lone fishing trawlers, their nets held by a crane arm at the stern. Lulled by the hum of the engines and motion of the boat, I fall in and out of sleep, disturbed by middle-aged women in long coats, handbags on laps. The only thing louder than the factory-settings ringtone on the first and last mobile phone they were ever bought is the volume at which they talk into it. "Biz denizdeyiz!" one shouts loudly into her handset. "We're on the sea!" And hat over my eyes, trying to doze, still it is hard not to smile.

This sea, separated from the Aegean by that passage through the Dardanelles, represents a key atrium in the heart of the Turkish state and its economy. In Istanbul, as well as in its satellite cities along the Gulf of Izmit to the east and Tekirdağ to the west, there motors around a third of the Turkish economy. To the south, in Bursa and Bandırma and Yalova, a string of smaller thriving cities prop up the economic belt above them. Across this region stretch highways and rail tracks, rolled out beneath smokestacks rising with the skyscrapers and central spans of suspension bridges. A third of the Turkish population lives in this greater region, and their numbers, combined with industry and a warming climate, now test the limits of the sea itself. In 2021, the waters of the Marmara were overwhelmed by a slick of so-called "marine mucilage" that carpeted the coast for weeks before disappearing just as quickly.

Sewage, fertiliser runoff and an excess demand upon the sea are a reminder of the limits of nature, of the need for Türkiye to make itself more geographically democratic, and to spread its economy and population across all its regions.

The Marmara region is also an outer chamber of the European economy. Were Türkiye an EU country, it would be its sixth largest economy – larger than the tax haven of the Irish economy, and the manufacturing economies of the Swedish or Czech states. The Turkish economy, skewed westwards as it is, means that the Marmara region alone has an economy four times the size of Bulgaria's. Bulgaria nonetheless joined the EU in 2004, even as Turkish accession soon after that began to stall. The Marmara economy is about the size of the Danish, and in all this lies a seldom-spoken truth about the Turkish path into the EU. For while Islamophobia fuels Western assumptions of a country too poor and too backward to join the EU, the reality is quite the opposite. The Turkish economy is not too small; it is too big. Türkiye is not too weak, but with some 10 million Turks already EU citizens, with its close relations to Germany and the German-Turkish community, for many in the European Union, Türkiye inside the EU has the potential to grow too strong. That the two entities would perhaps both enjoy greater global influence together is for now a narrow view, but one that a rapidly approaching future might yet favour.

I often consider my British-Turkish origins through the prism of the EU. Two countries both for now outside it, one by choice and the other enforced. One half of me granted the pseudo-privilege to leave, the other debarred from the pseudo-privilege to join. A British exceptionalism that thinks itself apart from Europe; a European exceptionalism that thinks itself apart from Türkiye. I recall some years ago, in the depth of the Eurozone crisis, asking a Turkish friend if Türkiye still wanted to join the EU. "I think soon the EU will want to join Türkiye," she replied. That confidence has diminished, but also gone is the idea that the EU is the arbiter of Turkish destiny.

I remember too the UK referendum campaign of 2016. How quaint it was to see the centrality that Türkiye gained in leaflets dropping onto British doormats. The Leave campaign alleged, with some exaggeration, that Türkiye and millions of Turks were on their way into the EU, and – once inside – would find their way to Britain. The Remain campaign counterclaimed that this was false, and, more to the point, the only way to ensure the Turks did *not* come to Britain was to remain inside the EU and block Türkiye's entry. In plain sight, what united the otherwise polarised camps of Leave and Remain was an imperative to keep the Turks out. They simply disagreed over how best to do so. And this was Britain; Britain which in Ottoman times argued against the break-up of the Empire, and under the New Labour of the nineties pushed for Turkish membership of the EU. Britain, arguably our closest European ally. Much could be written about how Muslims and Turks – the perception of them and obsession with them – have in fact taken over the Western mind to such an extent that the triumph of Islam, a full Reconquista, if such were being attempted, was long ago complete. But an announcement is coming through the speaker. The shore of Bandırma nears, the dock cranes and freight containers grow larger, we must disembark. There are kilometres to be ridden.

Bandırma

With the Bandırma port and coast appear the grain towers of a well-known confectionery brand, its name painted on the curved matt steel. To one side is the Erdek peninsula, dauntingly tall in its dark outline against a sky misty white with sun. A crowd of fishing trawlers line the dock, and again all along the headland above are the rotating turbines of windmills that power the industrial operations below.

As I prepare to disembark, a man maybe a little older than myself says hello and gestures to my loaded bicycle. He asks in hesitant English if I'm Turkish, to which I answer in Turkish, and return the question before he begins to talk of his previous journey by motorbike around the country, and the break he is now taking from his marketing job. I suspect his English is better than my Turkish, and we switch again as we walk off the boat together. He carries a dry bag and is dressed casually in a bodywarmer and trousers covered in pockets: the style of metropolitans around the world who prefer clothing and equipment that exceed the needs of their daily life. A sign of their preparedness for a life where more exciting things happen: I work in marketing, but inside, believe me, I'm a rock climber. He tells me he was in the US a while, studying. He asks if I've eaten, suggests food, and although the afternoon is drawing on, and part of me is eager to get moving and reach Çanakkale tomorrow, he's a nice guy, and I should be finding opinions of the country held by others, not only my own.

"I haven't eaten yet today," I think aloud.

"Me neither," he says, so we walk uphill from the port, agreeing that somewhere with a choice of stews and rice sounds good.

In a restaurant window a block away, we see blanched courgettes and minced lamb with aubergine. A moment later we are inside and watch our trays loaded with a plate of stew, a plate of rice, and another of salad. We carry our meals to the short tables and stools outside the restaurant. We have both taken an ayran, and both instinctively make satisfied sounds at our first sip of the yoghurt.

"I was in the US some time," he says. "California. I studied public policy at Berkeley. I guess the rest of the US is not like Berkeley. It's a hard place, I think. So I came back to Europe, to Copenhagen."

"I spent some time in the US," I say, thinking how to put it delicately, to let him know his opinions are safe with me. "I don't like it."

"It's brutal," he says.

"There's no love there," I add.

We break bread, nodding in agreement.

"I worry it's becoming more like that here," he says as I eat.

"In Türkiye?" I clarify, through a mouth of rice.

"Yes. That we are trying that model. More capitalism, the market, more religion."

"But here there is a social contract, and Islam is maybe part of that." I try to disagree gently. "I'm not sure it is like that in the US. There is more poverty there. Homelessness. More addiction. Violence. Here there is a society."

"It's true," he says. "Here there is a safety net. Even if it is your family and your community."

We take it in turns to speak and eat.

"My friend teaches at a private school here," I add. "Elite kids. He says the US appeal is wearing off. The young see the US more accurately now, what it's really like. Trump helped. They worry about shootings if they study there."

The drum of the street rattles beside us. The snap of men playing cards, a man pulling a trolley on solid wheels, its metal clattering.

"You vote here?" I ask, and he nods.

"So you did your askerlik?" The Turkish word, renowned everywhere, for "military service".

He shakes his head.

"Not even the short one? Four weeks or whatever?"

He shakes his head again, and in this I learn something of his class background. That's quite a chunk of money, even in euro terms, to get out of it entirely. There again, university in California perhaps already dispelled any doubts I might have had there.

"I regret not doing it now," he says. "My friends all say that the main thing they got from it was a feeling of being grateful."

"Grateful for what?" I ask.

"For what you have. Because army life is very simple. So you appreciate what you have. And even after it, you appreciate things more."

"I can imagine that," I say, before returning to the original part of my question. "So who do you think you'll vote for next year?"

This question is asked after the application of numerous filters: we are speaking English, he has studied social sciences at a Western university, he lives outside Türkiye. As such, I can pinpoint with a degree of accuracy the epicentre of not just his own political views but also his entire family's political views.

"I don't know," he says. "My mother says she appreciates how AKP created all this public transport the last ten years in Istanbul. She accepts the CHP would not have done that. Like they expected your vote. They were complacent I think."

"That's exactly what they were," I agree. "But I think it's changing with CHP. Like they respect voters more. They are more respectful of Kurdish voters. They know it's OK for women to wear hijab. They got better. They know they need to make a real difference in people's lives."

"Yes," he says, then pauses uncertainly, like he's about to say something important. "But I think I would probably vote HDP." He pauses again and adds:

"It is important we get Demirtaş out of jail."

He looks at me, as if he's just confessed something. Let me bring you up to speed.

*

HDP was the Halkların Demokratik Partisi: Peoples' Democratic Party. It was an overtly socialist-leaning political outfit that from its inception had an unswerving policy to advocate for a peace process between the Turkish state and Kurdish militant groups. With a commitment to the peace process, the militants could lay down arms. With a commitment to the view that there was no need to redraw borders for some idea of a Kurdish state, that all could be equal, fulfilled citizens inside Türkiye, the state could rest easy. Being left-wing and in favour of diplomacy as the only way towards peace, the HDP had suffered the same fate as that political tradition globally: they were decried by the state and helpful media as terrorists and terrorist-sympathisers. With militant Kurdish separatism erupting across the border during the Syrian civil war, backed carelessly by the United States, the Turkish state had decided it couldn't simultaneously have an ascendant pro-Kurdish democratic voice within the country *and* an ascendant Kurdish militancy without. Demirtaş had ended up in jail, and we did need him out, for his true crime was to be a large-hearted and charismatic leader of the sort Erdoğan was watchful of. Much like Sinn Fein and the IRA in Britain, some old connections between HDP and the PKK might have existed, but the former was necessary to engage the latter and help to represent Kurdish regions, so that they might see some of the development that the rest of the country had enjoyed since the new millennium. There was no reason for Demirtaş to be in jail, something that had been achieved by an act of political clumsiness when the CHP agreed to a law lifting criminal immunity for elected representatives, in the mistaken belief it would take down some AKP ministers for corruption. Unlike Demirtaş, those guys proved untouchable.

*

Across the table I see my man shift a little, as if his principles oblige him to tell me this part of who he is, but he is unsure how I'll react. I may be one of those diaspora types who has never lived in the place itself and so instead clings to every stitch in the flag's hem.

"Yeah," I reply, "if I were voting. I'd probably vote HDP." I pause, decide to make the conversation more interesting. "Or AKP."

He does a quick double-take, smiles a little that he needn't have worried. He's surprised at the combination of the two, but I'm safe.

"We do need Demirtaş out of jail," I say, "and we need the HDP in politics so that party doesn't have to be reinvented every decade and start again."

He rolls his eyes, "BDP, HADEP . . . there were so many. But I'm surprised you say HDP or AKP."

I haven't thought this through. In truth, talking to a guy who went to Berkeley and who I could have guessed was HDP, I've confessed to more than he has.

"I just think AKP do really want to move the country forward. It's like your mum said, about public transport. I think their economic policy is right too. Social spending, public investment, wage increases. I don't want the CHP doing whatever Western banks ask them to do. I worry CHP is too interested in Western approval. And I don't accept this idea that the West is concerned with Turkish democracy, or genuinely cares about Turkish people. They're worried that Türkiye is asserting itself more now, acting more independent, in its own interests."

He nods. Looks like he might genuinely agree.

"And I have this nostalgia for, you know, Ottomanism. When you look back at what's happened to Iraq, in Palestine. I think it was all better before. I think it could all have been avoided. And I think it's good Türkiye took four million refugees from Syria. That was the right thing to do. That was humane."

He nods. "It was that many?"

I'm almost surprised he doesn't know this figure. "Yes! Maybe three and a half million from Syria. Then Afghans. Iranians getting away from sanctions. Ukraine, Russia, Iraq. The West made war on all of our borders. It's everywhere. It's like refugees are five per cent of the population now. So many people who are traumatised. It's good that they were welcome here, even if it is difficult for the country."

"Yes," he agrees, "but I worry he wants to give these people the vote now. And they'll vote for him. Because they are grateful. I don't know. It feels transactional to me."

Damn, but if there wasn't a more valid reason to vote for someone.

"Yes," I say diplomatically, "I've heard that reasoning before."

And I have, though only ever from CHP types, those liberals anointed by Westerners and thereafter free to be as illiberal as they like – refugees welcome . . . right up until they start forming opinions of their own, getting ideas, putting on airs. I wonder whether or not to continue, decide to do so.

"But these people are not safe in Syria. They are not safe being sent back. So they should stay. And voting is political participation, which has to be a good thing. I don't know. Scotland changed voting laws to let asylum seekers vote, and that was seen as progressive, and I think that's a good idea. So I'd feel I was a hypocrite to think differently here about Syrians."

"That's true," he agrees as we make ready to leave. The conversation has run its course and only the gravy of the mince is left on the plate. We've had about as much conversation as a passing meeting will allow.

"AKP, though," he concludes, "they're getting flabby, you know. They have some people who are corrupt. They don't do anything. Change is good for this."

"Yes," I agree, "change is good. You need the mechanism to work."

We both smile. As if this is a fair resolution to reach, the best we could have hoped for. We finish our meals, both suck the juice from the remaining lemon resting on the edge of our salad plate. I need to be in Çanakkale by the end of tomorrow. He wants to reach before dark the village where he's spending his city retreat. At the same time we realise that in an hour of talking we haven't introduced ourselves.

"My name's Erdem." He sticks out one hand and picks up his dry bag.

"Emre," I reply, one hand on my bicycle and the other reaching for his.

We shake hands, eyes meet, express thanks for our conversation. And we are gone.

Bandırma to Lapseki – 25 October

Out of Bandırma the sense of industry continues. There are more grain silos, cement works, refineries. Once again, everything is flanked by turning wind turbines. On a far hillside the earth looks serrated and a deep marine blue, so I guess that what I am seeing are solar panels that face the sky. An unceasing convoy of trucks occupies the road, day and night, as constant as the second hand of a clock.

The city limits are lined with new apartment blocks, more modern than the small properties in brick, concrete, tin, with some plants in the garden, that used to be thrown up on the edges of towns and cities, but also more suburban and bourgeois. The older dwellings are still visible, charming to those who don't have to live in them, and need only romanticise someone else's simple life. Erdem's fear is also realised: the US model or its idea of aspiration is evident. Some of the apartment buildings are gated, with a look of high security that is alien to Turkish daily life, in a place where people do not fear one another in the fashion of the US. On one of the new developments, still unsold, the offer, the lie-cum-promise, bears the name Elit Apartment, and it occurs to me that Türkiye has had to import the English word "elite".

As I ride out of Bandırma, two fighter jets roar over the city, rolling together in simulated battle as they go. The sound of their engines tearing at the peace of the countryside is an addition I could do without, but their passage through the blue sky seems to resemble the course the country is now on, hurtling forwards on a trajectory to which it has total commitment, and from which it feels like there is no going back.

I eke out the last of the daylight, wringing it like water from a cloth, conscious of November coming, days shortening. I covet the kilometres under sunlight, a precious form of riding. If you could have shown me then what the breaking of December would bring, I would have hurried all the more.

From a short bridge crossing the highway, I watch a dusty orange sunset pressed down by the blue of first night. The highway cuts between two hilltops, splitting them as the jets did the sky, and one by one into the horizon the trucks keep up their convoy. A minaret stands silhouetted in the village beside the road, where on the asphalt arrows indicate the lanes. Like everything else they have only one direction: forward.

In the main square of the village, a köfte restaurant's sign gets my hopes up, but the place has since closed down and been shuttered. Two men sitting in a large tea garden sip glasses of çay, and when I ask after food they point to the far side of the mosque. I ride in that direction, passing the large steel tanks of milk being pasteurised next to a line of milking sheds that look like the village's main business. Ahead there is a light on in a window, a tiny tray of coals, tended by a man while his daughter plays. Wearing glasses and a pink headband, she runs around and talks to herself as, arms spread and knees up, she flattens herself against the restaurant wall and pretends to climb it. The chef welcomes me. There is rice. There is chicken. There is lentil soup. It is a good list. I order all three.

We talk as he brings my food, asks where I'm going. He wears glasses, has tattoos on his arm, a polo shirt and a nice pair of trousers. I ask if he's from here.

"I was in Istanbul. Twenty years. But everything there is so expensive. I was a chef anyway, in Kadıköy. So I started doing that here." He nods back inside, his eccentric daughter still pressed at the wall, mid-climb.

"My child is happier here too, she likes it. Last year business was good. Inflation this year. Not so good."

"This was your memleket?"

He nods. "Originally. So I came back."

Another customer arrives, goes inside to wait.

Chef points to the bike. "Where do you stay?"

I point to the bag. "I have a tent."

As he goes back to his kitchen and customer, he gestures at the mosque beside us. "Sleep in the cami. In the garden. If you want."

Hunched over the bowl I drink my soup. Perfect seasoning. I slide the bowl out and plate in. I eat my chicken. Perfect seasoning, perfect tenderness. Here in this small town is the first of many examples of how a food culture should be judged not by the best meal you can find and how far you travel to it, but by how hard it is to find a bad meal. Michelin guides and the French have it back to front, and in Türkiye bad food is all but an impossibility. Here in Sinekçi, with only one restaurant and no competition since the other went bust, still this chef makes sure everything is cooked to perfection, because how else would you cook it?

In the hour I sit there, the chef comes and goes. He cooks, then steps out to a motor scooter with a pannier. He jumps on the kick-start and takes off with a *pap-pap-pap-pap* of the exhaust into the night. The restaurant door is left wide open, and I consider how his business model of small restaurant with local delivery depends on his being able to leave his premises unattended. All around, trust circulates.

Beneath a quince tree in the garden of the mosque I set up my small tent, climb straight into it. After nights spent inside in Istanbul, I am alert again to the noises outside. There is a heavy thud next to me, a clumsy footfall coming my way. Strangers, certainly. And then I realise, only a quince falling from its branch. I sleep. I wake to a dog, barking at having found my tent. Next morning I'll see him as he picks around the bins with an almost guilty look in his eye, as if he knows he overreacted. But now, after dark, the arrival

119

of this strange shape is all that matters to him. Lying awake, I can hear his bark; loud, right over me. I can hear the size of his lungs. Deep, large lungs. A larger dog than I'd like, calling out to all the other dogs, warning that something's up. Over the years I suppose I have come to understand a little of dog, and know he is barking a version of: *Gather now, or, mark my words, it will drive us out.* From the other direction, a small dog yaps support, but a fence intercedes. I consider opening my tent and throwing a quince, decide against it. Let the thing make noise. I'll be gone in the morning.

Sinekçi to Çanukkale – 26 October

The roadsides of the country open to me, their asphalt like the long and singular page of the only report I trust. The morning is cool, and the heat of midday steals up on me. I remember that these are still the hot months of the year; that I have been careless with my time and soon will be caught on the skirts of a mountain range in the afternoon sun. Beside the road are fields, the crops harvested. On the road itself a few dry aubergines have fallen from carts, each a sad loss at today's prices. In Istanbul, people are dismayed that aubergines have become expensive, it is a grievance that eclipses all the rest, and explains that these are strange times.

Sights familiar from my first rides in Türkiye return to me, written above the truck cabs and trailers. *Allah korusun.* Allah forbids that something bad happen to this journey. *Maşallah* is also common, the word and sentiment behind the well-known evil eye in blue glass, and its call to Allah to watch over something incredibly precious. Normally a baby or a child, but here a truck, and before I reach the eastern border of the country, a few gentle souls, talking to me as I ride, will utter the word as they pass me and find out where I have ridden. "Maşallah." It is not that these sentiments are especially profound, but rather that even the everyday of Türkiye has a spirituality to it, a presence as unmistakable as the road itself. Republican motifs also appear in some of my vehicle companions: Atatürk's face and *Ne mutlu "Türküm" diyene.* Happy is the one who can say "I am a Turk".

In a large town I stop and drink coffee, the smell of which attracts a pair of wasps to my cup. Opposite me and the wasps is a bust of Atatürk, on a plinth in one of the town's main squares. I am so used to this sight that it almost warrants no mention: it is as obvious as breathing, and the fact that I barely notice it makes me question what else essential to understanding the country I am neglecting to share with you. I talk to the waiters, and faced with the regular dilemma of speaking Turkish inexplicably well for a foreigner, or inexplicably badly for a Turk, I opt for the former and accept their praise, in so doing also saving myself the story of my parents' marriage some half-dozen times a day.

The mountains I crest are perfect – forested in pine, rolling high. There are beehives in filing cabinets below me, the occasional ploughed field and age-old Anatolian oaks that must have seen so much, whose green acorns are scattered round them, like marbles rolled out on the bronze earth. An eagle sits on a road sign. I watch it out of the corner of my eye so as not to startle it, catching myself just as I am about to turn my head.

Across the misty mountaintops is peace, tender and precious peace, though precious all the more because it came close to being lost. In these hills are gold deposits that are unusually close to the surface and so unusually easy to recover, so long as you first fell the trees, break open the earth and rinse it with a cyanide salt solution to separate the gold. I see all this as I ride, cursed – not for the last time – with the habit of seeing politics in nature, even if that is perhaps sometimes only as it should be, and how nature is preserved. The so-called "right" to mine these mountains was bought by a Canadian mining company, and the hills remain pristine before me because the farmers and villagers of these hills protested. Because they blocked roads, because they refused to move. The city types of Istanbul, who come to these hills for their retreats and to replenish a little of their urban-blasted wellbeing, heard the concerns of the rural people, and in that perfect union of city and country, where good things happen because those from different walks of life walk a moment together, the Turkish government conceded. They listened to the democratic expression of an outraged population and revoked the mining licence, protecting these perfect Anatolian hills from the Canadian miners.

At the time of writing, though, this story is not over. The Canadians are taking the Turkish state through the courts of arbitration, attempting to seize – not from these particular hills, but from all Turkish taxpayers equally – a billion euros in lieu of what they feel they were denied. This may be but one small instance of it, but the story shows how it is often only when a state learns how to say no to Westerners – when it moves to protect its resources from mining, when it speaks of a free Palestine – that Western concern for that state's democracy becomes most pronounced. With those states most adept at silencing dissent, signing over resources and toeing the line, the West knows how to get along just fine.

Into the yawning heat of the afternoon I ride, so hot that my mind begins to soften. I should have bought another bottle of water on the way out of that last town. I stop at the roadside. I have a few more biscuits in my handlebar bag, possibly a mouthful of water for each of the – I count – four dry cookies. Nevertheless, right now, a banquet. I revive a little, return to pedalling. When I say that I return to pedalling, I mean it. My pedalling right now is constant. As I write, I realise that where so far I have translated Turkish into English, for a time I must translate Bicycle into English.

A suspected break in my freehub has destroyed that infinitesimally small and yet crucial part of a bicycle that allows you to freewheel, particularly relevant on descents. Unless I keep tension in the chain by pedalling, then the chain jumps about violently in an effort to escape the sprocket turning under it. So now I have to pedal continuously, if just to move the chain. There comes a grinding sound of bad mechanics – somehow delicious, like scratching an itch – whenever I stop. I tried to repair this developing fault in Greece, but they said it was fine, and like a lazy fool, though I knew it was not, I left it and went and sat in a café instead. I throw in this mechanical detail only because it informs events up ahead.

The road winds on. I sweat, but from the sea comes a breeze of winter, of the north, that chills me. And so I keep on my shell and sweat some more. Salt runs into my bleary eyes. All temperatures are imperfect, you just choose the least imperfect. Small semicircles of blue appear through the trees as the Sea of Marmara narrows behind them, closes into the Dardanelles Strait. I glimpse it now and then between high mountain bends in the road. And I am tiring. The days in Istanbul have cost me my condition. I take it easy, no hurry, just keep the wheels turning.

Soon enough, a couple of buildings appear up ahead: some shaded benches, large plastic boards in red and white that advertise an explosion of ice creams and prices, dispatched to Anatolia and roadsides around the world by a multinational conglomerate. An old man comes over to me. Bald, golden head and happy round belly. In plastic sandals he leads me to his storeroom filled with decades of stuff: old newspaper, rolled-up carpets, crates, oil cans, rugs laid on top of the deep freeze to help keep the chill inside. Grade A clutter. Three freezers are either broken or switched off to save energy until business picks up again. Together we go through the frost and ice crystals of a working freezer. I choose my ice cream and he brings down the lid of the cold trunk, replaces the sides of cardboard and rugs over the top to conserve every kilowatt. He follows me back to the clearing in front of the shop; a square of old picnic benches with used glass bottles as ashtrays in their centre. I sit with my first ice cream, wondering which will be my second. He sidles up to the adjacent table, pulls the material of his trousers up over his knees, and heavily takes a seat. It is one of those moments where I'm reminded of my inner Westerner: I'd like to sit alone, but Türkiye knows only community, company. I remember a family friend visiting his sister-in-law, an academic in London. He said how nice it had been to travel on a London bus, where nobody talks to anyone, while in Türkiye everyone wants to know your business, wants a piece of you and conversation is non-optional. It's funny, the things we romanticise simply as a result of not having them.

The patron and I talk. We exchange where we're from and our

purpose. He opens mostly for the summer; two more weeks and he will shut for winter.

"Who comes through here?" I ask.

"People like you, travelling. Istanbulites. Truckers. Tourists."

"Are there more people now, with the new bridge?"

"Nobody is using the new bridge," he says. "The ferry is cheaper."

"The price for crossing is too high?"

He nods. "Maybe others are using it. Maybe foreigners."

"Türkiye is not so rich right now," I say gently.

A belly laugh. A sigh. "Maybe in the palaces Turks are still rich, but the people are poor."

I eat my ice cream, pondering what natural socialists Turks are. I think of what to say, opt for the big picture.

"Yeni yüzyıl geliyor ama." But a new century is coming.

"Evet." He nods, gives a chuckle at my knowing this.

"Maybe the second century will be better than the first. Easier," I offer.

"Evet." He smiles, not without optimism. It is, after all, easier to be optimistic than pessimistic, because optimism is the path of least resistance, and for all their love of melancholy, Turks are, I'd say, optimists.

A man walks over to us from an adjacent house. He has seen that the late-afternoon gathering has begun. It is a couple of hours now since the morning gathering finished, so why not? He hears from the patron that I am from England. His face lights up. His phone comes out. Right in my face appears another face. "Oğlum!" he calls out. His son! I have known this man but seconds and his son is now looking at me. "In Fulham!" Ah. I'm not sure what to say, so tell the truth.

"I don't really like Fulham."

He doesn't mind. Puts up three fingers. This isn't about Fulham.

"He owns three cafés. In Fulham!"

I laugh. Well done that lad. Dad scrolls through photos, shows another photo. Red-bound. Passports.

"British citizen!"

"What's the other?" I peer. "Croatian?"

"Evet, evet . . . Croatian! Many years there. My son," six fingers up, "he speaks six languages. Smart child."

And he beams as I smile. The pride in this man could light the night.

1915 Çanakkale Köprüsü

Riding west, I think of Türkiye, the poor country, as across the top of old wrecks in a boatyard I see the uprights of the bridge come into view. It is now the longest suspension bridge in the world, having surpassed the previous record-holder in Japan. From Anatolia to Thrace it stretches, meeting the Gallipoli peninsula and continuing on towards Greece, Bulgaria and Western Europe. Whatever the storekeeper's remarks, some are certainly saving time by using the bridge. I see the shadows and shapes of trucks driving over its five-kilometre length, with its central span of 2,023 metres, which you must assume was also approximately the necessary distance for the span, but was certainly chosen to honour the centenary year in which I write this book. The shop owner suggested it was little used, but it's possible that was only the healthy scepticism of the Turkish public, bedfellow to the unhealthy scepticism of the Turkish public. People are always eager to give you a contrasting view, to let you know that they are in possession of some secret knowledge that without them would be hidden from you. Or perhaps, more simply, it is a sampling error: those not using the bridge were those who stopped for an ice cream en route to, or waiting for, the ferry. They explained why they were not using the bridge, bemoaning its price. Those who used the bridge were never in Lapseki for questioning because they were on the bridge, and gone.

Whatever the truth, there is something else to consider. The bridge may save its drivers and passengers and freight a handful of hours, but in Türkiye those hours of labour remain cheap. For now, at least, those hours will cost less than the bridge tariff. I recall a conversation from far away, a sunny afternoon in Astoria Park,

Queens, with Begüm, a scientist who was waiting to take up a new job in New York. I asked about the prospects in Istanbul, her home city. She said there were no jobs there, then corrected herself. "There was one, at Boğaziçi. But only one, and the university rector," she rolled her eyes, "he will pick his favourite."

As the bridge grows nearer, magnificently tall, its red arches silhouetted by the setting sun, I feel a connection between its usage and a Turkish scientist choosing instead to work in the US. Both point to the need for Türkiye to enter its next phase of development, the added-value phase, where the hours saved by a bridge are worth comfortably more than the tariff for crossing it. The country can continue to find efficiencies in making basic goods and sending them faster to markets further away, but there are limits to both the value of this growth and how much it can ultimately expand.

Beneath me on the waterfront, a man prepares to push out the small rig of floating pontoons on which he will farm mussels in the shallows. A tractor delivers its load of sawn branches to the baker for his oven. A shepherd leads his flock, dogs bringing up the rear, down a dusty track with the occasional clank of a bell from around an animal's neck. Written in spray paint on an old concrete hut is *kurbanlık koyun* with the number to call if you need a sheep for sacrifice at Eid al-adha, Kurban Bayramı. All through the country, families will cook the meat and what they do not eat will be distributed to the poor. And up ahead, over all this, is the world's longest suspension bridge, all five kilometres of it. I long for all this to coexist, for Türkiye to develop and then share the profits of a more prosperous economy, but never at the expense of those who farm and work the land and seas.

On the approach roads of the bridge as I ride by, I see workers labouring among bare-steel rebar, metal waiting for its concrete in supports still being completed. On the far Gallipoli shore, wind turbines turn in the dusk. On the near shore, where the bridge begins, a hospital has been built. In its shadow is a new secondary school. Looking out at the bridge from their classrooms, I wonder what the students think of the country taking shape in front of them.

Çanakkale – 27 October

As I said, we have a mechanical problem developing. I have now been pedalling non-stop for two days. The freehub is done-for and in need of resolution. I continue to curse the mechanic in Selanik who said it was fine. Part of me has considered constant pedalling all the way to Armenia – I have got used to it after all – but I have no idea of the descents up ahead and I will come to be grateful that I dismissed this ridiculous temptation. Now in Çanakkale, I cover dead kilometres around the city, acting on bad recommendations of bike shops that can assist, riding south to a suburb, past the smell of fish and the soft white steam billowing out from the chimney of a tuna-canning factory. Finally I head back to the city, with nobody able to help, and most not even sure about the nature of the problem. The many bicycles of this small, flat, relaxed seaside don't often have their freehubs ridden through. In fairness this one has done Britain to Türkiye a few times, London to Paris many times, been once to Berlin, made a couple of laps of the UK and one of Palestine. May this hub's be the last death at Çanakkale and in the service of the Republic.

As morning turns to afternoon there comes a final recommendation in which I instinctively have no hope. I make my way to the suggested store with bikes outside, including an expensive-looking downhill bike with full suspension, which could be seen as encouraging, but in reality bikes such as this are found all over the world, ridden only around town and with their owners clueless if anything goes wrong. Owning the bike shop itself, sadly, is no insurance against this. In the doorway of the shop stands Egemen. He gives a nod of hello, then turns back to a child's scooter, squats down in front of its handlebars and goes on repairing the steering.

When I stand there a moment longer and turning at the crank, Egemen gets back to his feet and walks down to me and the bicycle. It is Friday noon, and the shop is opposite a mosque, where the ezan is calling in Friday prayers at volume. Although the grumble of my rear wheel when I lift it off the ground to spin is far from quiet, Egemen and I wait for the minaret to fall silent before I do it a second time and he looks at it enquiringly. He cradles his stubbled chin. I point at the cassette, the sprockets: "These are new." At the chain: "New." And then at the hub: "Inside," I say. "Freehub," I say in English.

"I think a new freehub is necessary," I conclude.

Egemen waves at other bikes. "I can't do it now," he says.

He gets up from a perfect mechanic's squat, the squat of one who spends hours, days and weeks in that position. He goes into the shop, rummages in a box, comes back out with an old freehub.

"We could try it," he shrugs, offers, "but later. In an hour?"

I nod gratefully. This is the first person even to understand what a freehub is, and it says something of Türkiye that a mechanic asks apologetically that I should wait an hour before he does a not-trivial repair to my bike.

"No problem. Later. I'll go for food," I say. "Back in an hour."

He gives a thumbs-up, returns to the scooter, squats beside it.

An hour on and my bike is in the stand, back wheel out and between Egemen's knees. A chain whip is beside him on the floor, the cassette is off, but the largest Allen key beside him doesn't fit inside the freehub to remove it. On top of that, the spline on the spare freehub, which the cassette slides down and onto the hub, is visibly different from mine and so – like trying to open a door with the wrong key – the hoped-for swap will not work. Unperturbed he goes to his bench, gets a flat piece of metal that looks like a worn technical instrument. Egemen places this into the grooves inside the body of the freehub and tries to unscrew it. The narrow end of his tool is too narrow – it slips – and the broad end too broad. I sit back and wonder if perhaps it's over already. There is no spare part, and we haven't the tool to take my hub apart.

I am familiar enough with hubs to know that inside it are springs that push out small metal paddles – pawls – that intersect the hub so that the sprocket doesn't have to turn when the wheel does. This is what allows freewheeling. And so, as we crouch together in the shop, I do see roughly what Egemen sees, although most of me now believes that the bike shops in Izmir are the only option. On the hills ahead, steeper than I yet know, I will learn that to turn the pedals all the way to Izmir would be impossible. Egemen moves to the back of the workshop and gets out an angle grinder. Never a good sign. With a screech its stone-cutting disc comes up to speed, and a tail of sparks flies across the workshop as he puts the disc to his metal instrument, in order to narrow the broad end that would not fit inside my freehub. Intrigued but doubtful, I still feel gratitude that his commitment to my hub is such that he will irrevocably alter his tools. He comes back to the hub. Still too broad. Angle grinder screeches. Sparks. It fits. Something in this commitment to fix the thing, from our society of throw away and buy new, strikes me as almost eccentric, quixotic. He sizes up the task, possessed of that certainty of purpose that is either mad or a sign someone knows exactly what they're doing. Returning from the angle grinder, his adapted tool now fits the grooves in my hub. Egemen leans in. Pushes with all his might. Without the hub giving an inch, his tool slips, throwing out a spark of its own and a whiff of smoke, like a flintstone. He pushes again with all his might, breath held. And again. Finally, a deep cracking sound shoots out as one fused piece of metal breaks back into two separate parts, and as the freehub opens Egemen makes a sound of ecstasy that really belongs somewhere other than a workshop. I am beginning to sense that he can see the insides perfectly in his head, like a technical drawing. Egemen has a method.

We talk as he works. On the wall is a framed, embroidered prayer from the Quran. A photo of Egemen in green military fatigues, a barracks. Snow. I ask if this was his askerlik. He nods. In Ankara. There are small plastic and metal plates with his rider numbers for the races and competitions in which he has ridden. As he begins to look at the bearings in the wheel, his cat pads through the oil and tools. Bit by bit, Egemen takes everything apart. Inside are small metal washers, but one has been steadily mangled by use, disintegrating within the hub and impeding movement. This freehub has done its time. I peer inside the grease and metal and see the sheen of steel ball bearings: the essential image of industry. I spot a piece of debris, like a grain of twisted steel. I point to it and Egemen gives a sharp intake of breath, uses tweezers to pull it out, then removes the corresponding pawl from its spring. "This," he says, "it's this."

The paddle is broken on one end. It has a chipped tooth, so can no longer engage to allow the wheel to turn without the cassette. Egemen lifts out the debris and resets those pawls that aren't broken, leaving three rather than the initial four.

"Three's enough?" I ask.

Egemen smiles at me. "Don't worry. DT Swiss hubs only have three."

And my trust is complete.

As Egemen begins to reset bearings that refuse to stay in position, a middle-aged woman appears brightly at the door holding a bag.

"Merhaba!" she says loudly.

Egemen's head doesn't move and as if on autopilot he says hello back.

"Merhaba an-ne."

He turns to me with a kindly look of explanation. "Annem." My mum.

She goes to work with as much purpose as her son, only hers is the work of a mother, which in Türkiye, no matter how old the offspring, is never truly done. From her bag she pulls out three hurma, keki fruit, in their thick and waxy orange skin, pinched together by the barbed remains of their stems.

"Look! They're ready," she says, half to Egemen, half to me and anyone who'll listen. Egemen takes out bearings that jump to his small magnet, and his mother disappears to a tiny scullery and cooking space at the back of the workshop. Her permed hair and smiling, lipsticked mouth reappear from around the door frame to say, presumably of the hurma, "When they are ready they are very good." She disappears again.

Egemen smiles and shakes his head, replacing bearings in the bed of grease. "Annem," he repeats to me, like this is just the way she is.

A few minutes later she is back, the hurma peeled, sliced and lying soft on a plate, each piece of fruit with a cocktail stick in it. On another plate are biscuits. "Eat, eat!" She smiles and I enjoy the hurma while Egemen, squatting with the wheel and its open hub, gestures that he has no hands free. His mum leans down and takes a biscuit, Egemen turns his head, and she places it whole into his mouth.

I smile. "Your son is a very good man."

She takes him by the shoulders. "Oğlum! Oğlum!" she says. "My son!"

As he works, she cups his head in her palm, cheek full of biscuit, as if even after all this time she can't believe he's real.

"Everyone in Çanakkale says this! Every bike shop sends people here."

Egemen nods, almost wearily. His mum turns to me, phone out. I know what's coming now: photos. She tilts the screen to me.

"Bak! Look! This is Egemen's sister. My daughter." She keeps scrolling. "And this is his sister, and this is Egemen's wife." Mum looks round at me.

"Beautiful, no?"

I nod. She is beautiful. Egemen smiles, as if he knows. Superficial as it might be, Egemen deserves nothing but beauty.

"Where's your family?" she asks.

"Ingiltere," I answer.

"Brothers? Sisters?" Important stuff.

"Anne!" says Egemen, trying to stop the inquisition, but just as night follows day, some things cannot be stopped. His mum realises she's forgetting herself, cuts to the chase.

"Where's your mum?"

"Ingiltere."

"Your dad is in England?"

My least favourite question on earth.

"He died."

Her face drops. She looks almost as devastated as me. The one thing that in Türkiye always atones for the unwelcomeness of the question is that the emotion is somehow shared, despite our having just met. Still, though, unfortunate as death might be, she must go on. These aren't just formalities. As a mother she needs to know me, the human, every bit as much as Egemen as a mechanic needs to open the freehub.

"When?"

"Anne!" calls Egemen. She ignores him.

"Ten years ago."

"How?"

"An-ne!"

I smile, we're into this now.

"Kalp," I say. "Heart."

"Kalp krizi?" she asks.

"Patladı," I explain, which as a word still feels more apt to that event and its moment in my life. I am, after all, also a Turk. "It exploded."

She looks so sad. And together we eat fruit. Silence but for hurma and Egemen and the tapping of metal. We move on to my journey.

"And you're going to Kars?" she checks.

She asks if they can follow on social media. She offers a slip of paper for me to write my name. I suppose this might now be it, even if my surname is not so common. I write *Julian Sayarer*. She takes the paper and looks at it. "Sayarer," she says, smiling. Like the world's a small place and English and Turkish aren't so dissimilar.

"Sayarer," she says again. "Sigh-a-rare. But it's like a Turkish name."

She turns to her son. "Bak! Look! An *er*, like a soldier."

I smile and come out with it. "My father's from Izmir."

She smiles, then starts. "You're a Turk?!"

"My Turkish name is Emre."

"Emre!" She loves it.

"Yes, the family were from Izmir. But my grandfather was originally from near Florina, in Greece. They had to move to Izmir, in 1923. Mübadele. The population exchange."

"You're Rum?" she asks. "An Anatolian Greek?"

"No, Turk, but my grandfather came from what is now Greece. Like Atatürk. With Selanik."

She is sad, she is amazed. "Us too. Our family came from Bulgaria, after the war. Everywhere is so mixed up."

She turns to Egemen, who is still squatting with the bearings. She says quietly, as an aside, as if to ask why he had not told her, "You knew he was a Turk?"

"No, anne!" He sighs.

She turns back to me. "And your mother?"

"From England. She and my dad met in Istanbul. They fell in love and moved to London."

She smiles, warmed by the story. "Life is good in England?"

"I don't know," I say. "I like it more in Istanbul. England has big problems. How's Türkiye?"

"Türkiye has the biggest problems. It used to be OK. But now . . ."

I decide to venture towards politics, feel we now know one another well enough to warrant it.

"Who do you think you'll vote for in the elections?"

"Uuuffff!" she exclaims. "It's difficult. We were always AKP. Always Tayyip Erdoğan." She waves at the street. "Round here everyone is CHP, but we were always Tayyip Erdoğan."

"Now?"

"I don't know." She pauses. "I think Meral Akşener maybe. What do you think?"

I consider the question.

To recapitulate: the CHP are the party of Atatürk, the Republic, but they became something of an elite. The AKP taught them something about hard work, and, to give them some credit, I think they're learning. Meral Akşener is a dislikeable nationalist, but there are worse. She believes in the legacy of the Republic; as a woman in politics she even in some ways embodies it. She's a racist and a potent nationalist but not a thug; she believes in a system and not pure power. I saw her poster a couple of days ago, facing off with Devlet Bahçeli, the virulently far-right MHP leader. It stood to reason that in a place like Çanakkale, with its strong history of nationalism but not entirely well off or liberal, it should be the nationalists who would gain from the generational decline of the CHP, especially now the AKP are having to nurse a coming global crisis. Still, if Türkiye could turn Akşener's İyi Parti, the Good Party, into its political right wing, even that would be a useful step for the country, would represent a cleaning-out at the bottom of the cupboard.

I pause, then venture:

"I think Tayyip is better than Akşener. He has the right idea about the economy. I think the refugee policy is good."

"But he's doing it wrong," she says. "Inflation!" she says. "Eighty per cent!"

"All the world has this now. Britain is a rich country and inflation is twenty per cent. Argentina has increased interest rates and inflation is one hundred per cent."

I add, "Türkiye isn't a rich country, unfortunately. We have to import all our energy."

"And now Arabs are everywhere," she says. "People working

without insurance! Thieves! Afghans! People who've never been to school! They don't speak Turkish!"

"Refugees," I say, "people who escaped from war."

"Working without insurance," she goes on, "working for nothing, for no money! Thieves! You understand? Yes, they escaped a war, but life is hard here also. Tayyip says, 'Everyone is welcome in Türkiye, come! We are all Muslims!'" She claps her hands together in mock unity. "But that is not enough!"

"*Anne!*" puts in Egemen, looking up from seating the bearings in the hub and trying to calm his mother. "Leave it!"

She does have half a point though. All the Person of the Year accolades bestowed upon Angela Merkel for accepting a million refugees into Germany, while Tayyip Erdoğan insisted it was a moral duty to accept four times that number but couldn't escape being made a demon in the eyes of the same people.

I appease Egemen's mother. "The problem is that Türkiye has all the refugees. We have four million. In Britain, there are ten thousand from Syria."

"This is the truth!" Egemen voices his agreement, as if it's about time someone said this. He finally gets the bearings to sit in position, then tightens the hub back together.

"Evet," says his mother – this much we agree on. "Yeter," she says. "Yeter." It's enough.

With the hub restored, cassette back on, spinning free again. I prepare to leave and thank Egemen with all my heart. He smiles, his mother grabs his shoulder and, in case I haven't got it, repeats. "Oğlum! Oğlum!" My son! And now she steps towards me.

"Emre . . ."

She grabs my shoulders.

"You are always welcome here, OK? Tamam mı?"

I smile, but she is deadly serious.

"Really! If you are ever in Çanakkale again you come to me, you stay with me, tamam mı?" She hugs me close a moment, then straightens her arms again so that she can hold my shoulders while looking me in the eyes.

"We're waiting for you, Emre! You're always welcome. There'll be no money. There's food. A room. Everything! You just stay with us! OK? Tamam mı? If you're in Çanakkale again, you stay with us, tamam mı? You understand me? Tamam mı?"

Çanakkale to Dikili – 29 October

The day is 29 October. Turkish Republic Day. I write this on the ninety-ninth anniversary; I write it for the hundredth. As I ride south at the entrance to the Dardanelles Strait, I see a flotilla of ships – gas and grain – sailing north to the Bosphorus. On the far, sparse shoulder of the Gallipoli peninsula are the stoic, upright columns of the monument to those who died here in 1915, defending the country from a joint British, French and Russian invasion in which the British gallantly let their subjects from Australia and New Zealand do most of the dying on their behalf.

Riding on, I think of the words of Atatürk upon the successful defence of Çanakkale against that invasion. There he achieved what is so often and so mysteriously the hardest of accomplishments: the gracious victory. In so doing, he ensured a fond place for himself and Türkiye in the collective memories of many an Australian and New Zealander.

> *Those heroes who shed their blood and lost their lives . . . you are now lying in the soil of a friendly country. Therefore, rest in peace. There is no difference between the Johnnies and the Mehmets where they lie side by side here in this country of ours . . . You mothers who sent your sons from faraway countries, wipe away your tears. Your sons are now lying in our bosom and are at peace. Having lost their lives on this land, they have become our sons as well.*

In it, too, is an important lesson in leadership: know when

you have won. Know when to stop fighting. When it serves your interests better to be gentle than firm. Your enemies are dead and in the ground, their quest sits in failure. The deed is done, the day was won. The need to win more, to win harder, is a feature of bad leadership, for it will only set the will of others against you.

As dusk turns to night, I sit upon the Assos seafront. I hear the jubilant music, the marching songs of the early Republic. "Yaşa Mustafa Kemal Paşa Yaşa!" blares out triumphant and people sing and dance and clap and sway, drinking small and not-so-small glasses of rakı, pale and white, to the words "Long live Mustafa Kemal!" For today and tonight, at least, the concerns of the economy cannot touch them.

A fire burns in a brazier nearby. Looking up at the sky, I think of the War of Independence. I think of the Revolutionary War and I think of the Revolution. In reality, the war that ended on 29 October 1923 was all three. The old Ottoman order was removed, along with the sultan and the foreign invaders who tried to prop him up.

You still see the depth of it in even the peasant's ramshackle roadside hut, next to the orchard and one or two goats: the small triangular Turkish flag flies from the roof. Although they have little, it still makes them a stakeholder in the Turkish state. Outside a café in a quiet village, men talk about their animals and market. Inside, the snap of tiles from rummikub is the only noise; nobody says a word. Later, two men talk of gas exploration in the Mediterranean, of problems with Greece. They move on to the gas find in the Black Sea, on stream in 2023. I notice that they say, "*We* found the gas," as in, Türkiye found the gas. In this village, the men still see themselves as stakeholders also in the Sakarya field. It belongs to the nation, and their relationship to Türkiye is one in which the nation is an extension of their village. They envisage the find making their lives easier. It is good news. Neither the discovery nor its benefit has been released to that amorphous, all-encompassing entity in most modern industrial states: *they*. Some months later, during election campaigning, Erdoğan will announce free domestic gas, from Sakarya, for up to a year. When I hear the news I think of these two men, who it appears in their instincts were correct.

In 2023, Türkiye remains a revolutionary state. Even the country's first effort at building an automobile in the 1960s, a fully state-backed project, saw the car named the Devrim. Revolution. The process begun by Atatürk – to end foreign occupation, to consolidate a Turkish state and identity – has been continued in the economic policies and nation-building of the AKP. The industrial strategy, the reduction in imports, the growth in exports. The effort to rebuild Ottoman relations and spheres of influence. An autonomous Türkiye, capable of holding its own in a changing world. To get back, in full, the seat at the world's table that the Ottomans held and then lost.

These revolutions within Türkiye also mirror those in the world without. To go from the bipolar world of the Cold War to the briefly unipolar world of US hegemony, and now to a more democratic, multipolar world of multiple powers, is a revolution on a global scale. It is a revolution in how our planet acts and interacts, and it will engage new parts of the world that the West has never learned to look at, or learned only to laugh at. Even as a war in Ukraine sees Russian energy sources diverted and sold east instead of west, it is the Turkic countries of Kazakhstan and Azerbaijan that Europe taps first for new supplies. The Organisation of Turkic States becomes relevant; a niche but resilient twentieth century idea of Pan-Turkism becomes relevant.

There are risks in these transitions, in sudden political and geographic movements, in the act of balancing and rebalancing. But for all that this is so, these trends are more dangerous if left undescribed, or if a hegemon is allowed to describe equality as chaos, or fairness as threat. The world must exist in a state of balance, because domination is unsafe, unjust and unsustainable. Maybe this change – balance rather than domination – is hard to accept after you have grown accustomed to control, just as in water we cannot instantly swim, but if we do not panic, we soon learn to float. In this world I maybe hold an advantage over many of you, because when I was very young I went to visit my grandparents in Izmir for the first time, and before meeting them I was told we would not be able to understand one another, but they loved me very much, and I meant the world to them. This, I sometimes think, is the essence of a multipolar world. I cycled vulnerable across much of that world. No one did me harm, and so many acted with such kindness that I learned trust. This too is the essence of multipolarity.

In navigating this, a sense of revolution is the single most important quality that a state must preserve. It is its engine, it is a people demanding to be heard and a state understanding that it must listen. I think of the Tunisians I knew who partially welcomed the Kais Saied coup of July 2021, because parliamentary protocol was sucking the life from their revolution, which had won ballot boxes but not – as it needed to – smashed the oligarchies of Tunisian elites and French corporations that still keep the country down. The spirit and work of the revolution remained incomplete. I think of the people of the US, who know that revolution is their heritage but no longer understand what it is they must revolt against, so simply revolt against themselves. "No taxation without representation" is reduced to the simple whine and bellyache: "No taxation."

A war against foreign aggression can be a revolution. A civil war can be a revolution. A revolution against domestic elites is the only version that is formally labelled a revolution. This can create a misdiagnosis, as perhaps in the case of Türkiye, if people are looking at a revolution but believe they are seeing only a war. Revolution, correctly harnessed and understood, is an opportunity rather than a threat; it simply needs to identify the correct targets. Revolt against foreign occupation. Revolt against domestic elites. When both are gone, revolt against deprivation, against ignorance and poor schooling, against sickness and ill health. Technically, these should be the simplest of revolutions to lead, for they are against structural conditions rather than coercive enemies. Still, their hold can be among the strongest.

On the eve of the War of Independence, Türkiye is mired in

all of these ailments. Chaos reins and the country is struck dumb before circumstances that none would have wished, and options for its future that none would wish to choose between. Countries are novels in constant need of authoring. If you don't write your own then others will write it for you, but they will not write it in your interests. In search of understanding, I return to the memoirs of Sabiha Sertel, describing Türkiye as it waits to pick up its own pen.

The Friends of England Society argues that foreign policy should follow Britain's lead, while the Wilson Society pins its hopes on a US mandate. Most intellectuals are gloomy, and some claim that we must give up parts of Turkish territory to maintain our national independence. But the Turkish people sense by intuition that the imperialists will not tolerate an independent Türkiye and that independence can only be won by fighting another war.

Meanwhile the imperialist states of the Triple Entente have already agreed to divide the country. The internal confusion only emboldens them. They have been exploiting Türkiye's economy for centuries, and now they are preparing to carve up the country itself and establish control over the resulting pieces. Never before has Türkiye been so close to dismemberment and destruction. The Ottoman sultan is only concerned with preserving his own rule. Politicians and public figures like Damat Ferit and Ali Kemal grovel before Harrington and Bristol, eager to carry out their orders. They despise the CUP Turkish government and are ready to place the country under the British yoke.

Britain wants to gain control over Türkiye, just as it did with Egypt. Its main rival is the USA, which is lobbying among intellectuals, presenting itself as Türkiye's guardian and trying to set up a mandate in the country. Some luminaries prefer a US mandate to British rule. They claim the USA has no imperialist ambitions and will bring democracy.

Coup

A yellow truck passes me on the road, pulling slowly ahead, and I see it has a piece of history peeling back from a large sticker on the rear of its red trailer. A photo shows Taksim Square, a crowd and the Turkish flag. Above the photo are words written in English: *Democracy Wins in Türkiye.*

It is 15 July 2016. Rogue elements in the military attempt to stage a coup in Türkiye. They fail. Tanks roll onto streets, soldiers attempt to take the Bosphorus Bridge. Pilots from the air force, the military branch most prominent among the putschists, bomb the Turkish parliament. But the coup fails.

The coup failed because the first rule of a coup is to take over the broadcasters, and the second is to get people to stay home. The coup failed because the first rule of democracy is to get people on streets, and Türkiye came out onto its streets. I cannot help but feel that in this is a lesson so relevant to Westerners it bears repeating: that media control and the reluctance of people to take to their streets are the two primary conditions required for a coup. There were other factors, too. Soldiers stayed loyal to the country. Chief of Staff Hulusi Akar, even with a belt around his neck, refused to give the order to implement martial law. Media freedom came to the aid of an AKP who had often been hostile to the very things that helped save them; a broadcaster put a phone to a studio camera, through which Erdoğan addressed the nation by video call.

Memories of that day. An estate agent in Istanbul told me of his relief at the failure of the coup. "I went next morning to buy bread, to the shops. And I was happy, because I know that there are still laws. After a coup, the only law is the rifle." Memories of that night. My friend Yeşim, from Ankara, told me how she lay in bed looking up at the ceiling, holding herself as she heard the explosions from parliament. "I said to myself, 'If I survive tonight then I am leaving this country.'" (Happily, she didn't.)

In the evening light I watch the truck pull away, the road climbing up towards hills. I read the sticker again: *Democracy Wins in Türkiye.* It makes me smile that this man is so proud of the outcome of 15 July that he feels compelled to advertise it in English on the roads of Europe where he drives. I agree with him, too. Whatever the excesses of a political party or government, it is always preferable to the military, because what brings a political party to power is its popularity, or at least a pretence of popularity. What brings the military to power is its guns.

The words stay with me: *Democracy Wins.* It is true that the AKP and Erdoğan are a democratic phenomenon. They were Türkiye's first political party run as a professional operation, they knocked on doors nationwide and told people they would be respected in the lives they wanted to live and votes they wanted to cast, that the military was gone. It was not only conservative, religious people who wanted this deal. Many of the secular, left and liberal also came on board with a new country ready to be built, tired of a politics in constant disarray because the army didn't know how to back off. The CHP lived for most of a century on the laurels of Atatürk, whereas the AKP had to generate its own laurels and did. This process finally taught the CHP that they too needed to work harder to earn votes, to earn trust, and it was in their learning this lesson that Turkish democracy grew stronger. Perhaps it is odd to read all this of Türkiye, because it is not what you are used to. While the Western world talks much of democracy, in truth it seldom shows much stomach for the confrontation that democracy entails, and in foreign states it prefers acquiescence.

To understand more of coups, look south to Egypt, to 2013 and 14 August, the Rabaa Massacre, where a thousand democrats are killed in a day by General Abdul El-Sisi seizing power. The bodies overfill the morgues. Erdoğan spends years saluting crowds with four fingers in the air and a thumb folded in, the symbol of Rabaa and a refusal to forget. You can be sure that the indifference Erdoğan goes on to show to Western rebukes against him are fortified by the fact that a coup could see a thousand Egyptians murdered in a day with scarcely a wrinkle in Western attitudes to Cairo. El-Sisi imprisons, El-Sisi tortures. Türkiye has the decency to break off relations with this Egyptian abomination, who in 2020 boards a plane from Cairo to the Élysée Palace in Paris, so that Emmanuel Macron can pin to his bloodstained breast . . . the Légion d'honneur.

No doubt the El-Sisi coup goes further than the West would want. They start out with the provincial organisers, the religious, those guys with not a word of English nor friend outside the country between them. But because the only law of the coup is the gun, and because its only morality is brute force, when Giulio Regeni, an Italian labour researcher from Cambridge University, shows up for his fieldwork in Cairo, he too is tortured, his parents too will feel bereavement, will learn what it is to lose a son. El-Sisi starts imprisoning the Anglophones who speak to us eloquently in our own language, imprisoning the graduates of Western universities, the dual nationals too. Alaa Abd El-Fattah is left to smuggle out his prison diaries. The putschists go too far, of course they do, but no Western state breaks off relations, because, and let me break it to you, they do not actually care. The violence of the coup might embarrass them, but it does not in fact offend them.

For a moment, I allow myself to think that, after all the coups of the twentieth century, if the military can never again carry one out against its politicians, then Türkiye is perhaps at its most democratic in this century. Then I realise that it is not so, because if people are expected to be grateful simply for the fact that the military cannot perform a coup, then the spectre of the coup persists, and has not yet been fully dismantled.

Riding through the evening, I rue how thankless a task it is to balance all of this. A West that talks democracy but doesn't truly want it. A democracy that forgets some who helped build it, who want to strengthen it. There is nothing I write that won't be unfair to someone. No sentence that read in isolation won't let down somebody, that doesn't fail to see another person's hurt or fear. Sometimes all I have is uncertainty, doubt, but if I give it to you successfully, then perhaps you have learned a little more of the truth. Perhaps we do not understand a country until we are confused by it.

At the roadside, farmers bring in an olive harvest, tractors deliver it to the factory press, and the air smells of virgin oil. The road slopes upwards, the last hills demanding the last of my attention. Rosemary grows from beneath the rocks. A fig tree, as always, finds a way. The smell of pine lifts the spirits, and needles and cones carpet the ground. The roll of the wheels in the warm light of evening is conducive to optimism, if only because, like history, they keep moving forward.

Dikili to Izmir – 31 October

Across the water, the sun falls from the bottom of a golden sky and goes sinking into the horizon. The outline of a Greek island stands large beside the coast. I ask a couple of Turkish pensioners, carrying home their folding chairs from the beach, and they confirm that it is Lesvos. A moment later they correct me and call it by its Turkish name, Midilli.

I watch it as I ride, as a line of three fishermen fish, their rods silhouetted against the gold. I was there, in 2018, when refugee numbers were at a peak, after the Iraq War finally spilled across into Syria and both countries collapsed. I remember the life jackets piled on the beach, belonging, you hoped, to the luckier ones who made it across, rather than the many thousands who did not. I remember visiting that volunteer camp, where European youths taught bike maintenance and swimming lessons to those traumatised by water. I remember a makeshift gym with skinny boys doing pull-ups and trying to bench press. I remember an Iranian teenager and his Yemeni friend, one of them running from a state the West was happy to vilify and the other went running from a state the West had been happy to destroy, because the money was good and the responsible regimes were called "friendly". And I remember, soon after that, the videos of Greek coastguards opening fire in the sea around the boats, and bullets spraying in the water.

Riding south, I cross a narrow causeway. To my right the Mytillini Strait. To my left a salt marsh, with mountains of salt piled at the far end of it, and a pair of flamingos standing in the shallow water. Farmers with roadside stalls sell mulberry juice, pomegranate molasses. I wonder what lives are now being lived here by those who in the end never made the crossing, or who were forced back.

Again I wring the last of the light from the day, a favourable wind pushing at my back, making the flags point south. Around me another day's olive harvest is brought in. Families beat at trees; the wealthier farms have a special machine resembling a large, soft whisk that slaps the branches, causing the olives to fall with a patter onto the nets below. At larger processing factories, the air smells lush, like newly dressed salad, fragrant with the oil, and men rake forecourts then shovel branches into threshing machines.

On the edge of Dikili, I follow back roads along the coast, where stray dogs pad among summer villages abandoned for the coming winter. Riding into the town, I see the flames of ovens firing pide for a few diners. The small van of a mobile florist is parked at the kerbside, its tailgate down and functioning as a work surface, where a florist slides her knife down the stems of roses and strips them of their thorns. By a small, empty café, a young woman dressed in leggings is working the evening shift alone. She turns her back to the mirror and looks over her shoulder to check – approvingly – the reflection of her bum. I think of all the lives we do not see, but which quietly make up this world.

At the docks a large cargo ship is anchored, its cranes working late under floodlights to load the hold of the boat. I hear the loud and booming heave of metal, and, nearer to hand, the softer clunk of heavy chains as a child swings high in a playground, so that the chains go limp at the end points of his arc, before snapping taut again as he swings back down. An old lady stands alone among the municipal exercise equipment. She grasps a wooden dowel in each hand and with them turns the circular dials on which they are mounted, huffing and puffing through her routine. Determinedly she goes about her exercises, then steps back with a hearty sigh to watch the sea.

It is after Dikili, a little north of Izmir, that I feel Anatolia begins.

There is a sweet and fragrant smell in the air: of dried grass, tinged yellow, mixed with scents of oregano and thyme. I leave the coast road, and immediately face bigger and steeper hills. A fair-sized lizard runs across the road ahead of me, its angular legs spinning fast under it like bright green cartwheels perpendicular to the upper part of the leg. On the trees the olives grow plumper and blacker. I squeeze one between finger and thumb and out bubbles a purplish juice. Villagers are in the fields, where men and women alike have scarfs tied around their heads to ward off the sun. The women wear flowing pantaloons in patterns of rich purple and orange, contrasting against the blue sky and pale green leaves. It is a sight bright with the colour and hope of harvest.

Over one rise, larger than all the rest, it changes again. Laid out on a giant tarmac runway are sections of steel columns and, awaiting collection on the forecourt beside me, the twisting carbon-fibre composites of wind turbine blades newly moulded in the factory. On the opposite side of the road, a cart track leads to a small farm-house where eggs are for sale, and a black hen pecks around the yard. Yet again I wonder at this collision of the rural and industrial: the turbines spinning over these hills, the farmyard hens and the olive press in a space where it seems all might thrive together. As if to confirm my optimism, a blue flag with its orbit of yellow stars marks European cycleway Eurovelo 8, which adjoins the road just beyond the farm. I think of who may have come this way already. I think of who will follow.

Over a final rise the bay returns and I roll back to the coast I have spent most of the day parted from. Tankers are at anchor and chimney stacks mark a refinery in the port town on the outskirts of the city of Izmir. At a small café I eat a fish sandwich and drink a soda water. Kittens brush against my ankle, and they too, it seems, are optimists. Scraped, fine-boned skeletons litter the floor near my table, remnants from diners more generous than me. After eating, I ride into town, heading for the metro station at the end of the Izmir train line. Built a short walk from where the train tracks stop are blocks of new apartment buildings waiting to be sold. From their style and location, you can envisage their prospective buyer: bourgeois, white-collar job in Izmir, but priced out of the city and looking for space and a quieter life. Aliağa, north and on the coast, sleepy but not too sleepy, is perfect. Train each morning and evening. The need now for the Turkish state is to create jobs in Izmir that justify the apartment price, and also jobs in Aliağa itself. A few blocks from the station is a statue of Atatürk, though for once his arms are spread and fingers pressed together, one knee lifted as he dances. He looks jubilant. I'm not sure I've seen him dancing before – his statues usually show him poised and pensive. Here, it seems, the spirit of Izmir is contagious.

From the platform edge, I watch wooden-bottomed freight cars roll empty through the station, headed for the Port of Izmir where they will be loaded with container units. I confess, I'll ride the metro into the city. I will do so to skip the traffic, but also because the metro fills me with excitement at just how much has changed, at the future being built. I roll my bicycle along the platform, looking for a ticket. I find only an empty office, and, peering in, see a room with a chopping board and a half-bulb of freshly diced garlic. A generous handful is waiting in a frying pan on a small electric hob. My heart fills and I wish that, no matter how much Türkiye is to "develop", as they call it, this sight should never be lost. The station master will also always have a hob in his office, where he can chop and sauté the garlic that begins the cooking of his evening meal.

Station to station, the train fills up. On the hillsides are long lines of satellite dishes: bowls and their antennae all pointing out to space. We pass through university towns where dock cranes are visible above the hills on the coastal side of the tracks, and apartment buildings climb up mountains on the inland side. A man in the chair next to me sleeps like a baby with the rocking of the carriage. An adult asleep on public transport is one of my favourite sights: a state transporting people where they need to move, a public trust in which people can sleep as they go.

A man rests his hand on my bicycle and smiles a small thanks at me for the perch. Looking down the carriage, I am reminded that the Izmirli are maybe the most relaxed of all Turks. Couples cuddle a little closer, the girls from the university wear a little less. There are more piercings in everyone's faces, more leggings. It is true that you will find all this in those enclave neighbourhoods of Istanbul – Cihangir, Kadıköy – but you won't in Eyüp or Fatih. In Izmir, it is the same at every station along the line, for here this is the fabric of the city itself. Izmir is just Izmir, whereas Istanbul has its Beyoğlu but also its Beykoz. In this way, it is Izmir rather than Istanbul that more resembles a New York City, London or Shanghai: a city with an air of *we're different*, in an age when a person's chosen metropolis helps form a part of their identity.

On the city's streets the ezan is heard more seldom, because in Izmir there were always as many Greeks as Turks, so mosques were no more numerous than churches. Off the train, downtown and near the waterfront, large brass statues show women with their hair open to the wind, headscarves filled like parachutes behind their heads. It is a vision of emancipation which forgets that many women wear a hijab due to religious freedom, not its absence, but this is only the sort of soft bigotry common among the Izmirli, who in other ways are maybe the least relaxed of all Turks. This conservatism is the stark opposite of and yet exactly the same as that found elsewhere in Türkiye, and I wish for a world where compromise does not have to be found, inelegant, at the midpoint of two extremes.

Enjoying being in a city again, I push my bike through bustling streets as the day ends and the sun sets. It is ten years since I was last here. Perhaps thirty since my first visit. A woman with a shopping trolley for a storefront knits baby clothes in another of those businesses that will reliably put food on a table while never showing up in an official statistic. Under her clacking needles, booties and hats and bibs take shape or are commissioned new by mothers and aunts. In a small square, a line of people has formed in front of a stainless-steel mixing bowl of batter and a machine that forms and drops balls of it into another pan, this one of bubbling oil, a fryer that turns batter into doughnuts. A man in an apron with a strainer lifts the tulumba, the tiny balls of sweet, cooked dough, from the oil. On a whiteboard at the front, in marker pen:

Merhum – Avni Karagül. Ruhuna Fatiha.

Deceased – Avni Karagül. To the soul a prayer.

I love the gravity of the words, the warmth of the gesture, and that the whole community, everyone and anyone, will tonight have doughnuts one last time on Avni. This is what we do when people die, our own small way of keeping them alive. I head down to the water's edge. More lights, more skyscrapers than I recall. It's glorious, beautiful, the vast Gulf of Izmir with its naturally deep water that made it such a fine port across the centuries. Music plays, people drink and eat mussels stuffed with rice. A tram rolls through, wheels rattling rails. I'm sure this place wasn't so thriving before. Beside me are rows of rods. Men fish. Husbands and wives fish. A woman weaves through in an electric buggy, selling çay. Two men push a trolley with glowing coals under a samovar, all spouts and chambers. I see two tents on the promenade, curse that even here has come the blight of homelessness, then see rods protruding from the openings of the tents, lines, a thermos being passed between the two. It is only night fishing. Stand down.

As I wait to cross the road, a bus rolls by me in the street and I jump when I see its destination. It is rush hour, and on the bus filled with passengers seated and facing forwards, one woman stands alone in the aisle, dressed in a long coat, holding on to an overhead rail. She looks out at the city, catches me staring at her bus rolling by, curiously stares back, one of those moments in a city where our total separation – by glass and distance and travel – means for a moment we stare at one another in total intimacy before the city carries everyone on. She will never know the reason I stared: that the bus was headed to the neighbourhood where my father lived as a boy. I stand there and I miss my father so much it still hurts, where I had hoped that by now I'd just be numb.

From deep in my memory I recall that first visit to Türkiye, to Izmir, when I was six or so. I remember little. I remember my grandparents and their excitement. The computer game that my elder cousin Yalkın allowed me to play with him. Other than that, I remember the street outside my grandparents' apartment. It was such a steep street, and the road surface was pocked and dusty. I remember loving simit, and the magic that from the apartment you could let down a wicker basket on a string, and simit would come back up in it. The money that went down in it was an immaterial detail to me at that age – exchanging paper for simit seemed too perfect a swap. Instinctively I loved it all, but I remember too a poorer country. It was not the place I see before me now. It may be the luxury of the comfortable to disdain the idea of skyscrapers as a sign of progress, and the comfortable may not be wrong, but perhaps I have in me more of a poorer country, and more of Türkiye, than I'd realised. Because right now, looking at the skyscrapers of Izmir, I feel, unexpectedly, sort of proud.

On a bench I sit and watch the scene. A woman nearby has Atatürk's signature tattooed on her forearm. Having a man's name tattooed as a feminist statement may seem odd, but again it is such a normal sight that I almost forget to tell you. The square is full of moustached men on low stools drinking from curvaceous glasses of çay. One half of me sees and thinks to describe this fine Anatolian scene. The other half of me just sees men in the early evening. I walk into an establishment and I speak Turkish. I order my food, or I enquire after a room. Nothing happens, only the transaction. Other times, I decide to speak English to prompt conversation: this reminder of the outside world is a reminder also of the existence of Türkiye, rather than us simply getting on with life inside it.

Two thoughts nag at me. The first is that I am reporting on Türkiye, and who this serves depends on who this report card is handed to. The second, more fatal to travel writing, is that I am here but there is no discovery to report, for I am at home and it is not new to me. It simply *is*. The people I sit among are Kerim and Bahar and Bülent and Zeynep, there are smiles and there are frowns, young and old, raised voices and whispers, an optimist and a pessimist. Suddenly the idea of depicting *a people* or *a country* strikes me as a gross imposition against the right of people to be individuals. It occurs to me that the broad strokes of the best travel writing often rest on nothing more than the immodest suspension of this courtesy and the confidence to reveal that, before you arrived there, you knew nothing of a place.

Izmir – 1 November

The sun shines bright white off the blue of the Gulf of Izmir. People sit and gather on the seafront: they drink çay, they eat simit. The road still to come is long, I cannot spare many days, but I must rest a little, walk around, visit family. There is a calm upon the city, despite its size, its forest of apartment buildings and houses climbing up each hillside as far as the eye can see. The tram slides round the bend of the coast behind me, its bell clanking at two people up ahead who loiter as they cross the tracks. Palm trees sway in front of seafront apartments painted cheerfully in pink and yellow. Turkish flags and Atatürk flags hang from balcony windows for the Republic Day just gone, as if nobody wants to be seen to be the first to take theirs down.

On the wide promenade, a child pedals enthusiastically on his bicycle, but with an energy that is for now beyond his balance. The bike goes down under him, spills him – hands outstretched – to the ground where he gets first to his knees and then to his feet, climbing slowly back upright. He immediately looks round to his parents for their reaction, as if to check whether something bad did just happen. There is fear in his face. His father smiles, and a second later, hesitantly but happily, the child smiles, and trusts that he is OK. I try to take this same lesson in writing this journey: to match energy with precious balance, with restraint. But who is watching me?

As I pay for my morning coffee, a café owner takes an interest in my accent. He asks quite proficiently if I speak English and so we switch. He worked many years in retail, supplying the hotel trade, and finally got out of that line of work to start this café, just last month, as he had always dreamed. He reaches below the counter to pull out a box of notes so as to hand me my change. A face is tattooed on his arm in pale ink: a man with curly hair, his head on his hand, a pensive expression. It looks to me like the famous Turkish poet, so I ask, "Is that Nâzım Hikmet?"

In the moment of my asking, I realise my potential error, remembering why a man's face may be tattooed on his son's arm. Familiarity with the reason and its emotions at least dulls my sense of guilt.

"No. It is my father," he confirms.

I smile my condolences and ask, "Is he still with us?" although I know the answer from his face.

"No, he died," he says.

"Mine too."

We smile at each other, together in our grief, by which I still believe the world would be improved if only we realised we were all in it, or had been in it, or one day would be in it.

"My dad was also from Izmir," I decide to tell him.

"Really?"

I nod.

And he smiles. "They are watching over us."

Şirince – 2 November

On the mountain road up to Şirince a minibus had passed me. On its bonnet was a crest: an orange shield with a black rooster on it. The words Matematik Köyü moved quickly through my line of sight. At the crossroads, I see the same crest on a wooden sign, pointing to the place I have come to see. I follow its arrow, walk down the track that leads to the village, and after a few turns its buildings come into sight, all of them so very handsome in a mixture of stonework and red brick, of timber-framed structures with wide wooden windows that flood halls and broad floorboards in light. I see a dining room with red and white checked tablecloths, a terrace outside with a chimney and stone hearth. Branches of bay have been piled in the fireplace, leaves shining and waiting for the flame. A stone tower with a small pointed roof surveys it all: the surrounding mountains and the cabins and washrooms built into the terraced hillside above this, the Mathematics Village. A golden retriever pads out to meet me, sniffs my hand. On a trellis overhead, the leaves of a climbing plant turn yellow to autumnal red. A cat jumps onto the trellis in pursuit of something, and down flutters a scattering of bright leaves.

The Maths Village is known across Türkiye and increasingly outside it as a utopia-cum-haven for mathematical discovery and the application of maths to social problems and needs. I call it a utopia but of course it is literally not, for it is here. And now so am I.

I first heard of it some years ago, on a bus in Istanbul, as I headed out with a friend to Bilgi University, where he was working at the time. It is an institution that has always had strong links to the Village, a connection formed through Ali Nesin, once a professor at the university and the son of famed Turkish writer Aziz Nesin. Ali had used the inheritance from his father to start a trust, establishing a small campus in Istanbul that taught maths, and then, at the beginning of the millennium, beginning construction of the village now standing over me. Volunteer mathematicians from around the country laid the first stones on this hillside plot, an early days of a new nation kind of thing, and in it something reminiscent of the Köy Enstitüleri, or Village Institutes, that also once spread a utopian idea across the Republic, and which our road will soon explain. I consider how much the world has changed since then, not so much the determination of people to construct a better world, an impulse still strong in Türkiye, but more the thought of making enough money as an author to build an entire village.

The Maths Village had been built in the spirit of *ask forgiveness, not permission*, and apparently lacked the necessary building permits. This legal point seemed to be held in reserve against the Village by the authorities, despite its vast social and national value and the many hotels and mansions of dubious legality that line the Turkish coast and avoid such scrutiny.

That day on the bus out to Bilgi University, stuck in Istanbul traffic, we met a mathematician called Chris. It must have been around 2017, and in the era of post-coup anxiety he'd briefly been detained by the authorities, owing to the politicisation in that time of, well, basically everything. The architect responsible for the village's beautiful buildings had recently escaped from a jail and headed straight for the Greek island of Samos. Looking out at the village now, I think back to our conversation. My friend had asked how things were going, down in Şirince.

"It's fine," Chris had said, relaxed. "They don't really like it, but the AKP has always recognised the value of education, and they recognise that the village is good for education. It's helped produce so many great minds."

As I walk down the stone path towards the main buildings, I see a woman rolling a cigarette. I ask in English the way to reception, wanting for some reason to come as an outsider: a guest to both village and country.

"We don't have a reception," she says, smiling over the paper full of tobacco, "it's quite informal here."

"Is it OK if I walk around?"

"Of course," she says, and tucks a thick curl of black hair back behind her ear, then licks the gum on the cigarette paper.

"You work here?" I ask.

She nods, and places the cigarette between her lips. She holds out a hand and smiles, introduces herself.

"Ceren."

We shake hands and I try to figure out how to begin a conversation.

"It's so peaceful up here," I say.

"It is quiet today. Our group is visiting Ephesus. But tomorrow we have a new group of five hundred arriving."

"Five hundred?!"

She nods, happy and subtly proud of what she is part of.

"Do you mind if I sit?" I ask.

She gestures to the opposite bench and I take a seat.

"You look after projects and things here?"

"I'm a kind of programme coordinator, for some years now. We are twenty permanent staff."

"And things are going OK?"

"Yes," she says. "People are coming. There aren't too many problems."

"You're local? From Şirince?"

She shakes her head. "No. Far. From Ağrı. You know it?"

I shake my head and she points into the distance, as though pointing a long way away.

"East. Ağrı is Mount Ararat, although its name in Kurdish is Karaköse."

"Karaköse," I repeat slowly. "What is köse?"

Ceren holds her hand under her chin and looks for the word. "When you don't shave."

"Ahhh . . . Beard! So Dark Beard!" I say as Ceren exhales smoke, pointing her cigarette at me with a smile, as if to say I've got it. "I think that's a good name for a mountain. You have many students from there, from all over Türkiye?" I ask.

"Yes, now there are more. First not so many. But now people know about us. It is half from the west of Türkiye. Half . . ."

We both sort of pause, smile at this awkward division of the country that's so familiar and yet false, unhelpful, a more potent version of the British instinct to describe everything outside London as "the north".

". . . half from east. We do a lot with local schools here too. If students can afford to they pay, if they are poor then it is free."

"Just anyone who loves maths?" I ask.

"Yes, but we also teach other things. There is also the Philosophy Village here now. We teach sociology, physics. People are now coming from outside Türkiye. Here is sort of the only place like this in the world."

Again her tone is matter-of-fact, but also quietly proud of the work being done.

"And it's going well?" My enthusiasm for it all is restrained only by a self-consciousness about asking so many questions. "It is sustainable? It makes enough to keep going, from those who can pay fees?"

"Yes," she smiles. "And many people now volunteer time to teach here. We get donations of books too, for the library. Some from Ivy League universities, MIT sent some. Some from the UK, I think." She points to a work team beside us. "Now we are extending the kitchen."

I laugh. "That is important in Türkiye!"

"Very!"

"And politics now? The government have relaxed a bit? They are leaving you to do the mathematics?"

She laughs. "Maybe not relaxed, but it is OK."

"They must realise it's good for the country. That everything they want – education, economic development, building the country – needs places like this."

"Yes. They know this. But here we also promote critical thinking. And I think they are still afraid of criticism. It is like they see us as a threat, because we have a different view of how to do education."

"To be honest, this would also be a problem in other countries also. France is very against independent schools. Like a parallel school system."

"Yes." Ceren pauses, as if this is not a new consideration here. "And this is why we are not a school!"

"Right! You are a village!"

She nods kindly, like I'm slow but getting there. "Being a school is a lot of paperwork. Here is just a place people can come to."

I smile at the broadness of being "a place people can come to".

"I know the architect who designed the village went to Greece. The Turkish-Armenian guy. What was his name?"

"Sevan Nişanyan."

"Can he come back now?"

She shakes her head. "He is banned."

A sadness sweeps over me, as if there has been some awful mistake. It is hard to imagine a more sincere act of patriotism – a demonstration of a person's love of Türkiye, their concern for its wellbeing and betterment of its future – than this village.

"I guess it was a crazy time," I say, "the coup attempt, Daesh attacks, Gezi Park."

"I would love to know what you think about this, about Gezi," she says. "It was a special time. It was so important."

"Of course," I sigh, "because the most important thing in a democracy is for the government to know that people can become angry. Gezi would not have happened in the West," I tap my head, "because people are already dead inside a little."

"That's interesting." She starts rolling a new cigarette.

"But I do think Gezi was successful. It wasn't a failure. That is why people are in jail. If something is like a revolution, and it goes across a country like that, then people go to jail. I think sometimes Turks think they are not free, and this kind of freedom exists in the West. It doesn't. People in the West are in jail now, for protesting against oil, for protesting against racism. Assange is in jail in Britain for reporting US war crimes. I don't think this view of the world, that the West is a place of freedom, is good for Türkiye. The West is just a place where people are more obedient."

Ceren smokes, lets me talk, as if this isn't a common perspective here. I tread carefully, conscious of my privilege in being able to drop in and out of the country.

"I think too that the AKP, Erdoğan, you know ... in Türkiye, where the army was always happy to carry out a coup if the West did not like the government. If you are the AKP you worry that you lose control, the military does a coup, and you go to jail. Look at what happened to the government in Egypt ... so many dead, the prime minister dies in jail. The AKP are aware of this."

I pause a moment. "I just hope these days they feel safer, so they can let go of the control a little. So they don't feel they have to control things so tightly."

Ceren exhales smoke, the words following it in an instinctive response.

"But at some point their safety makes me unsafe. It cannot be like this."

I realise that in these words, Ceren has just explained every-thing.

"How do you feel unsafe?" I ask. "As a woman, as someone Kurdish?"

"As a woman ... as someone who is not religious ... yes. They make me unsafe. The problem is I think they want to control everything."

"Yes. This is bad for the country," is my reply, obvious as it is. I am conscious that she declines my offer of Kurdishness as a category in which she needs to be validated or protected. I think aloud, summing up my own thoughts.

"Everyone's safety has to be balanced. Or it is not safe."

She nods, as if this conclusion is obvious enough but inoffensive. I look up, awkward at what I'm about to ask, knowing it is a stupid, patronising question, but still having to ask it.

"Everyone here wants to help with education, though? To build the education system, for society? People here like Türkiye, are proud of it?"

Ceren smiles, putting out her cigarette and pulling the sleeves of her hoodie over her hands, uncurling from under her the leg that she is sitting on.

"Yes. We are proud. But for us, to care about a country means sometimes you have to criticise it also." She gets to her feet, looks a little apologetic. "In Turkish I could talk about this for a long time. I wish we could."

"Me too," I say, meaning it more than she realises.

"I have to go now, but please walk around. There is a lot to see."

In the air is something of the sacred. Sofas are set out under small shelters, overlooking a view of hills and olive groves. Classrooms with blackboards are dotted in tiny courtyards, some with their equations wiped clean, others still displaying their opaque language of numbers, symbols, brackets and alignments. A semicircle of empty chairs encircles the boards, the sort where a small wooden ledge, the shape of a kidney, is joined from the hip of the chair to offer its incumbent a little desk. On a terrace is a dining table half a tennis court in size. The whole setting embodies nourishment of mind and body.

All around is the energy of a place usually filled with great life, but for now emptied of it; perhaps something like a family home after its children have left. The workers labouring on the new kitchen break for çay and cigarettes and freshly baked açma brought over to them on a tray. They speak together in Kurmanji and Turkish, some with accents that sound halfway between the two languages anyway. They joke, talk money, and gather round a phone to laugh at a video from the internet of builders like them suffering misfortune elsewhere on earth. I eat the açma that Ceren has brought over to me with a glass of çay, take the empty plate to the kitchen, where a young volunteer, sleeves rolled up, stands and does the washing at a sink full of suds. I wander out and up the hillside, through cabins and washrooms and the library. I make my way to the village edge, down its stone passages to the tower.

At the base of the tower is a small bust of Sevan Nişanyan, and I hope for him to return, to take the place of his bust in watching over his architectural creation. I climb the spiral staircase of the tower, its metal steps sounding a warning to the young couple at the top, listening to music with a bottle of Şirince wine and tiny cups. I have interrupted, no doubt, but hospitality still rules and they offer me a cup of their wine. We share a little drink and she and he explain that they are both musicians, bassists. They play covers in bands in Kuşadası, where life is good. The Istanbul music scene is too competitive, they tell me, and the rent scene too uncompetitive. One day he wants to buy a van, drive across the country, to the east and the rest of Türkiye, playing his music, but he worries he will be judged in conservative parts for his eyebrow piercing and ponytail. As he speaks, I smile at this bohemian Türkiye, which appears now and then in buskers along the west coast. She smiles too, but more at the idea, I think, that there might be room for them together in this van.

Şirince to Aydın – 3 November

Everything moves by so fast. My legs turn in front of me like the spools of a tape deck playing Türkiye, and folk music blasts from the open window of a truck. I ride through Aydın, where years ago, during a longer journey, I stopped at a bus station in a small and dusty town. Everything seems to have grown larger and more modern. A red, white and blue passenger train – the Izmir–Denizli Express – rolls by, followed by freight trains bound for the Port of Izmir. Students gather on streets lined with shiny, new apartment buildings. Only the dust is as I remember. The rivers are low, as they seem to be everywhere, at least in this autumn of my riding. I am not complaining, but it has yet to rain on me even once. Although that might mean forfeiting a day of cycling, I could use the chance to stop and write. And the earth needs it.

In the Aydın valley it is clear that industry and agriculture exacerbate the dust. Cotton farming is extensive, and at the end of the day I see an old man with a bicycle and empty wine bottle sitting on a concrete platform to watch the sunset over fields of picked plants. I ride by a maze of steel pipes and a few small towers from which steam escapes a geothermal electricity plant, a renewable energy technology for which Türkiye has become one of the world's biggest growth markets. Deep in the earth, water is pumped onto naturally hot rocks, with the resulting steam driving turbines to make clean power. Already this has saved the country billions in energy imports, but removing the water from the land makes for drier earth. One morning as I eat my breakfast, I see a column of smoke in the distant hills. I point and ask the waiter, who informs me it is a chicken factory, yet another demand on the water table, like the cows, forever thirsty, that are reared for the livestock market. All around grow olive trees, that miracle of nature which needs no irrigation and yet will still produce. Sleeping dogs lie in their shade, as farmers hit at branches and ripe olives drop to sheets spread below.

As I go, I meet the people shaped by the last century and those who will shape the next. History acts on us, and we act on history. People who believe themselves powerless before it are those most at risk of dispossession in their future. Sometimes I can hardly believe the energy of those I meet. The young woman from Bursa, studying international relations in Aydın, who says she chose the wrong course and university. To support her studies, she waits tables three nights a week at a roadside restaurant in the middle of nowhere, and her situation is part of that cocktail of judgment calls, errors and determination that makes up all the world. Eager to practise her English, she says of the economy, "Türkiye is desperate."

"Everywhere is desperate."

"Yes, perhaps. It is not good for us to join the EU now, I think. They don't want us to become strong. To build up our companies."

"You don't think so?"

"Of course they do not." She looks at me softly, as if I'm a kind fool but with no understanding of competition law, the EU, or industrial strategy. "This is not how it works."

"What do you want to do after university?" I ask.

"I would like to work for TOGG. You know it?"

"Turkish Auto Group? Don't they have a new electric vehicle coming out?"

"Yes. They need political scientists, economists, to make an export strategy, to understand international markets."

She goes away and returns a moment later with my soup. I wonder what the future will hold for her, whether she will bring food to tables or a global export strategy to a Turkish automobile company.

Briefly one morning I meet with Ayşe, an old friend from Istanbul who moved to the countryside to be closer to the earth. That the city is full we agree. That the economy and population needs to spread out across the country we agree. Now she wants only to grow things, to have her hands in the soil, like she did as a child. She brings me a paper bag of pickings from her garden: walnuts, figs, apples, quinces, a pomegranate. She has bought a small plot of land with her boyfriend, a German-Turk, from Frankfurt. Like her he craved nature, though he also craved Türkiye, a pull factor accentuated by the push factor of a rising fear of the German Neo-Nazi movement. We talk of the future in Türkiye.

"I think Türkiye will be OK," I say.

"Me too," Ayşe agrees. "There is a calm here, in the countryside. People live simply, they know how to cook. How to plant things. How to save. They have lived a lot. There is a deep strength here, it seems to me. But sometimes I think it is a dangerous thing, because people do not expect much."

Her eyes shine as she says it: she says both the good and the bad, describes the strengths but also voices the criticism that slowly builds greater strength. In her eyes is not hope, but something deeper than that. Something more like faith.

I ride higher into the mountains and sleep again in the grounds of a mosque. I wake to four young boys with road bikes. They are dressed in lycra too big for their skinny limbs, but nonetheless proudly wear the jerseys of Aydın Cycling Club. Click-clacking in cleated shoes, they scarper about, the youngest nine, the eldest thirteen. They tell me they have cycled twenty-five kilometres to get here, from near Aydın, and will cycle back. Fifty kilometres, the eldest says proudly. I am still in my sleeping bag, brushing my hair out of my face, as the eldest then asks if I have a wife, and the youngest calls over, "Do you want a pomegranate?"

I watch as he reaches as high as his little arms will go into the tree, which snaps back when the pomegranate is plucked from its branch, and a shimmering haze of dew is catapulted off the leaves to shine in the climbing sun. They wait for me to say something – I'm the adult and that's what adults do – not realising that, for all my appearances, in the Turkish language that we speak, I am not so much older than they are. I leave them to play as I pack up my tent, and they run into the mosque, where eight cycling shoes are lined up on the mat out front as I walk over to say my goodbyes. From within comes the thump of heavy-footed running, of jumping on carpets, the sound of no parents, of independence, that gift the bicycle delivers so well to young people everywhere.

"Are you praying?" I ask the eldest, who is sitting outside, and despite the noises, which suggest not.

"No," he answers seriously, "we're playing."

He pauses, returns the question. "You pray?"

"Sometimes." I pause. "In my head."

At the roadside I stop for a break at a stall where a man presses pomegranates in a machine. He places a cup beneath to catch the juice for my drink. On the shelf beside us, honey is for sale. I say I heard last year's forest fires wiped out beehives round here. He shakes his head, as if it's news to him.

"Maybe on the Muğla side the fires did. Round here we were OK."

My imagination rolls with my wheels. On a helipad just over the road I see a helicopter, the old kind for aerial observation, its cockpit a single glass sphere, its tailfin proud and its rotor blades drooping on all sides. On the road I see a dragonfly, its head a single sphere of two eyes, its tailfin proud, its wings drooping. The higher hills and sparser villages make life harder for the stray dogs, and they pay a high cost on the highway for their curiosity. One dog has been opened up on the butcher's table of the road, its sweetmeats crimson and still somehow intact, as if the wheel were a surprisingly deft blade. The teeth of another, a large, skeletal bitch, are bared in a grin, as if she died doing what she loved.

A truck has swerved off the side of the road and into the wide drain of the highway. Some of its cargo of asphalt has spilled, but mercifully the truck has come to rest on the high motorway wall, and stands propped against it as if steadying itself. A crew of men is already there with shovels as I cycle by, waiting beside the van that brought them, ready to reload the spilled cargo. A flatbed truck arrives on the scene as I do, carrying an enormous digger, the sort used for quarrying. Its towering arm is having straps and hooks attached to it in order to lift the truck back onto its wheels and, in turn, onto the road. The speed of the recovery response, the availability of labour, is the other side of a high official unemployment rate. The cargo of asphalt is no doubt official, it exists, but the arms called upon to rescue it and get it to its destination are not. The cash they will be paid for showing up, the story they will tell friends over çay this evening, is another of those instances of employment and spending that appear in no official statistics but sustain vast quantities of the Turkish economy, that keep the country moving.

Gara Guzu – 4 November

A dog sleeps outside a hangar. Opposite is machinery for stone cutting. Small yellow winches and chains for lifting rock stand ghostlike, covered in the white dust of cut marble. Next door are trucks with their chassis exposed and cabs tipped forwards to show their innards. Mechanics in overalls and oil are about to finish a morning's work.

The door to another hangar on this industrial estate is rolled open, revealing the familiar sight of brushed, rounded steel cylinders for brewing. I see another familiar sight, stencilled on a wall: a dark sheep with a stem and ear of barley held in its mouth. A man walks across the unit, steps over a couple of wide hoses and a drain in the floor.

"This is Gara Guzu?" I ask, and he turns towards his visitor with a smile.

Gara Guzu, ten years ago, was the first craft beer to break the Efes monopoly on the Turkish beer market. A decade after its arrival, it is still the best. Twenty minutes later we sit in front of the brewery, each with a half-cup of beer that I watch Ataç pour direct from one of the giant tanks that stand in the main brewing room. Stuck to them are stickers from the craft beers of the world. Some I know from London – from Hackney, from Brixton; others come from Poland, from the Czech Republic and the US. I break the news that Brixton Brewery was acquired by Heineken in that wave of craft beer being bought by corporate beer when the fashion first boomed.

Out front the chairs are little more than sections of pallets and a couple of cushions, but with the sun shining down, and now and then a cloud to cool the temperature, everything is perfect.

"The thing is," says Ataç, "people don't appreciate quality here. At least, they don't appreciate quality beer."

"I looked in the shop on the estate, before I found you, to see if they had any Gara Guzu. But it was only Efes."

"They don't understand it. I sell more beer to Japan than to Muğla."

I smile at this notion, simultaneously inspiring and dispiriting. Ataç hands me my beer. We toast: "Şerefe!" We sit, he crosses one leg over the other – a nice pair of jeans – and pushes a well-cut crop of black-silver hair back into place.

"Because in Japan they understand craft. They respect it. With Turks, if they can have double the quantity for the same money, but half the quality . . ."

He lets the silence finish his sentence. I drink my beer, flavoured with just the right amount of hops. The flavour, after days on a dusty road, is in every way superb. I consider his point, which the quality of his own beer disproves.

"I suppose people don't have much money, so they prioritise."

"The more money people have, the more it is like this. The elites are worse. People here like to consume. And they want to be seen consuming. You go into a restaurant, everyone is on their phones. Sharing – or they think they are sharing. And they want to be seen consuming. I was just in Istanbul. A rakı-tasting event. Türkiye, Istanbul just got its first Michelin-star restaurant—"

"I saw!"

"But everyone who goes," Ataç makes as if to fasten a tie, "wants to wear a suit." He points to his own red trainer, tips his foot onto his toes and lifts his heel. "The women are wearing high heels, cocktail dresses. Because this is what it's about to them. The restaurateurs don't understand it, because it is supposed to be about the food." Ataç slaps his chest: a T-shirt under a bodywarmer of fleece and down. "You can go to a Michelin restaurant dressed like this, if you are going for the food."

We drink. A dog wanders across the industrial estate.

"Same with olive oil. Mostly our olive oil is not good. Because you cannot just collect the olives and press them. The press is important. The temperature is important. We don't do these things."

This, I know, is not true, or not entirely true, but Ataç is committed to his point, and there is something in it, so I leave him to make it.

"Our wine!" he laments.

I jump in. "It's got better!"

Ataç, already smiling, says with the nod of a connoisseur, "It is not good!"

I laugh, and Ataç gets to his real point.

"And it is not good for the country either. The Greek wine industry started at the same time as ours, but now is a thousand times bigger. They get all the exports. We have nothing."

"Could it be because the Greek brand is easier to sell? You know, like the Chobani guy? A Syrian-Kurd from Türkiye, he goes to the US and makes yoghurt, calls it Greek yoghurt and now he's a billionaire."

"There is this, but no. It is the quality. Like the man who likes to drink tea but does not care about the leaves. He does not care if the tea sat for a long time, if the tea is bitter. He doesn't care about the quality of the tea," Ataç returns to his original thesis, "because he does not care about quality!"

Ataç sits back down from a trip to a different cylinder, hands me another glass, this time a bright red ale. We toast: "Şerefe!" He draws out a pack and lights a cigarette. A bird sings on a ledge above. A thin cloud drifts across the sky, drops a little mist of rain down towards us, and leaves a rainbow over the opposite hills.

"We need more than this," he says. "Normally by November, December, everything is green again."

"It is very dry." I take a mouthful of ale. "Could you ever farm barley here, for brewing?"

Ataç shakes his head. "There is malted barley in Türkiye, but it is all Efes. And I prefer to buy mine from Germany. Hops from France, from Czechia."

"Could you grow hops?"

"That would be hard, especially with the dry weather. Cargill and many of the big agriculture corporations got out of Türkiye a long time ago, because of the drought. The weather and future do not look good for farming here."

"Is there nothing that can be done?" I ask, thinking of sustainable agriculture, of rain harvesting, something optimistic in the face of doom.

"No." Ataç looks my way, a little surprised and confused, like I seem bright enough but perhaps nobody has told me. He breaks the news.

"It's the climate. It is like this now. Maybe in thirty years we are lucky and we start to have a lot of rain. But I'm not sure."

Ataç hands me another bottle. Jet black. Porter. We toast: "Şerefe!" And we drink. I gesture at his brewery.

"You've got a great set-up here. The canning line too, it's bigger than others I've visited. You know Taybeh, the brewery in Palestine, near Ramallah?"

Ataç shakes his head. "Introduce us!"

"I will!"

I reply enthusiastically, the alcohol starting to hit, everything a good idea and all the brewing world a single family. I sip the porter, still but smooth.

"Is any of this equipment made in Türkiye?" I ask.

"The brewing units are from Denizli. Before we had to buy them from China, but now they are made here, and the quality is better."

"That's fantastic," I say, as Ataç smiles back with the nonchalance of an intensely relaxed person, as if it is neither good nor bad, but yes, I am probably right, it is more good than bad.

"The canning line is new, from the United States," he goes on. "With the lira now it is an expensive machine, but it is worth it. Glass takes so much energy to make, and it weighs so much, so shipping costs are high, which is bad for us. With the cans we will save money, and save energy too."

"You run the whole business from here?"

Ataç nods, draws another cigarette. "My wife does the book-keeping. I do the brewing. A friend in Izmir did the design work, the logo and the labels. We moved down from Istanbul fifteen years ago. We started a family. We'd had enough of the city. It is not always easy, but we are happy here."

I raise my glass to his progress. "And I guess you don't have to pay for beer anymore."

He laughs sardonically, lifts up his own glass.

"The most expensive beer I ever drank!"

I smile, not surprised to learn I've romanticised the journey of even a successful craft brewery.

"Why Muğla?" I ask. "It's your memleket?"

He nods. "Yeşilyurt."

The name of a tiny village, five kilometres away, that I saw on a sign. Everything around is all so impossibly small, so rural and agrarian, that it feels as though artisan beers, imports and exports, belong to a different world.

"Yeşilyurt!? It must have changed so much!"

I assume that it, like everything, has grown, but such change is not linear.

"Yes! It disappeared! When I was a child it was seven thousand people. Now, two thousand. Before it was a big farming town. Bigger than Bodrum, bigger than Datça, all those places that tourists come to. In those days Fethiye was the only one that was big, because Fethiye always had fishing."

I marvel at this: the emptying of rural Anatolia. Prosperity moving from farming to tourism, to foreign money.

"Where did everyone go?" I ask. "What happened?"

"The 1980 coup was bad. After that the military, the government, they did a lot to make villages weaker, because Kurdish fighters were strong in villages. So they made the villages weak."

"I suppose globalisation too. The world moved from villages to cities."

"Yes," Ataç blows smoke, "that too."

We sit here, near Yeşilyurt in Muğla, by the Aegean, talking of a policy necessitated primarily by events so far away in eastern Anatolia.

"It's interesting that there was just one policy for the whole country. The state didn't separate east from west."

Ataç ponders it.

"Maybe," he says. "We still have the same pattern today. People go to the towns. Now the government makes lots of public sector jobs, like here in Muğla, because if you create jobs people vote for you. So now Muğla has become a big town; before it was small. We used to have a good electrician in Yeşilyurt, and a good plumber." He points up the hill. "Now both are in Muğla, in public jobs."

"I guess it is good to have a regular income every month, and farming out here must be low-paid work."

Ataç shakes his head. "You can make good money here. But it is hard work, and people now, they do not want to work hard."

We toast: "Şerefe!" Together we raise another glass. Amber. Crisp, fresh, with a colour true to its name.

"It must be good that it's growing, craft. People must notice. The government must be aware. That it's creating jobs, companies are spending money on equipment. Paying tax revenue. It must help make it accepted."

Ataç gives an emphatic shake of the head, as he often does to my notes of optimism, which he seems to think are misplaced.

"We do not work together. Turkish craft. So we are small. Craft beer started in Greece at the same time. Now they have a craft beer association. They are seventy! We are ten. This is because they work together."

"They have a bigger market?" I suggest. "Drink more alcohol?"

"Their population is eight million. Our drinking population is eight million. Probably more. It is only because they work together.

Craft has grown in Türkiye. We have other good breweries now. Üç Kafadar. Knidos. Antakya Brewery in Hatay. I always tell them we need an association, but they just want to do it alone. So we don't grow. For me, this is not craft thinking."

"I saw those beers," I say, "mostly in supermarkets."

"Yes! For years I worked to get craft into supermarkets. They were not sure about craft. Then the supermarkets say 'OK', but they ask me to sell at this price." Ataç places his hand flat and low. "It is not a good price, so I say, 'Why should I sell at this price?' For years I do not sell, and then they accept my price. But now the new guys accept any price from the supermarkets." Ataç throws up his hands. "For me, this is not craft thinking."

I sip my beer, which adds – until next morning – clarity to everything. I wonder at this distinction. Craft as a process and way of being. Or craft as merely an aesthetic, a gentrified facade of rebellion attuned to all the existing structures of power. The aesthetic of craft is maybe enough for the individual, but to build the spirit of it demands the collective. Ataç sips his beer; a handsome man and neatly dressed but quite ordinary to look at, sitting here on a Muğla industrial estate close to the village where he is raising his young family. Meanwhile in Kadıköy are those with tattooed knuckles and pierced septums, flesh tubes in earlobes, checked shirts, talking of new worlds as they drink their artisan beers; all of it has the appearance of some new and radical dawn, but is not yet able to stand up to even the buyers of a French supermarket chain.

"It is because we don't work together," repeats Ataç. He points at the brewing cylinder. "It is made in Denizli, but the company is in Germany, they only manufacture here. Because we are only ten breweries, we do not brew enough to develop this kind of knowhow."

"Does it help you, being in Muğla," I ask, "on the west coast, where people drink more alcohol? Where culture is more open-minded about beer?"

He gives a sigh. "This is not open-minded. It is only alcohol."

As someone from the West, where alcohol is so often treated as a yardstick for liberal values in Muslim countries, I smile to hear such a sentiment from a Turkish brewer. The substance is only the substance; the values attached to it entirely random, just as the aesthetic of craft can also be attached to a business model that has in it nothing radical. Ataç turns to me and gives a smile, raises his glass a little my way, like he wishes it could be easier. We drink to days when it may be.

"Why do you think the other breweries don't want to cooperate?"

He shrugs. "I used to run rafting trips here," he waves a hand, gesturing towards his other life as if it were an age ago. "Rafting and mountaineering, at Ağrı, Ararat. I did rafting in the United States also, California. And my friend from there, a New Zealander, he came once here, to Türkiye. He saw the industry, the consumerism. He says to me, 'Wow Ataç . . . it is really like a little America.'"

We go all day. Dusk comes for us in our chairs made from pallets. We cycle amber through blonde, pale ales, red again, more porter, a summer ale. A little more rain falls. We talk out the day. A small dent has been made in the contents of the towering cylinders. Ataç returns from what we agree should be a final trip to the cylinder, hands me an IPA. We look each other in the eye, as we have throughout, but more purposeful this time. And though, or perhaps because, all we have done is drink all day, there is a quiet determination in our look, a conviction that everything we have discussed will come to pass.

"Şerefe!" We say a last time. To honour.

Menteşe Mountains – 5 November

Hills turn to mountains. I ride upwards. Mountains grow larger. I leave the pretty town of Muğla, cut out of a mountainside in cold grey stone, and then, having passed through a few villages, I begin the true ascent. Where the old road is warped a new one is cut, and the pine trees flank lengths of rebar pointing straight up and waiting for the concrete pour of new viaducts that will replace ageing switchbacks. Much has changed in this century and more change is coming, but still an old lady dressed in a headscarf and pantaloons sits on her cushions under a wooden structure at the roadside, one knee raised and one arm rested on it. Kettles with winding spouts twist upwards like the road. The kettles bubble and steam, and with an arm shooting up as she sees me, she calls out: "Çay!"

So long as this remains, all will be well.

On the highway I notice signs imploring drivers to keep our road clean. *Karayolumuzu temiz tutalım.* It strikes me that just as *we* found gas in the Black Sea, it is also *our* highway, and *we* should keep it clean. For all that the country has a sense of rugged individualism, it is run and is being built as a group project.

From a layby I look out across Türkiye. Everything is green forests, the horizon buried under deep hills as far as I can see, like the cardiogram I once saw in the hills of the Palestine skyline, and have never since been able to unsee. Here though, in Anatolia, the skyline beats twice as high, and the enormity of the country begins to impress itself upon me. Next to where I stand is a rickety old table, scarcely more than a box, abandoned, but testament that people will always make a place to sit and drink warm drinks amid beauty, as if this is the only way to truly comprehend it.

Smoke lifts out of small houses by the road, from the villages set among the hills. Roadside signs promise figs, but, even this far south, the season is over. From one of the roadside kiosks a man emerges in moustache, flowing pyjamas and his own small head-scarf, dressed, I think, much the same as the village women. "He" and "she", I feel I should tell you in your Anglosphere of gendered pronouns and all their newfound strife, are in Turkish the same: both only the perfect letter and sound, O.

His pyjama trousers also make me think of Mossadegh, the Iranian leader the US brought down with their 1953 coup to ensure British control of Iranian oil, and while they were at it kill off the perceived threats of socialism and Iranian democracy. In their stead they installed the fake monarch, Reza Pahlavi, as shah, and to repress the population gave him an Israeli-trained secret police, the SAVAK. The long flowing trousers of my man in his village remind me particularly of the reported disbelief among Western diplomats that in their meetings Mossadegh would wear pyjama trousers just like these. How could a man so dressed be permitted to manage Iranian resources for Iranians? To stop the British and US from doing with those people and resources as they pleased? By what right did a man in pyjamas expect to be taken seriously by the British and US delegations stuffed all proper inside their suits? This was the culture by which the empires justified their coup. Once it was done, the Westerners dressed their shah in a military tunic and epaulettes, trussed him up in a suit just like their own.

Although it was driven by insiders not outsiders, and motivated by a desire to leave behind the weaknesses of Ottomanism rather than to suppress, much of Turkish fashion was similarly trans-formed, along with what it said of gender, during the move from the sultanate to Kemalists. It is only in recent years, and under the AKP, that the Turkic identity, and the Ottoman identity, complete with their aesthetics, have become fashionable again in Turkish culture.

As I ride over the hills, I consider the region's history. After World War I this territory was not handed to Greece like Izmir, but instead the province of Antalya and its nearby islands were given over to the Italians, who were allowed to manage Turkish resources and population for Italian profit. Between 1919 and 1923, Türkiye was, though it immediately resisted, a colonised space. Between the years of 1953 and 1979, Iran was a colonised space. Since 1948 under the Israelis, and before that under the British, Palestine has been a colonised space. Colonialism is a disease, and it is curable, but the longer you spend under it the worse shape it leaves your body. Nor is it only a word belonging to history, but one that governs the world and millions of lives, whether restricted or traumatised by it, still to this day. Türkiye, alhamdulillah, knew pure colonial struggle for only four years, but still it leaves its mark.

To be colonised, even for a day, instils a vulnerability and sense of inferiority that can be hard to shed. Why were we dominated? How did it happen? Will it happen again? The dissent of a society can also be harmed, because so many legitimate demands – more federalism, religious tolerance, social liberalism, economic justice – have been used disingenuously by colonisers: to instil division, to help shape propaganda against a country. One of the most pernicious features of colonialism is that, because of it, a state can come to reject even the words of its own patriots, because they align with the insincere scalds of the coloniser. It can lead, too, to an infantilisation of society, where you blame others, outside, for failings that are well within your own control. To decry all dissent as originating in the coloniser is a final and resilient form in which a country can remain colonised.

The Little Prince, Antoine de Saint-Exupéry's beautiful book, is loved in Türkiye. As a schoolboy my father would have found it in the national curriculum, because in the first half of the book an Ottoman professor visits the academy in Paris to present his great theory. He is dressed in his Ottoman clothes, and is laughed at. In the second half of the book, the professor returns in a suit, and the academy applauds. This is the ideal response to colonialism: where you show the gaze of the colonialist, rather than seeing yourself through it. Having in 1935 crashed his plane in the Libyan desert, and been saved from death by the traditional rehydration methods of the Bedouin who found him, Saint-Exupéry knew well not to belittle the knowledge of indigenous people, but it is rare that a coloniser learns this lesson so directly.

Village Institutes

The hillsides feel like mountains. I would call them that were it not that to do so would leave me no word to describe the larger things appearing ahead. Colossal boulders guard the road; sometimes the remnant of a small village hunkers among them: houses of stone, the door and window frames long gone, leaving only holes in stone walls. The stone gables just about manage to hold in place the upper parts of the houses. Roads lead to nothing, to old histories now gone from the land.

These then, I think, are the lost villages of Anatolia. The villages that emptied in the second half of the twentieth century; emptied first into the cities, and emptied for a second time out of Türkiye altogether. The British after World War II rebuilt with Indian and Caribbean labour. Turks meanwhile rebuilt Austria, the Netherlands and, most of all, Germany, so that now, a half-century later, I ride through empty Anatolian villages. Their populations, entering their second and third generations, are today in Neukölln, in Kreuzberg, in Wedding, in cities all along the Rhine. The words of John Berger, ever a friend to the Turks, come to me. On why a man leaves his village to earn his living elsewhere, he wrote: "The opportunity to earn a living; to have enough money to act."

It was not always so empowered as this. The photos of the Gastarbeiter, the guestworkers, at Haydarpaşa station in Kadıköy, Istanbul, show Turks and Kurds, stripped to their underwear, standing on scales and beside measuring rules. The images are part Ellis Island, part European colonialism brought closer to home. Too short: a man is rejected. Overweight: a man is rejected.

Underweight: a man is rejected. The colonial process of selection and rejection dies hard. A half-century later and Mesut Özil, a Turkish-German footballer at the time with Arsenal and Germany, says, "I'm German when we win, immigrant when we lose." Özil spoke these words as he took early retirement, vowed never again to pull on the shirt of the German national team. You can be a millionaire many times over, lift countless trophies in silver and gold, but the Gastarbeiter in you dies hard. If such an amount even exists, your bank balance needs to get an unfathomable number of figures from zero before you know for sure you will be let off the Haydarpaşa scales for good.

If from this it has become a phenomenon that the Turkish diaspora of Germany, Austria and the Netherlands are nationalists, are likely to have supported the AKP these last twenty years, are likely to vote as Turks and for their flag and faith, then that is because that same generation had stamped into them the fact that they were Turks, and stamped out of them the idea there could ever be any cause for pride in that. In the automobile production lines, factories and domestic appliance conveyor belts of Stuttgart and Düsseldorf, these men had pride pressed from their souls on the factory floors. Amidst the spinning of cogs and growling motors, Anatolia was pulled out of them and reformed in cables of steel. Banned from having wives or family join them. Blacklisted from work if they mobilised or unionised to be accorded their basic rights. At night they lived in two square metres. By day, they glued a million soles onto the shoes that then walked all over them. They laced copper piping into refrigerator units, laid dashboards onto cars, all of it so mechanised and repetitive that to the factory owners these men became little more than machines themselves. Out of this, it should come as no surprise that when a Turkish political project is brought before this diaspora and says, "Be Not Ashamed", those same people decide that it sounds good not to be ashamed, and they turn out and vote for not being ashamed. None of this is destiny; European societies have in them the potential to learn from their mistakes and improve. Second and third generations have new expectations and will not tolerate the treatment of their Gastarbeiter parents and grandparents. But such histories unwind slowly, and never without effort.

As I ride, I remember how, for a time, a small statue stood on the Kadıköy coastal path in Istanbul. Cast in iron, it showed a man wearing a flat cap and blazer, holding a single case, his arm raised in a farewell. It was called *Journey to Hope*, and commemorated the Turks who had set sail from that dock and out into the world. It marked the contributions of those who had left: their part in rebuilding Europe after the war, their remittances that helped build the Turkish economy, their contributions to art and science and thought in Europe and beyond. One afternoon I copied down the inscription beside the humble statue:

> *This monument was made in memory of the beautiful-hearted people of Anatolia who went to a foreign land full of obscurity, entrusting their loved ones to their homeland in the hope of a better life, and leaving their hearts with those loved ones.*

The path is now empty of its statue, but it pointed to a confidence that, though still being built, is surely growing in Türkiye. In its message was such a very tender mixture of assurance and vulnerability, a self-knowledge that is the true foundation of strength. I remember most of all its final lines, which, I suppose, though I didn't grasp it as a child, described a little of my father's struggle, but maybe also my mother's, returning to her country after making a home in Türkiye. The purpose of the statue, the inscription said, was "in order to remember this great labour migration and to respect the first generation, which carried the burden of being an immigrant".

As I ride through the empty villages of Menteşe, I see another strand of history, a way that might have worked better for everyone. There was, as there always is, another way. In 1930, there began the system known as the Köy Enstitüleri, or Village Institutes. The programme recognised that, at the end of the Empire and beginning of the Republic, the villages that formed the backbone of the Turkish state were not in a good way. Illiteracy was rife, agricultural methods inefficient, and the knowledge necessary to thrive in the twentieth century was lacking. The Köy Enstitüleri, then, was a nationwide educational programme that introduced new methods of farming, tool repair and maintenance. Innovation and problem-solving in the needs of village and field were encouraged. There was group study, municipal buildings were erected and agricultural cooperatives established. Life in the villages showed that same improvement that tends to follow when people gain control of their own destiny.

As with all the best political programmes, it was not merely functional: people learned crafts, they took music lessons. The violin was particularly favoured because it was suited to playing the music of both East and West. Underpinning the programme was the belief that arts, culture and intellectual pursuits belonged as much to the village as any city. If the aim of the Institutes was to improve village life, make villages more productive and encourage participation, social expectations were also upended. Peasants were taught that they were not subordinate. In the Kurdish majority region of Bingöl, the Köy Enstitüleri member Mehmet Rauf Inan interviewed many people, asking them about the Institutes. He reports the words of a peasant who said: "Look, until today no official came to us talking like you did. They never considered us as humans. They called us to their place, gave orders or sent gendarmes. So now we understand that we are also humans. You showed us this!"

It may be unnerving for both nationalist Kurds and Turks to hear that Turkish state-building helped formalise Kurdish political consciousness as never before. The programme focused on class and self-improvement, however, and its vision was a universal one, reaching beyond both ethnic distinction and religion. For the decade the Köy Enstitüleri existed, they brought the far reaches of Thrace and Anatolia into contact with the Turkish state in ways that were, despite not needing to be named as such, socialist.

The programme had to stop. Throughout the twentieth century, perhaps the only thing so entwined as the Turkish state and its military was the Turkish military and the US. As the Institutes developed, Turkish membership of NATO was also being brought to the table, and the US wanted certain things in return. The Köy Enstitüleri, though it was no formal objective, were essentially helping embed socialism across rural Thrace and Anatolia. Even more dangerously, the Köy Enstitüleri inculcated socialist expectations that were incompatible with US expectations that global capital be made safe in both its existence and ideology. The Köy Enstitüleri did not just aspire to improve material conditions, they also promoted a dream of a world built by and for its people. The Köy Enstitüleri did not, as the saying goes, just give a man a fish, they also taught him to fish. But nor did the programme stop there either: pretty soon it was making its own fishing rods, scaling up rod production, and giving lessons in the way the fishing industry operated. That this effort in upbuilding the population was an aspiration both morally correct and essential to social progress was beside the point, for that is not how the United States operates.

Though Türkiye has often been seen as a bridge, the reality is that it is more often, at least for the West, a bridgehead, or a drawbridge that can be raised at will to leave no way of crossing the moat. If lately the West perceives the danger to be Arabs and Islam that are best kept a bridge apart, in the mid-twentieth century the danger was ideological and red: communism, socialism, the idea that there might be more important things on earth than money.

In Türkiye, a US-loyal military found common cause with religious conservatives, who for their part grew worried that the Köy Enstitüleri were also encouraging excessive mixing between men and women, and a spirituality where the name of Allah was coming to be used alongside the more secular word for God, Tanrı. And so, a decade later, the Köy Enstitüleri were no more. Both the military and the religious conservatives got their way, and with a battalion of Turks dispatched into the Korean War to die for the US on the cold roads out of Pyongyang, Türkiye joined NATO. Sometimes I cannot help but consider the words of the great Argentine footballer, Diego Maradona: "I hate everything that comes from the United States. I hate it with all of my strength."

The result of the winding-down of Köy Enstitüleri is the empty villages I pass as I ride, considering how much a revived version of the project could still benefit the country. Such a substantial programme helped build Türkiye in ways that are both difficult to measure and that could not be undone quickly, but it is hard not to think of what more they might have achieved, and what their return could bring today.

Çavdır to Antalya – 8 November

When I asked after the road to Antalya, down on the coast, the woman running the guest house in Çavdır outlined how it would go. One of those answers that gives full confidence, on account of its precision, that she knows the road to perfection. Normal for ten kilometres. Then up. Then normal for thirty kilometres. Then a little up. And then sixty kilometres. Down, down, down. Big down. Palm flat and elbow raised, she made a slope, all the way down to Antalya. She smiled at my obvious appreciation of this answer, before getting back to the task of dipping a ladle into the bowl, handing me soup, pointing to a bag on the kitchen counter and instructing the boy beside me to fetch the bread. He jumped to his feet as, one by one, she served dinner to the family, before taking her seat at the head of the table. Although a woman like this is not always visible at my roadside precisely because she is running the homes of the country, do not doubt that there she is in charge of everything.

And nor was she mistaken about the descent to Antalya. Damn but she was not mistaken. I go screaming down and through the hills, the road seeking out the lowest point at which to cross each ridge and all the time just as she said. Down. Now and then the road slices through an ova, a small plain inside a bowl of mountains, and inside it there is enough growing to sustain all life. There are crops, a couple of pomegranate trees, hay is bailed, a farmer calls an order to his flock of goats, nibbling plants in the rocks that buttress the road. Where the earth is ploughed, it is a black so rich you can see its fertility, the minerals it contains, the snow that settled on it then melted in warming sun to water the earth.

And still the road continues down. I don't think I've ever seen a road so vertical. Looking up I realise that to make a hard shoulder on this mountainside would have required blasting off a further hundred metres of mountain above to gain the necessary three metres of width around its lip. And so just two lanes of traffic and I go careering down into another corkscrew, me doing my best to avoid a rumble strip of indentations in the asphalt and a concrete barrier above a ravine. Up ahead in my own lane is slow-moving traffic: a truck carrying timber, absurdly heavy, logs of orange hardwood just visible beneath the tarpaulin. The weight of the truck combined with the steepness of the descent makes it clear no man-made brake will ever stop the thing should it reach a certain velocity, and so the driver is on and off his brakes. I tap my own to get a sense of what to do, and a sense of my own speed: too fast to sit behind the truck, and for now too slow to join the relentless traffic in the fast lane. Still, I have no choice but to go for it, and I watch over my shoulder for a gap. A car flashes by and I heave into a pedal stroke behind the truck, reach the tailgate and pull into the outside lane. I pass the truck's back wheels. The smell of cut timber comes to me. Front wheels. Cab window, revealing a driver having no fun at all. I zip ahead, anxious to slot back into the lane before the next car shoots by. The sun is shining bright but chill winds blow down from the mountains, from a place of true cold. Were I listening close enough, I'd make out the laughing words on the wind: *You ain't seen nothing yet*. I barrel down the descent but another small, limping lorry lies ahead, brake pedal to the floor as the driver's heavy cargo – sacks of cement – resist his attempts to fight gravity. Less hesitant this time, already moving at most of the speed limit, I hop out of lane and overtake, hop back in but now there's a tanker up ahead carrying LPG. On the road under me are tyre skids, black rubber laid down, a pockmarked surface that has either been caused by, or caused, impact and fire where some smoke stains the asphalt. I rumble over the divots, ride by the tanker and look in at the driver with his flammable cargo just behind his seat, he gives me a nod as together we flash through old castle walls that once guarded this valley. Pulled in at a rare layby, I see a truck with *Murat Lojistik* printed, semi-professionally, on its canvas side. In the cab an exasperated man is talking on his phone. Looks like it might be Murat: a man both his own boss and nothing like it.

Every few kilometres of hard shoulder is a small pile of rocks, scattered where they have clearly been wedged under a tyre to lodge a broken-down vehicle in place and take some of the strain from the handbrake. And then forgotten. I fly past a larger rock, shaking my head a little, the thing sizable enough to destroy another vehicle or spill a cyclist over his handlebars. This rock, left on a modern highway, is perhaps where Türkiye is now: somewhere at the midpoint of an industrial development that still has features of the village. I don't think it is out of selfishness that the driver leaves the rock; more likely it is exhaustion. The truck broken down, the consignment late, the boss irate, the rock forgotten. There is no greater cause of accidents than poverty, for poverty is obliged to accept unreasonable demands. Poverty breathes down your neck. Poverty is forced into risks. And poverty creates tunnel vision.

As I career downhill, I think more of this idea of Türkiye as a Little America. Many things certainly keep Türkiye safe from such an awful fate, but in it too is a truth. There is in the country too much respect for hard work, which makes people work harder, and allows the creation of expectations that people should be working harder even where they are already at their limits. Sometimes, even, there is an affectation of hard work or haste, born of the idea that this is what work is supposed to be. The boy on the scooter accelerates down a city backstreet because that is just what he does. Then comes the moment where the boy crashes his scooter after a risk too many, a gap too small. The truck topples off the road in an absent-minded minute: a phone not just checked but an entire message sent while driving. The highway is closed after the crash. The coal mine is closed after the blast. The hoped-for profit or gain is swallowed up a hundredfold by disaster. In Türkiye, society and community are paramount, but there is also a great respect for the myth of the rugged individual who pulls themselves up. The opposite of rugged individualism is a smart society: community above individual, a community that aspires to remove obstacles rather than necessarily triumphing over all of them.

With these thoughts I pedal forward towards Antalya. The exhilaration of racing a bicycle down a fast descent, towards glittering sea and under emerald forest, is perhaps different things to different people at different times. But for me, here, odd as I maybe am, it writes manifestos in my mind. I am suddenly conscious that what Türkiye now needs, as its highways are smoothed or replaced by railways, as its ports fill and its imports are substituted for domestic production, is to become an economy based on knowledge and not the extraction of resource. It is capable of this transition, and it needs to make it because knowledge is a thing that makes better money with less danger and fewer limits. Turkish chemists shouldn't end up inventing vaccines for German pharmaceutical companies. Türkiye needs to build an economy based on the collection and deployment of information and not just the collection and deployment of resources. It needs to do this so the rivers can refill, so the soils can replenish, so the air can clear, so the people can breathe, so the men can come out of the mines, and a boy from Hakkari you've yet to meet in Mersin can do more than make wraps for a living. It needs it so the drivers can rest, and so that when the many fine minds of this country express themselves, it is understood as part of our culture of knowledge and critique and analysis. With the same definitive clarity as the descent itself, it occurs to me that if the first century was a success, then it follows that the second has to be easier.

1. Preparing to set out from the childhood home of Mustafa Kemal Atatürk, in Selanik/Thessaloniki city centre.

2. Greek roadside adorned with graffiti, most of it from far-right groups.

3. Nearing the Turkish border, riding through the rich delta region of the Nestos River, named Karasu in Turkish.

4. Crossing the Meriç/Evros River, and the border of the European Union, at dusk.

5. It is hard to imagine a city that cares for animals quite like Istanbul.

6. Crossing the Bosphorus.

7. One of the fleet of drillships purchased by Turkish Petroleum to develop offshore gas fields in the Black Sea and Mediterranean.

8. Posters of Recep Tayyip Erdoğan outside a football stadium in Istanbul - "Turkish Century, Starting".

9. Swimmers relax as a cargo ship powers north up the Bosphorus.

10. Ortaköy Mosque, with the Bosphorus Bridge behind it - one of the most iconic sights in Istanbul.

11. Dusk settling on Balıkesir Province.

12. A boat yard with the world's longest suspension bridge, Çanakkale Köprüsü, in the background.

13. A father and daughter sit on swings at the Çanakkale beach.

14. Bringing in the olive harvest, a common sight in late autumn.

15. A couple in Izmir do some relaxed night fishing.

16. Izmir close to October 29th and Republic Day. Flags of Atatürk and Türkiye hang from every balcony.

17. Breakfast in a mountain village, complete with many glasses of çay, and lots of homemade jam.

18. The picturesque village of Şirince stands in the hillsides of the Aegean.

19. Four young riders from the local cycling club find my campsite in the grounds of a mosque.

MALT IS THE SOUL OF BEER HOPS IS PERSONALITY AND YEAST IS THE HEART.

20. The Gara Guzu craft brewery ships artisan beers worldwide from a small premises in the mountains of Muğla.

21. Regular irrigation from melting snow leaves rich fields for farming.

22. Börek – layers of thin pastry filled with potatoes, spinach or minced meat.

23. November 10 marks the anniversary of Atatürk's death, commemorated here at a monument in Antalya.

24. Melon harvest lines the highway in autumn, with the crop sold to passing drivers.

25. The city centre in Osmaniye, just months before the earthquake that devastated it.

26. A woman takes her children down to the water at the Port of Mersin.

27. A driver heads down from the mountains, as a new road is built alongside.

28. Wind turbines surround a truck stop in mountains above the Syrian border.

29. A bicycle joins the crowds at Abraham's Cave in Şanlıurfa.

30. HDP bunting in Diyarbakır, Türkiye's largest Kurdish-majority city.

31. The River Tigris flows beyond the Diyarbakır city walls and towards nearby Iraq.

32. Two young men sell the last of their pomegranate harvest.

33. Near Bitlis a maverick sheep takes the long way round.

34. Lake Van reflects the sky at the city of Tatvan. In 2020 the lake saw tragedy when a boat sank with 61 Afghan migrants on board.

35. The second-highest mountain in Türkiye, Süphan, stands over a small house with "Nation First" written on its side.

36. Behind me, the snow-capped mountains that mark the Turkish-Iranian border.

37. Ishak Paşa Sarayı, a seventeenth-century Ottoman palace, in the mountains near Doğubayazıt. Just east of here begins the old route of the Silk Road into Asia.

38. In the city of Kars, tables are pushed back as Cossack dancers perform in a local restaurant.

39. The ruins of Ani beside the Turkish–Armenian border.

40. On my way back to Istanbul on the Doğu Ekspresi, or East Express, an overnight train that runs through Anatolia, between Kars and Ankara.

Part 3
Antalya to Şanlıurfa

PART THREE

N

TÜRKİYE

Gaziantep

Şanlıurfa

Antalya

Mersin

Adana

Alanya

R. Euphrates

CYPRUS

Lefkoşa
Nicosia

SYRIA

MEDITERRANEAN SEA

0   200 km

0   200 miles

Antalya – 10 November

Inside the small pension where I slept, words from a loudspeaker come into my waking dreams and a lingering half-sleep. An announcer is saying something about Adalet ve Demokrasi. Justice and Democracy. In the square outside, the opposition coalition is staging a gathering. Lying there, possibilities of sleep retreating, I think of the not-dissimilar name of the AKP: Adalet ve Kalkınma. Justice and Development. The words of politics, the big ones, are not much more than a crowded but open buffet, where some words are more popular than others, and some fit the mood of one time better than another.

In the West, the word "change" is the most desired and contested, precisely for the absence of it. There the tactic of the politician is to conjure a sense of change for the people while assuring the powerful that they will not alter the status quo. It is a process of organised delusion and then disappointment that eventually erodes faith in democracy, at which point the narrators of the system lament that the public has lost faith in democracy, not that the system has been stripped of democracy and the public has subsequently done the logical thing of losing faith.

Türkiye is yet to reach this cynical stage of political maturity, but still things have changed. For Turks at the turn of the millennium, after the national debt crisis and currency write-off, Development sounded good while Justice was sought by all who'd been denied political representation under successive governments and military coup. After twenty years of improved living standards and no change of government, Democracy starts sounding good again, begins returning to the menu.

From the pension I head out towards the main square and ask a man what is happening. "Atatürk'ün ölüm yil dönümü," he says, taking a photo of the wreaths in front of which we are gathered. Anniversary of Atatürk's death. The AKP may have run the country for two decades, but the wreaths show the full spectrum of the Turkish political space. Türkiye's youth, environmental, workers', liberal, women's and nationalist parties have all placed their tributes of flowers and braided laurel.

Looking at the line of wreaths and the vibrant, diverse breadth of opinions behind it, I think of how politics is made up of votes and of voices. Votes are formally recorded but are mostly private affairs, while voices shape the thoughts of all who hear them, and all who speak them, but are not formally recorded, so that sometimes we risk ignoring voices in preference for votes. I remember the 2017 referendum, won by the government, which transferred more powers to the presidency. I stood outside a gallery with Ali, a Syrian painter, and we sipped our coffees together as he smiled at the sight of protest which to me – at the time, and however spirited the scene – felt like the opposition going through the motions. Ali, though, marvelled at the sight.

"You don't have demonstrations in Syria?" I asked.

"Small ones, maybe," he said, "but not like this, in the streets, demonstrating against what the government wants. This is not possible in Syria."

I watched a Syrian man almost laughing at this sight. Since that day, I've realised that, by going through the motions of democracy, you do slowly build a democracy. Moreover, making a demand, and feeling entitled to your demand, can be an act more integral to democracy than voting. If all you are allowed to do is complete a ballot slip once every five years, you become like the customer forlornly demanding to speak to the restaurant manager who has long ago decided that it is safe to ignore your meek protestations because you can be trusted to keep returning to the restaurant despite professing not to like the food. Perhaps you have even reached the point where you prefer complaining about the food to seeking out good food. Perhaps you have stopped complaining because to complain is to admit that something is wrong, to admit that there are no other restaurants in town and you have forgotten how to cook.

If a person is content to live within a permitted but narrow range of options, then it is safe to say that freedom will never be a problem to them. I consider Rosa Luxembourg's words: "If you don't move then you don't feel your chains."

Turks, like Iranians, Palestinians and so many others, do not like chains, while Westerners have perhaps come to interpret as freedom what is in fact their reluctance to move. Saudis, Emiratis, Egyptians, and Bahrainians do not like chains either, but because Western states get their oil there, because they moor their warships there, it is not in the national interest to discuss these chains, or the struggle of millions to break them.

Westerners have come to view – and *view* is the operative word – the rejection of chains as a sign of repression, where in fact it is a sign of freedom, if not of liberty. It is true that, of all of them, Western chains are often better-padded. They come with a currency and passport that unlock not the chains but much of the world. Westerners have been raised in an information system that teaches them theirs are the finest of all the world's chains, and therefore many will wear their chains more like medallions. But as Westerners discover that even their chains within this system are to be fastened tighter, as the padding on those chains wears thinner, the reality that they too are in irons begins to show.

Riding east along the coast I think of Atatürk, the roadside today presenting even more opportunity than usual to remember him. It is testament to the unity of Türkiye, for all its polarisation, that such disparate political persuasions still see a place for themselves in what Atatürk represented. Many stake a claim upon his memory. Erdoğan, too, as the post-pandemic currency crisis in the lira began to break, rallied first of all not around Islam or tradition, but in stating that this was a new War of Independence moment. While Atatürk was not only *a* Kemalist but *the* Kemalist, the idea of Türkiye he helped create has become a home even to those outside of that political tradition.

I think back to a journey by cargo ship I once made between Istanbul and Odesa. As we sailed out late one night, up the Bosphorus towards the Black Sea, I stood with a Ukrainian sailor who was travelling as a passenger home to the Donbas. We talked together on the bow of the boat, gliding under illuminated bridges and out through the glowing metropolis. At some point in our conversation, as he stood there in his thick, denim dungarees, one of those huge men that never gets cold, he hit his fist into his open palm and said, "He was a strong leader, Atatürk. He was good, wasn't he?" In response, I said that yes, he had done good, but had sometimes been too firm, which created problems of its own.

"Sometimes history needs men like this," the Ukrainian said. "Atatürk was like our Peter the Great. I think he was a good man for Türkiye."

And that was his conclusion. I think about this as I ride today, and there is truth in this sentiment, but it is also false. There were also errors of judgment, too great a fear of ethnic diversity, the ban on headscarves. Kurds fined by the word for speaking Kurmanji. A friend from Kahramanmaraş, himself no pious Muslim, would boggle that men of his village still worked the fields when Ramadan fell in summer. He told stories of men fainting as a result of fasting even while they laboured under hot sun, but he would also bemoan Kemalists desecrating mosques, saying that they would walk mules through them to insult Muslims. I have never found reports of this episode, but – just as our conversations in Greece about that which is written or spoken – not everything that happens is reported, and sometimes perception is everything, because if a man thinks something happened and is willing to act as if it happened, then in some ways it may as well have. This is why it is important for states to be good, because grudges can very easily taint or even outlast them. It is also why giving accurate information to society, ensuring society thinks critically and seeks to verify what it is told, is often in the long run an asset to a state, and not a threat.

I don't doubt that Atatürk understood this. In him was the unmistakable force of progress, but one that was tempered by a philosophy and even an affection which had its roots in Sufism, Mevlana Rumi, Yunus Emre and all the poets. The Atatürk quotes on roadside posters today bear it out. *Seni özlüyorum*, says one, tenderly. I miss you. *Sevmek yetmez, anlatmak lazım* says another. To love is not enough; it is necessary to explain.

It is worth asking why Atatürk remains so prominent in Turkish life. Is it healthy or does it hold the country back? On one of my first visits to the country as an adult, I asked a family friend if one day the portraits of him would be removed from so many rooms and offices, so that the celebration of leaders would maybe abate a little. I suggested this assuming that my proposition would be a mark of progress, of a country moving forwards. Her answer was simple, "I hope I never live to see the day."

Antalya to Alanya – 11 November

Over the ridge of Antalya's mountains, the Mediterranean returns and with it the coastal road. It was from this port and these turquoise waters that the Mavi Marmara boat set sail in 2010, with Turkish activists determined to bring aid to the blockaded Palestinians of Gaza. As the Palestinian coast neared, Israeli forces lowered themselves from a helicopter overhead, shooting dead ten of the humanitarians on board. Therein ended, for much of the next decade, Turkish relations with the Israeli state.

As I pedal, a plane descends from sky to runway, the agriculture changes, and there is still the occasional polytunnel that perhaps holds tomatoes and aubergine, but gradually everything takes a tropical turn. Vibrant green columns of trees start to appear, their leaves melting down from them and whole arms of bananas turning green into yellow. Other trees have the bananas inside blue plastic covers that hold the heat around the fruit and accelerate the ripening. From a roadside palm, high above, there hang great garlands of orange ovals: dates waiting for the sun that will turn them brown and sweet. Turkish farmers are never shy of experimenting with foreign crops and seeing if the earth and sun with which the country is blessed will do the rest. Antalya has begun to cultivate avocados and mangos. Above a large greenhouse I see a billboard with a picture of a pink pitaya, otherwise known as dragon fruit, the latest tropical fruit to be grown here rather than imported from South-East Asia.

It is not only the agriculture that changes with sun and sea. As the plants and plantations retreat, Turks begin instead to harvest the lip of sand that shines white before the blue sea. The beach replaces the field; tourists become the crop. A bride dressed in white, with a long train to her dress, is instructed by a professional photographer where to stand against the sea view. Sun loungers are planted, umbrellas shoot from the earth as uniform as trees in the banana plantation. Private beaches spread beneath concrete hotels, and for a while I ride not through Türkiye but through Britain, Germany, Ukraine, Russia. Women sunbathe with the seriousness of office work. Eight and a half days' holiday. Make the most of it. Everyone is here, eking out the summer. From one balcony Turkish and Ukrainian flags hang together in support. From the one opposite, the Turkish flag with the Uyghur, in blue and white. Western tourists waddle up from beach tracks and down pavements, an air of confusion to them, sunstroke a term too gentle for what has happened here. Released from their daily lives, obliged only to walk back and forth to the beach, in crimson skin they alternate between the water and their rooms.

But it is not so innocent. These are no small family hotels; the entire coast is filled with cathedrals and citadels of concrete. Domed minarets are illuminated red and green, blue and pink. For mile after garish mile, the hotels command my attention like a grisly car crash. It is compellingly awful. I see animals coming towards me, camels towering over the pedestrians. Here I am, trying to dispel the myths of orientalism, and some fucker puts up a line of ten-foot camels in cast iron, a whole caravan of the things. In fairness though, these camels are less orientalism than capitalism, pure and simple: you give the people what they want, camels is what the tourists came for.

Shops stay open long into the evening. Knock-off jeans and bikinis and flip-flops are illuminated under white lights. A light outside the pharmacy offers Botox. Tattoo and piercing salons are more prevalent than kebab restaurants. People drive around in golf buggies, consider renting a quad bike for the following day. Such are the decisions of life here. Boat trip? Snorkel? Sea safari? A mother scolds her child in Ukrainian, or maybe it is Russian. I hope this book ages better than their conflict. An English woman squawks at her useless husband to hurry up, the show starts at eight. He replies that it's all right for her, not carrying the rucksack and all.

At the neighbouring table in a bar, Keith sits with a woman he seems to have just met. Both of them middle-aged, they order food, talk daily life. Keith opens up. "I buy large here but they're still a little small for me." We feel for you, Keith. Some German women, drunk as skunks, get up to leave, try to negotiate the narrow gaps between the tables. One of them treads on the tail of a dog, a Labrador. It yelps. She bends down to him, denim backside in the air, round and large and domed as a balloon lifting over Cappadocia. The dog seems confused, but she is delighted at her discovery of the hound, starts slathering in its mystified animal face, fussing at its jowls and ears. "Schnucki! Schnuckiputzi! Du bist ein guter Hund!" The Labrador is overwhelmed: a human more Labrador than it is itself. "Du bist ein sehr guter Hund! Du bist ein sehr gutes Hündchen!" I watch as the two creatures merge into one, her ecstatic mass slathering over the fur and form and tail of the Labrador until her friends pull her away and they wobble out into the night.

I head from the bar, go to see if I can find a shave, somewhere far from the tourist areas with prices given in foreign currency. As I walk down the street, a chef and a waiter at an ocakbaşı try to pull me in. Using their few words of the language, they call out at me: "English mixed grill!" I answer in Turkish and they smile, before, like informal border agents, demanding to know where I was born. Not answering, I put the same question to them, at which they take no offence. One replies that he is from Turkmenistan, and does not plan to go back. The other is from Mardin, a proud Arab and proud Turk for as far as his family line goes. Not for the first time, I wonder if the sense of offence at being asked where you are from is proportionate to one's awareness and experience of racism, a sensitivity proportionate in turn to the feeling of not belonging. For some, it is merely fascinating, essential information, part of the richness of the world. As with all truths, I feel that two are at work here simultaneously.

I keep walking, will continue until the word *hairdresser* and other signs in English have gone and *berber* or *kuaför* returns. Down a small street I find one. The barber is surprised at my having found my way to him, and I decide not to share the method of my search.

Huzar does a great job of my shave. He makes the usual small talk of barbers and hairdressers the world over, which I could do without. He asks why I'm here. I say a holiday. I ask how it is here.

"Beautiful. But expensive. No jobs."

"You've got a job, so I guess you're comfortable?"

"Yeah," he says. "Got a job. I'm comfortable."

He slides the blade over my cheeks, removing rectangles of white that turn back to skin. He shapes my moustache, then returns to the subject.

"But if I had a visa I'd leave, of course."

"Where?"

"Maybe Scotland. I've a friend there. A barber. We'd start a shop. They need barbers in Scotland."

Beside me at a bar sits Leon, a young Russian from Moscow, though originally from the Volga region. Strong jaw, neat haircut, a bit stiff in his manner, but also possessed of that quirky friendliness and warmth that with Slavs it can sometimes take a little while to find beneath the cooler exterior for which they are famed. As a result they are often misjudged by the world, but I've met enough of them that now I expect it soon enough, to show itself with a little patience.

Leon thinks by my moustache that I may be Russian, moves to English when it turns out I'm not. He is impressed to discover I know the city of Saratov, that I've visited it. He guesses it was a woman that took me there, looks confused when I say it was a bicycle and a journey around the world. He is here in Alanya to avoid the draft of able-bodied men for the war in Ukraine. "Do you know the word 'mobilisation'?" he asks. He booked a flight to Türkiye as soon as it was announced, explains that to get drafted you have to be served papers, receive them, and then take them to the army offices. He left his home immediately after the draft was announced and left the country four days after that. If you don't receive the papers, you're in the clear. He was relieved earlier in the week to learn that nothing had arrived at his house in those four days. He is off the hook.

"What do you do here?" I ask.

"I'm a programmer."

"What language?"

"Python. You know it?"

I nod, a little.

"It is good for data modelling, like these neural networks."

"I've heard that," I say.

"But here I am spending most of my time playing tennis."

"Table tennis?" I ask, knowing that programmers often like it.

"No. Big tennis," he corrects me, puzzled. "Why you ask table tennis?"

"I don't know," I reply, truthfully. "It was popular in Russia. I suppose."

"Yes. The Soviet Union. China also play a lot."

"Yes. They are very good," I agree, confused at our conversation.

"Yes. But I play big tennis here."

"OK," I answer. I'd like to improve the dialogue for you, dear reader, but it can't all be historical profundity and the sparse beauty of daily life. Sometimes you do just end up talking to a Russian in a bar about what sort of tennis he plays. For a moment I wonder whether to tell him that we don't call it "big tennis", or if this will just deepen the conversational hole we're stuck in.

"You think you'll stay here?" I ask in an attempt to escape it.

Leon shakes his head. "Here for me is not so good. Istanbul is beautiful, but still no. I have never been to Britain, or United States. But I think the service is better in Moscow."

I look confused, have to say it's a strange criterion. I reach for my *Post-Soviet Cultural Malaise Embraces Capitalism* generalisation, then remember my *Programmers Can Be Quite Dull* generalisation.

And I suppose I divide the two by Leon in front of me, another peculiar individual like the rest of us, and there's my answer.

"When I was young, I did not like Russia," he says. "I wanted to live in Germany, Poland. But I went there." He pauses. "And now I feel Moscow is quite good."

Interesting, Leon, interesting.

On the coast road I watch east and west draw closer: a half-hour of mountain disappears into each tunnel being blasted. I talk to Russians on the scout for cheaper cities in which to make a new home. They've been heading to Antalya for a decade or more, have bought up properties to a whole new level of price. I speak to a group of Russian men outside a bus station. Antalya is unaffordable. Alanya surprisingly expensive too. They're waiting for the bus to Mersin, the cheapest of the three, but they won't go further than that. After that the stream of roubles will thin to a trickle.

A girl talks to me as her brother sets my table, prepares my food. She smiles, her face bright in the light of the courtyard and in the frame of her headscarf. She smiles all the time. One of her front teeth is broken in half, but still she smiles, totally unselfconscious. I talk with her and her brother about their home town: not here. About my ride: far to go. He leaves, we talk more, Berika and I. Her name means "holy light", she explains, light from Allah. I feel guilty for thinking her so beautiful. She'd like to travel, one day, away from here. To where? Germany, she thinks. To where? She's not sure, she'd just like to travel. To see it. Maybe Hamburg. A beautiful city. Am I Muslim? Maybe.

"But I drink," I confess.

"It is not important." She puts hand to chest. Says softly, "Head is not important. Only in your heart. In your heart you know."

What does she do? Here in this town, at the family restaurant? She was a cook, but she had an accident, riding her motorbike. A car pulled out. She opens her mouth, points at the half-tooth I might not have noticed. She laughs and shrugs her shoulders, as if she had cosmetic beauty to spare anyway. She makes a chopping motion: she can't do this now. She rolls up a loose sleeve to reveal the purple scar on her wrist. She pulls out her phone, shows an X-ray: a bright white metal pin right across the wrist. It's still inside? Shakes head, it came out. The accident was two months ago. She smiles all the time.

Outside I sit at the table as inside the family eat their evening meal together. She brings me tea. Twenty minutes later brings tea a second time. Then once more she returns, finger to lips and *ssh*. Her brother Görken's birthday is today. "Gel, gel!" Come inside, she beckons. At the table is the whole family and still more beauty. They dim the lights. A UV light crackles as it kills a fly, glows purple. From the kitchen, sparklers flare. Candles. "Iyiki doğdun Görken, Iyiki doğdun Görken, Iyiki doğdun Iyiki doğdun, Iyiki doğdun Görken." Everyone laughs, claps. One candle accidentally sets light to a large, ornamental plastic flower on top of the cake. There is a smell of burning, we laugh again until Görken with a great puff blows it all out. And the smoke winds up.

Berika is a product of her family. They are all beautiful. All with a little of that light for which she was named. They are originally from Elazığ, Central Anatolia. We establish it is beside Tunceli, which they sometimes call that and sometimes its other name, Dersim. The two used to be in the same department, but now each has its own, adjacent. The mighty River Tigris, Dicle in Turkish, is the border. They ask if I'll visit, and I say I've been wanting to go to Tunceli but am not sure it fits this trip. "Fatih Mehmet Maçoğlu," I say simply. He is the communist elected as mayor of Tunceli, who since his election has set an agenda of insourcing council services and promoting social liberalism in everything from menstruation days off work to gay rights. At the table, only the grandfather has been indifferent to my presence; not unkind, just old and short on enthusiasm. At the name Maçoğlu, his head lifts up, then his thumb. His eyes shine as he says, "A good man." We agree on the importance of leadership, and so I mention that yesterday was the anniversary of the death of Atatürk. The grandfather says again, "A good man." He taps his head. "Zeki." He was smart.

As I leave the family and head into the night, I look back at them for a brief moment. Some are still sitting around the cake, others packing up their restaurant for another day. Berika and her mother and her mother's mother are wearing hijabs. A cousin is in that awkward phase and looks like she is on the verge of becoming a goth. She has long pointed nails, painted black. Another sister is in a short, pleated skirt. It makes me cringe at myself, but I feel the need to describe this scene. I ask forgiveness from my sisters for drawing attention to their clothing, the fact they are dressed in everything from short skirts to hijab, because it is all only clothing and choice, and as such unimportant and undeserving of such direct mention. There comes a point where working to undo the stereotypes of orientalism becomes its own orientalism, a struggle just to show how normal people are, how un-exotic. Like the opposite of belly dancing, like taking off all of your sequins.

Taşucu to Cyprus – 12 November

In the blue waters off the coast I see a familiar red-white boat with a giant, tower constructed in its centre: one of the drillships from the new Turkish fleet of offshore gas exploration vessels. Now and then in recent years they have been moored off the Haydarpaşa dock in Istanbul. By chance, a friend had the contract for English lessons aboard the ships, and I regret not taking up his offer of a teaching post for a few months on one of the boats. The fleet has a number of vessels, some with seismic exploration capacity, others for drilling kilometres down beneath the earth's crust. They are attended at times by naval frigates, to defend them from Greek naval harassment and avoid the possibility of an accidental escalation. At times, they are attended by other vessels, too, including barges that carry a certain type of mud which resists heat well and so is pumped down with the drill bit to cool it as it bores into the rock way beneath the sea. After drilling operations off Cyprus a few years ago immediately yielded much international controversy and few hydrocarbons, Türkiye switched to the Black Sea and hit the Sakarya field, due on stream – like everything else that was given the option – in 2023. It was the largest gas discovery in the world for the year it was struck, and its billions of cubic metres will meet a quarter of the annual Turkish gas demand, helping to displace coal power as the country moves to renewables.

One part of my heart mourns each hydrocarbon burned, but another recognises that Türkiye's reliance on energy imports, and the relative weakness of the lira against the currencies in which energy is priced, mean energy costs have the potential to bankrupt the country every time the world economy shifts from boom to bust. I will agitate for the Turks to keep their hydrocarbons in the ground only after the US, Dutch, British, Norwegians, French, Italians and Spanish have done likewise.

The plan goes beyond purely Turkish resources, however. The drillships were purchased at great expense from various sources: some from North Sea companies in Aberdeen, others from the Brazilian state oil firm, Petrobras. The role of English teacher that I'd have taken on was because, at the time, Türkiye did not have the skills of this sector. It did not know how to find the gas, drill the sea floor, capture the gas. An international drilling company was hired to train the Turkish staff, who for this purpose had to learn English, but once trained could drill Turkish wells independently.

Having begun the development of its own energy sector, Türkiye now looks to explore for gas supplies with Algeria in the west Mediterranean. It looks to partner with Libya in the waters the two governments delineated after Türkiye helped Tripoli fend off the warlord Khalifa Haftar. And so there develops – as happens so often in the fields of energy projects – a new basis for international partnership.

At the Taşucu port I see the Cyprus boat coming towards the mainland, the island less than eighty kilometres away, and the gas beneath this seabed only a footnote in that whole story. I stayed there once; ten days on both sides of an island needlessly divided. On my last evening I met with members of Turkish and Greek cycling clubs, both of which would have happily referred to themselves as simply "Cypriot". The ethnic distinctions belong only to lines that need not be there. Those who love the bicycle often seem able to maintain a love of the world and faith in how it could be.

The island of Cyprus, by square kilometre, is the most mili- tarised rock on earth. It hosts most of the British military in the Mediterranean, and while British–Turkish relations may be his- torically among the best of all European and Western states, still Türkiye has no enthusiasm for being militarily encircled. Cyprus itself was a British colony of largely harmonious Greek–Turkish relations until, determined to cling to power, the British waged a concerted divide and rule strategy of random killings and general brutality. British rule eventually came to an end in 1960, although the British military bases remained, and the Turkish Cypriot self-defence militias always feared that their fellow islanders – the majority Greek Cypriot population – might turn on them when the occupier was gone.

And so it went. But it was not only the Greek Cypriots who were to blame; the extremists of the island would have been far less potent without the 1974 military dictatorship we have already met back in Athens. Drunk on Hellenist fantasy, its leaders do not want an independent Cyprus; they want Cyprus inside Greece. The junta stages a coup so ferocious in its onslaught that the Cypriot president has to be evacuated to Malta by the British RAF still on the island. The Greek Cypriot militia, EOKA, which has attacked Turks for decades, is now so emboldened that even Greek Cypriots fear what its fanaticism means for the island. Cyprus will be Greek. For five days this is the state of affairs, with Turkish Cypriots shut terrified inside their houses, until Türkiye resolves to refuse this remaking of a new normal and the total violation of the 1960 Cypriot constitution. Ankara sends troops.

After intense fighting, the puppet regime installed by the junta falls, and the island is left divided by the intervention. Despite the coup on Cyprus, despite the outcome performing the un-alloyed good of bringing down the junta in Athens, Western history somehow sees the whole affair as the fault of the Turks, who are castigated for not acquiescing, for resisting, for having made a scene. Without that resistance ordered by Ankara, it could all have gone off smoothly. By now we'd need only a fifty-minute documentary with archive footage, perfect for the History Channel: a little remorse and sadness before work again tomorrow morning. As it is, thanks to the Turks, we've been left with a political impasse.

Many of us have our Cyprus stories. Dad was doing his military service in 1974 when the conflict broke out. He was on the next boat crossing to land troops when the ceasefire was signed. The family home of Rana, a friend from Turkish Cyprus, served as an army radio post. It was felt to be far enough north to be safe, but the attack from Greek forces was so forceful that in the end the family had to flee, their home evacuated.

That the junta in Athens began the war goes unremarked. That the Greeks did terrible things to Turkish Cypriots goes unremarked. That Turks did terrible things having been attacked is undisputed. War is terrible, which is why we must always seek to avoid it.

Still less is known in the West about the attempts to find a resolution. In 2004 there was a referendum on a UN-backed plan, painstakingly brokered, to reunify the island. Of the Turkish Cypriots, sixty-five per cent vote in favour. Of the Greek Cypriots, seventy-six per cent vote against. Doubtless cultural factors can be complex, but the outcome was not helped by the fact that among Greek Cypriots what can only be described as a stiff culture of bigotry has been developed. I remember crossing from South Cyprus to North and being asked by a kindly Greek Cypriot woman, amazed anyone would go at all, if we would be taking our own food – because Turkish food could be unclean. Dear Nikoleta, in that favourite of Athenian cafés, on the hill above Exarcheia: a true Cypriot, a true Greek. "Nasılsın?" she said brightly on learning I was Turkish. "How are you?" Nikoleta had begun studying Turkish because, she said, she hated the racism on an island she loved, and towards a population for whom it is also home. The man from the cycling club. I'll never forget the way he said it, confused and mystified, a Turkish Cypriot to a Greek one: "We know you're the enemy, our media is not good. But I don't think they tell us to hate you like your media does." The Greek Cypriot, a friend from the south of the island, nodded solemnly. "It's true."

In South Cyprus exists a supremacist current, not helped by the British military pensioners who stay for its sun, nor by the Russian oligarchs with their own nationalist ways and Christian supremacy.

That all this runs contrary to Greek Cypriot interests is unquestionable, because supremacy is a harmful drug. Supremacists make enemies and, true to their core belief of superiority, underestimate others.

That Türkiye will not be dislodged is not the point. The problem is that the North wants resolution, a full peace that South Cyprus will not consider. And why would it? The South has the keys to the state car. Gas from the seabed, they take it. Revenue, they keep it. Passports, recognised worldwide. All the time Turkish Cypriots are left quasi stateless, their passports recognised only by Türkiye, a mainland with which Cypriots are kin but on which they'd sooner not have to rely.

And what of external actors? Some outside mediation perhaps? Could the European Union help? *Ha!* It was recognised that no part of Cyprus should join the EU until the situation was resolved, for fear of making matters intractable. Fast forward to 2005. Flags flutter, trumpets blare: the European Union would like to welcome as its newest member − "the Republic of Cyprus". Far be it from me to make so bold a claim, but had the EU actively wanted to scupper resolution on Cyprus, I am not sure what they would have done differently.

Where are we now? Türkiye, along with North Cyprus, calls for a formal partition: a two-state solution with agreed borders and seabed. Western politicians bemoan that the Turks, who always wanted reunification but were denied that, now want to divide the island, an outcome none would have sought but for fifty years no one has worked with Türkiye or North Cyprus to avert. This is how you operate when you're a Western state: you deliberately marginalise diplomacy, then howl blue murder when people tire of being marginalised.

The latest is no more heartening. As tensions grow globally, in autumn 2022 the United States lifts a decades-long arms embargo on South Cyprus, designed specifically to avoid escalation. In this act lies maybe the most crucial and tragic thing to understand: a number of states, unlike almost anybody on the island, do not in fact want peace on Cyprus. When you are a distant state, the threat of conflict is not in fact terrible, but only leverage to be leaned on or released at will in achieving your own objectives. When you have peace, this lever breaks. You are left with only peace but no leverage. Cyprus becomes only an island in the sun again, beautiful perhaps, but useless to you.

Mersin – 13 November

In Mersin a change becomes apparent. The roads and pavements are a little more rutted. Where public works are being carried out, less care is taken to cover the gaping hole in the ground and the pile of steel rebar waiting to be woven and have its concrete poured. I get off my bike at the Othello Hotel, where the clerk knows about Shakespeare well enough but hasn't much enthusiasm beyond the basic reference. I say something about British–Ottoman fighting on Cyprus being the basis for the play. He just smiles in reply and says, "Room 207."

The port tick-tocks deep into the night, and seems even larger than Haydarpaşa in Istanbul. Looks larger than Izmir too. Ocean-going cargo ships are loaded. Ten large dock cranes work the quay, containers move constantly up and down. The promenade is less busy. There are fishermen with their rods, of course. Boiled corn for sale. Chestnut vendors toast nuts on hotplates, brown cases splitting to yellow flesh. When a large boat moves through the harbour, its wake occasionally throws forth a sudden wave. Sitting there, couples and friends smile in anticipation, poised to dash out of the way of falling spray, but somehow the curtain of water doesn't fall on the quay and instead drops back into the sea with a splash. This is excitement, Mersin style. In the harbour a couple of boats play music for partygoers, the vessels bobbing at anchor. Nearby are punchbags hanging inside glowing boxes, they wait to score the strike as the boys assemble to show off their strength. Girls with curled hair and high-waisted jeans lean in, ready to swoon.

I later discover that my arrival has coincided with a bomb

exploding in Istanbul, on Istiklal, the pedestrianised avenue of shops that makes something of a city centre, and where I and millions walk regularly. It is not the first attack on the street, but it is the first in years. The attack suggests Kurdish militants in the PKK and its offshoots, though it could equally be Islamic extremists. The state says it is a woman who is responsible, trained on the other side of the Syrian border I am to ride along in the coming days. Came through Mersin. Great. She placed a bag by a bench and ran. It is unbearable to consider a bomb in those crowds. I hear from Nesrin. Picking up some last-minute things before a holiday, she was in the shop beside the explosion. Her till receipt says 16.01. The explosion is given as 16.13. Such is terrorism, and the fear it generates, which always, as intended, has a footprint bigger than any blast.

Riding into Mersin at dusk, before I know about the bomb, I see a military position on the highway: a soldier standing behind concrete barriers. It looks permanent, but, given the bombing, I cut the Turkish state some slack, wonder if perhaps such fortified positions are in response, or perhaps just necessary, though I never want to believe the latter.

I walk the streets. High palms, needle-thin with fronds crossed, lean against the wind. The old stone city with its beautiful low archways abuts the new one of apartments. Into the shadows of a closed market I go, the smell of old fish still on the air. I hear music from above. Everything is shut but on some glorious rooftop, folk music bellows into the night. I hear violin, piano, songs sung with a full belly of feeling. The sound is everywhere but I must find its source. It comes closer, a dark stairwell with some coloured lights swirling at the top. At the entrance is a large photo of a woman smiling not entirely innocently, but, whatever, I'll follow the music in this quiet city. The room at the top looks empty but for the band who sit immersed in their music in a corner: three men, one violin, one piano, one singer. At my arrival I see heads turn, and notice three women sitting at a table beside the stage. A small but stout man rolls towards me and slaps my shoulder with a hand that lands like a club. I return the gesture as Ali pumps my arm; his shoulder feels like stone. He asks where I'm from, and I'm beginning to learn that with a moustache nobody accepts Britain as my answer anymore. Everyone takes me for a Turk. Ali tells me he's from Mongolia, the far, far east of it, and then demands I drink beer when I point to the samovar and ask for tea. Watching him work the floor, shirt tucked in over his large, wrestler's physique, it is clear Ali is the heavy in case things get rough around here, but he has the bearing of one who holds his power lightly. He brings me my beer. Another man, ungainly on his feet, clumsy, leads over a woman, the youngest and most beautiful of the three. "Drink 150," he says to me, pointing at her, to my surprise. "Buy drink 150," he repeats. I look firmly at him and apologetically at her and say I'm here only for the music. She stands up and we say an awkward goodbye. Ali tells the second man to leave me be, give me a break. I drink my beer as I listen to the music. It still sounds joyous but the mystery dulls a little, fades into the reality of how most of the money here is being made.

A couple more men arrive, they take a table and are given plates of fruit. They shout requests for new songs when one finishes, shout gratitude when the singer knows it and groan a little when he doesn't. I realise that tables with a better view of the women are saved for those who seem ready to spend more: sailors off the ships and with pay packets burning holes in pockets. An uneasy man who smiles a lot succeeds where I failed, and manages to be served a çay, not a beer. He sways and gyrates alone on the dance floor and is told in no uncertain terms not to look at the women unless he is buying a drink. He playfully covers his eyes, says he has seen nothing. With a stir and a hush a man arrives. "Patron, patron!" Ali says to me. The Boss. He does the rounds, shakes everyone's hand like it's a campaign rally. He comes over to me. Short, with a large jaw and smile, his shirt unbuttoned. He is middle-aged, inoffensive, unimpressive. Nonetheless, it is like a chieftain that he stands there and in English he demands, "Where are you from?"

"England. Where are you from?"

"Kurdish," he says proudly, not the first I've met but the first to stake his entire identity on it.

After the beer I get up to leave, though not before Ali tries to send a second woman to sit with me. We talk about Mersin, where she's been a few years. She smiles and I ask how the bar is.

"It's work," she says with a smile, unoffended, "just work."

For a while I walk the streets. The whole city is tense. I suspect the whole country is tense. Social media is down, so only official news is reported. I suspect that taking away social media from the country has an effect not dissimilar to if you took away its cigarettes. On television I see the Minister for the Interior announce more details of the bomber. I sit outside a restaurant and order soup, then watch as a loud argument erupts between a man and some cops, with the man eventually arrested. After a while I walk again, stop for çiğ köfte: a wrap of bulgur wheat cooked in tomato and pepper paste, served with mint leaves and cucumber, pomegranate molasses and salad. A plate of pickled chillies is handed to me for good measure. If Mersin has no bar scene then I will take advantage of its food instead.

The young man who makes the wraps begins to talk to me as I crunch through mine. He is wearing a smart white shirt. Impressively white at the end of what must be a long shift surrounded by tomato paste and molasses. He has short curly hair and a proud stance as, like everyone, he asks where I'm from but then adds, "Why come here?"

I answer straight. "I'm travelling with a bicycle."

"No, but why come here? If I could be in England I'd be in England. You can be in England but you come to Türkiye!"

"Türkiye is good," I say.

"Türkiye is crap," he says.

I sigh a little, then put the question back to him. "Why go to England?"

"Para!" is his answer, delivered like a word in a spell.

I roll my eyes, would normally be more respectful but am too tired, so reply, "There are more important things than money."

"Yes," he concedes, "but there are no good jobs here." He gestures at his smoothed heap of bulgur, ready to wrap. He's probably right.

"England is the same, though," I say. "OK for rich people. Same for everyone else."

He pauses, so I change the subject.

"Mersin is your memleket?"

Another terse reply.

"Hakkari."

Now my eyes open wide. "Hakkari?! Up in the mountains?"

"Evet!" He's happily surprised. "You know it?"

"Evet. I wanted to go, but winter. It's really cold, isn't it?"

"*Really* cold." He says it proudly, as if what he may lack in job opportunities he can make up for in understanding the true meaning of cold.

"But it is beautiful? Mountains. Amazing nature, isn't it?"

"*So* beautiful! Mountains!" He inhales sharp through his nose, enjoying his performance. "Air is so clean. Türkiye here. Iran there. Iraq there. Right in the middle."

He explains why I yearn to go.

"So you are Kurdish?" I decide to ask.

"Kürt'üm!" He thumps his chest for emphasis as he says it. "I'm Kurd."

A simple "Yes" is not enough. He says it triumphant. That thump perfectly executed for good measure. If all that mattered was the ability to thump a chest, they'd have ten states already, rule the world – though this is unfair of me, Turkish men aren't so bad at the chest-thump either. I consider the words so similar when written down. *Türküm, Kürtüm.* That T and that K transposed, but which goes first is all-important. I change the subject.

"And I guess there are no jobs in Hakkari?"

"Nothing." He turns indignant again. "Only thieves. Smugglers."

"Smugglers?"

"Evet!" As if it's obvious but he will explain it anyway. "Things in Iraq cost one lira. You sell them in Türkiye for three lira."

He rolls up his sleeve, shows off a big gold wristwatch.

"This is a thousand-dollar watch," he says proudly.

"It's beautiful," I lie, unsure about the price too. "And your family is there?"

He nods. "My uncle there has nine children. Everyone living together."

"So you came here alone?"

"No, another uncle. Dad's brother. He's here. This is his shop. So I came here."

"And you send money to the family in Hakkari?" I ask, presumptuously.

"No." He looks indignant. "It's my money I make here. Why would I give it to them?"

Maybe Anatolian families are changing.

Our conversation becomes more desultory. He tells me his brother would like to go to Germany, not England, but he prefers England. How is it? I tell him the food and weather are bad, the rent worse. But I wish him luck, wondering if there has been a shift: if people talk about where they would like to move, the country that fits their personality and tastes, but without entertaining too much hope of moving.

Mersin to Adana – 14 November

As I ride out of Mersin next day, a man passes me, delivering bread by bicycle, bags bursting with baguettes on each handlebar end. The sun sets against their perfect crusts, and the baguettes glow along with the windows of the jewellers that line the streets. Their shop-fronts glisten with gold bracelets, necklaces, rings, tiaras and any other arrangement of precious metal that can conceivably be hung from a body, limb, finger or toe. I notice the swaying pantaloons of the men as trousers are replaced by shirwals, an expanse of cloth that tightens at the ankle, a sign that here begins the more Kurdish and Arab parts of the country. The street itself is more Arab than any so far, but in ways that are integrated with the city, which is Turkish, Arab and Kurdish all together. I hear this observation in my colonial brain and reproach myself for it: my surprise, however pleasant, at coexistence. This fascination with ethnicity feels like a Western trait, where even to remark – however fondly – on a coexistence of centuries is in some way to presume its absence, to find coexistence notable rather than ordinary. People on a street full of people walk together, and I see only people.

The difference that begins here is nonetheless palpable. Coffee, grains, soup, spices, nuts; all of it sold throughout Türkiye but here with a greater sense of the souk. Two young men finish a conver-sation as I pass their café, they rise and rally one another to get on with the evening. I ride out to their words, "Yalla, yalla!"

The Seyhan river runs north–south through Adana, and for all that I might not believe in binaries, the river is as near to an east–west dividing line as I will find. On the west bank is most of the city, including the historic quarter with its clock tower and grand bazaar, all of it as beautiful in old stone as anything in Istanbul. The city, you suspect, has begun to realise this. Tourist maps show walking distances and places to visit, the historical significance of Adana, the visit of Ottoman explorer Evliya Çelebi back in the day.

Across the river is a near-immediate return to the tyre stops, exhaust repair and auto shops that line the outer approach to the city. The road is rutted, and concrete drain covers are cracked with twists of rebar protruding upwards like the shoots of tiny plants of steel. I ride perhaps a kilometre and then stop to order a portion of börek, some çay and a small biscuit of fig and walnut the baker pointedly advises is not fresh, insisting I should try the orange and hazelnut scone he has just pulled from the oven. I settle on a touring cyclist's compromise: have both.

Şaban sits with me, asks about my writing, my route, my marital status. Asks if I'm a Muslim, an identity I'm mostly comfortable with until I'm asked it pointedly and as if it mattered. Of course I haven't made it through over a thousand kilometres of Türkiye without hearing this question, but this is the earliest in a conversation it's been asked, and is another sign of the south-east getting closer, of regions becoming more religious. I marvel that, in Western depictions, what is arguably the most socially conservative part of the country was reinvented as the most "progressive", the most "secular", and all the other words that are quickly deployed when the Pentagon wants to fund some new ally in its eternal war, but still has to convince the US population and Western liberals to stump up the budget. You want Western support for a proxy group or coup in the Middle East, just tell people they're secular and you'll hear no more about it, including what that word even means. Throw in a hastily constructed LGBTIQ+ rebel battalion, armed with acronyms and heavy weapons, send it down the newswire to Reuters and it'll be blank cheques and pallets of cash forever.

Don't mistake me, having conservative religious beliefs isn't a problem in itself. Some of the warmest and most decent people I've ever met have been religiously observant to degrees I find odd; it is more the dislocation between Western perception and reality that worries me. Şaban asks me this question with no dogma in it; he is just asking about something that is important to him, something that makes up his world. It makes no odds to him what religion I am, and he'll be only mildly confused if I say I'm none, which looked at logically maybe is strange: why reject every route to salvation? It makes sense to choose one, if only as an insurance policy. I lay out my theocratic position.

"I don't go to cami," I begin. "I drink alcohol, but I think, inside, I am Muslim. Evet."

"This isn't the same!" Şaban laughs warmly, sits back in his chair and smiles. "Muslims go to cami, alcohol is haram!"

To be fair, he may have a point here. It isn't the same, and it could be jarring to learn that for any and all of his observations, for all those times he closed the bakery to go pray, in my eyes his spirituality winds up no different from that of a quasi-infidel like myself. But so it goes; they're the rules of faith and our own personal relations to whichever god, and however much or little of it, we choose to keep in our lives. "Religion is a link between Allah and the individual believer," said Atatürk, who claimed he prayed to Allah before each battle, but was wary of the potential for religion to become a superstitious force that could manipulate the public, a trait he believed lay central to the Ottoman downfall.

"It's exactly the same," I say, "beliefs are inside us! Allah knows everything!"

We both sip çay. Şaban hears me out, as if my invocation of Allah means I maybe mean what I say and I am a Muslim.

"For me it's OK to drink alcohol. It's OK if one man and another man are in love . . ."

Şaban laughs at the interpretations of scripture I'm willing to entertain, but he gives to my totally amateur religious scholarship a more serious and patient theocratic hearing than it deserves.

". . . because Allah understands everyone."

Şaban listens to me with an expression that feels strange, if only for the rarity with which we see it in others. He looks as if he is seriously contrasting my beliefs with his beliefs, and considering what this meeting of different beliefs should mean. He takes out his cigarettes, draws one for himself and offers me the pack. I decline with a laugh.

"You tell me alcohol is haram, forbidden, so I'm not a Muslim, but you smoke cigarettes, which are also haram, and say you are a Muslim!"

I smile, pleased with myself. Şaban laughs through the smoke, enjoys being caught out.

He points his smouldering cigarette at me. "It is true what you say."

"I know it's true!" I say with a laugh. "But Allah understands, he understands everything."

Şaban smiles warmly. We sit together in silence, and then we talk families. He shows me a photo of his son, aged one. He has a two-storey house, his parents live above. Do I speak other languages? A little French, a little German, but not really. Him? Some Kurdish. Kurmanji? He smiles that I know the name of it, I say I know Iraqi Kurds in London, say "spass", which is "thank you" in Sorani, and apparently in Kurmanji too. He smiles at my uneaten fig and walnut biscuit in front of me.

"I told you it wasn't fresh."

"You did."

"How's business?" I ask and he sighs.

"Not good. Inflation. People still come, but spend less. Ukraine war, all the world is like this. Flour prices always going up."

"It will get better," I say, and I think I mean it.

"Kısmet." He smiles as he says it.

My favourite of all the loan words. Kismet long ago made its way out of Turkish and into English, but is still not as widely known as it should be. It means fate, destiny – something you can always influence but not wholly control. I feel a warmth at the strength Şaban derives from this, though cannot also help but think back to my friend Ayşe's warm words in Şirince, the concern she expressed that although Turks can derive resilience and a calm from kismet, by that same token it puts them at risk of accepting too much.

My companions on the roads are now almost entirely trucks, as if the people stop at Adana but the goods travel on. Under the tin roofs of garages, trenches are sunk into concrete floors, and in them men work under the chassis of trucks and wagons, oil up to their elbows as they labour to keep the engines of Anatolia's roads thundering. Russians have stopped scouring the south for houses and new lives; Mersin is apparently their limit, they want the sea. Something in their migration reminds me of the US and the Midwesterners who eventually tire of snow and winter and move to California. Humans, the same everywhere.

I see bales of plastic recycling, identical to those enormous sacks that the kids walk the streets collecting for in Istanbul. Adana is the centre of the Turkish plastics recycling industry, which means, since China stopped accepting waste, it has also become the centre of British and European plastic waste disposal. Everything so casually thrown away in the West comes in the end to the Adana riverside or, melted down, is inhaled into a worker's respiratory system. A few years ago the government banned the imports, but clearly money spoke Turkish fast and fluent, and the ban was soon lifted. Another example that, be it a military intervention, a gold mine, or a waste contract, it is often the West that brings the corruption. It is the West that pays the bribe rather than change its ways.

"Ayıp!" A disgrace! I had exclaimed to Şaban of the plastic mess, maybe more incensed than he was that one of my countries should use the other as a dumping ground. "Ayıp," he replied, confused by my ardour but showing he was with me.

"Ama işler," he went on. "But jobs."

Here too, though, the unrecyclable finds its way to the roadside, the riverside. The dumping ground has its own dumping ground. The periphery of the periphery. Streams flow slow, the water appears thick, off-colour, now and then looking like something discharged, untreated, by a factory. All about me, industry whirs on. From an unfiltered chimney comes a dark smoke. The ruins of a castle and fortress stand proud atop a hill, while the adjacent mountainside is quarried clear away for building materials. Hills aren't what they used to be, they themselves can be pulled down. They won't protect you now. The air carries a whiff of solvents from where the scoops and dumpers of enormous quarry earthmovers are fabricated, the metal sprayed with coats of paint and lacquer.

Olive trees brave the stone dust, pale and ghostly. Riding in from Mersin I passed an enormous new petrochemicals plant: all pipes, chambers and chimneys, organs of industry readying to fabricate the feedstock for polyester, ensuring a domestic supply for the country's huge garment trade, keeping the money in the country and making Türkiye the world's largest producer of the stuff after China and India. Out to the east of Adana the spirit of enterprise continues, but feels different, more innocent. On the external face of a cemetery wall is painted the phone number of a man who sells marble. Beneath a pomegranate tree picked bare, a woman sells pomegranates. Capitalism is only a punnet. A rag and bone man kneels on the midpoint of a bent aluminium ladder, twisting at it in a slow effort to fold the thing over on itself so that it will fit with the other scraps of metal in his cart. More people ride bicycles. There are perhaps a similar number of scooters, but more passengers squeezed on each one. An EU-Turkish construction project is building a centre for those, it says, in times of crisis. The Arabic writing on the hoardings hints at the crisis. The entire Gaziantep region was lauded by Western donors and aid agencies for its welcome of refugees. They sent armies of professionals and white-collar experts, all of them out to unearth the secret of how to be less racist. Either they never solved the riddle, or they failed to carry its message back home with them. On the street I gradually begin to hear more Arabic spoken, by both Syrians and Arabs who have always thought themselves Turks anyway. I eat my first künefe of the journey, remembering it from breakfasts riding through Palestine. Soon it is joined by kadayıf, served with a glass of milk.

The first roadside chickens peck corn, dropped from trucks driving to the refinery. Farmers plough. I see a man on his knees in a verdant sea of green, cutting bunches of dill and tying them up with a stem. I smile, for in this country it is only ever a matter of time before there is a return to the village that will outlast everything. Long after the factories rust and the plastics industries are obsolete, the farmer will grow dill. A concrete column carrying a new road overhead is daubed in red spray paint: Işçi Partisi. Workers' Party.

Close ahead of me is the Syrian border, so they may be coming from there, but the increase in armoured vehicles is unmistakable. The gendarmes are more enclosed, behind concrete blocks, and I must accept this is not down to the nearness of Syria. At a roundabout I go straight, though I'm curious about the right turn, south towards Antakya and Hatay: a historically mixed Turkish-Arab-Kurdish-Christian-Muslim-Assyrian nook of the country. Here is a cosmopolitanism, so commonplace across Türkiye, which as I list it leaves me to consider the strangeness of the West's fondness for labelling people by ethnic group.

On a map, Hatay seems to hang as if from the underside of Anatolia. Again, though, the earthquake. Perhaps in this last year you have heard and seen more of Hatay, on maps and otherwise, although for once I wish you had not had cause to. The awkward shape of the province perhaps befits its history: "given" to Türkiye by the French in 1939, from their possession of Mandate Syria, in return for an assurance of Turkish neutrality in World War II. Even in the last weeks of his life, Atatürk continued to busy himself with the Hatay brief, giving his final weeks to the Republic, to resolve as much as he could before setting it into a future he would no more be able to influence. Whatever the ignominies of land being handed over by the French, of such colonialism, I am glad of it. The last nine decades probably gave the people of Hatay a better nine decades inside Türkiye than they would have had inside Syria, and I think – sadly for those on the other side – the future will hold a better nine decades, too. I care nothing for borders or territory, but everything for human wellbeing.

As I see signs for Hatay, I think of a night so recent and yet so distant. A few weeks ago, during my brief stop in Istanbul, drinking negronis in a Cihangir bar. A conversation with a guy from Hatay, Turkish-Kurdish heritage, working as a programmer in Istanbul but remotely since the pandemic began. He preferred Hatay: family, sea, sun, cheaper. Who wouldn't? At the end of the pandemic his bosses demanded employees return to the Istanbul office. The company was willing to negotiate: weighing its potential savings from the reduced wage bill for remote workers against potential savings from a tax rebate the government was offering companies that kept staff in Istanbul offices, a policy to help out the real estate market for urban office space. The guy was negotiating a reduced salary that would still leave him overall up on income, and able to enjoy more time in the more affordable city of Hatay. Türkiye has spent a century trying to move wealth and opportunity east, and now the internet will help, though not without that same tussle with Istanbul corporate landlords that will be waged in London, New York, Paris. As I cycled by Hatay in the weeks after talking to him, I hoped he had got his time there. And when the earthquake hit, with all my heart, that he had been in the office in Istanbul.

At a roadside stall I pull over, decide it is time for fruit. Under a modest timber frame stands a man with one large tray filled with apples and another with oranges and mandalinas. In the neighbouring field, inside a court whose rusting frame is hung with torn netting, boys play football. The sides of the court are overgrown with brambles that lean towards the touchlines. Together for a moment, the grocer and I watch them play, listen to the shouts and thud of boot on leather. I take an apple, adding a mandalina to it because if I ask for just one apple he's likely to give it to me for free. He looks at the two pieces of fruit, smiles and waves a hand. Gives me both for free.

He has fair hair and a yellowing moustache, a shirt of black denim over a T-shirt that is somehow still bright white against the highway's dust. His voice is rough, his demeanour hardy from standing always at this weather-beaten roadside. We talk about my ride and our shared road. I say there are a lot of truckers, that east of Adana feels different. He agrees, says there are a lot of truckers because there are few jobs, and so the men drive.

"But here is OK, Adana is OK," he clarifies. "We have farming."

"I think you have good soil here."

He nods, as if of this there can be neither doubt nor complaint.

"Soil's very good. Here we have fruits," he gestures at his stand, "but east – Siirt, Cizre – there they only have animals. Cows. Sheep. Goats," he says, looking perplexed on behalf of his countryfolk.

"Zor," he adds. "It's difficult."

I ride on, thinking again that east is a relative concept. Everyone has their own east.

Osmaniye to Gaziantep – 16 November

Today will be a big day. Today I must rise early and cover 130 kilometres over and through a narrow cordon of mountains, so as to make Gaziantep by dusk. On one side is flat farmland; on the other, flat farmland; in the middle, a spine of mountains that runs perfectly north–south towards Antakya. I look out at it from the hotel window in Osmaniye. A photo: hills climbing towards peaks, low mist in morning sun. Even without the earthquake that followed, the sudden belt of mountain I saw so clearly that morning looked like a fault line: peaks pushed up dramatically by tectonic plates. Now I can think only of that Osmaniye high street, and the café the night before where musicians played music as their bored children stared out the window, then slept on the sofa until the gig was over. And all I can do is hope that they are OK.

Out of Osmaniye the fields begin again, black earth turned newly over, gold chaff of corn sticking from it. Every house has a plough arm out front. Some of the promised livestock begins, and then we are into the hills. And then we are into the hills. And then we are into the hills. The hills are unrelenting, and bigger beasts lie up ahead. Bare, treeless rockfaces smile way above the earth. Across the valley a highway streams with trucks. I see them climb one long slow diagonal, like a ramp, up to a level where the road can be sustained. Once they are up, they are up. I watch as they disappear into tunnels opened through the mountains; tiny black holes with vehicles disappearing in and out like magic tricks, coins passed through a stone handkerchief. Bridges remove small valleys, crescent bridges remove large ones. The entirety of Anatolia has been made flat for them, each concrete span so confident on its enormous legs. I look at the stream of traffic, each bridge or tunnel saving maybe twenty minutes or half an hour, eliminating a dozen crashes a year on the perilous turns, preventing a handful of fatalities, sparing their families from grief. In front of me I see east and west moving together. In front I see distinctions of east and west disappear.

Across the tops of the mountains the wind turbines return; for the past few days they have been absent. I wondered as I rode if that was because the state was less committed to development in the east, in part because of a history of PKK attacks on infrastructure. More likely, there was just less wind. The turbines spin all around me, taking with them my overactive mind. Sun shines down through cloud, catching here and there a deciduous tree, a jag of yellow among the green of the pine. Blue sky is cut with small shards or dusts of light grey, dark grey, pure black and sheer white: a stained-glass window of colours, the remnants of weather leaving and arriving. Up ahead the mountains tower so high I can't make out if they are a line of peaks or a ridge formation of new and distant cloud way beyond the horizon. I climb slowly, pass a pomegranate tree with its last fruit unpicked, overfull with sun so that each fruit splits right there on the branch, its red pouches of rubies glistening. The road I ride is to be widened, and a flattened bed of stone turns the contours next to me, though construction has clearly been put on hold, and new plants grow indifferent to the plans and up through the road bed. The scent of wild sage rouses me.

None of it comes easily. The ascent will be the best part of eighty kilometres, winding around the mountain. Then the road will straighten up and make to cross the ridge at its lowest point, and here I will scarper across as if I were a mouse and the mountain a cat's paw. There the top of the pass, sheer rock, has been scraped desperately away, to save us a final few metres of elevation, though the mountain had plenty in reserve. A car engine stands defeated, stopped with bonnet up. My legs continue, though it takes its toll on the sinews of the muscles. Other forces act against me. I prefer the word "apprehension" but I feel something resembling fear when I think of the winter drawing nearer by the day, a process I will accelerate by riding northwards and to greater altitudes.

That winter nibbles also at my riding days. Pedalling after dark over long flats, or on more reasonable terrain, brings me as great a peace as I have known. But this is not reasonable terrain, this is a cycling travail. You ride on earth's terms. The sweat of the incline or hill, and the chill of the descent when it comes, are not appealing. The hundred miles a day I once felt able to cover without much ado have been cut down by Anatolia and winter to around a hundred kilometres. I have been starting late, and to ride them in six hours of daylight with sundown at five is harder than covering them leisurely in ten, with sundown at nine and a balmy twilight to follow. Nor, as I pass one town, is it twenty kilometres to the next one of any size, but more like sixty, and between them is little more than the occasional hamlet. A man looks me up and down in a shop. "Memleket?" is the first word out his mouth. But I have stopped answering this question, even if by it is meant no offence.

Inside me are too many thoughts: of the century past and the century to come; of the side of the bridge from which I write and that of those for whom I am writing. It is a divide I wish were not there but it is and I must be conscious of it. There is a similar divide between producing and consuming, and between you sitting there, reading, and the Turk I see on my travels, who does not know they are being written about. What right do I have to parcel their life in this way? The only justification I can think of is if you gain insight and empathy. Before I set out, a dear friend said, "Basically, it has to be perfect." It was a joke, but it was an accurate one, for any less and I will have failed.

I once made the vainglorious boast that I would set about this manuscript with the commitment and urgency with which Atatürk set out to Tripoli upon the Italian invasion of Libya. Nowadays the unremitting stream of thoughts tire me like the long slopes of the country. Guilts and doubts snap at me like the crackle of falling scree under the moving flocks, calling my attention. I think of Henry Hudson in the pay of the Dutch in upstate New York, on the river which later bore his name, the Algonquin who welcomed him until the Dutch returned with armies, and now the Algonquin are no more. It is not the same, of course, Turks are not the Algonquin, I am not Hudson and you good people are not the Dutch. We are prisoners of history no more than we are of geography; we can rise above both. But still there is the unassailable gulf between the one who explores and the one who is explored.

Sometimes after dark, at a café or if there is a small desk in the room where I find myself, I write what I can and feel myself climbing back on top of my thoughts, putting them in order so that I can mould them rather than they me. At such moments the proportions of what I am doing feel more manageable, and this journey of mine through a country and its first century becomes just another logistical arrangement – travelling with the quarried earth, the oranges and produce, the livestock and domestic appliances – on the roads of Anatolia this November.

Husnu and Kahramanmaraş

At junctions I see signs for the small city of Kahramanmaraş and I think of my old friend Husnu from a village in the province. We met at university. He must have been ten years older than me, was translating Kurmanji, Turkish and English at a local asylum-seekers charity I visited and he volunteered at weekly. We became friends. Each Friday we had tea or coffee in a park café, we talked of the world.

During the nineties he'd endured torture at the hands of the Turkish military. His small middle-class family, who ran a textile-trading outfit, had in the end saved the money to pay smugglers and, in the back of a truck, across two weeks, he'd made his way to the UK. Husnu was my friend, but he also taught me a great deal, simply by who he was. The idea of Kurdish nationalism meant nothing to him, which goes to show the stupidity and propensity for misdirection in state violence, quite apart from its implicit evil. He perceived the US to be the main force that had destroyed so much of a region he regarded as the place he was from, even if most of what we discussed occurred outside the Turkish frontiers. We talked of the US creation of Saddam Hussein who had attacked the Kurds so viciously, sending them into asylum in Türkiye. We talked of the US war against Iraq that throughout my university years was at large, with its unbearable force and ceaseless crimes.

Even if, beyond the borders of Türkiye, others had experienced far worse, in his own village Husnu had also seen terrible things. He told me the army had once thrown a man off a building, and I remember him asking, genuinely clueless, as if still looking for insight, "Why they do this?"

He went back once, for two weeks, many years after we'd first met, when he had a British passport and his right to leave and return could not be questioned by any border agent or Home Office bureaucrat. After that visit, too, he spoke plainly about what he'd found. The village now had pavements, he told me in disbelief. There were Kurdish TV channels, speaking Kurdish. He could not believe the difference. "This was impossible before," he said, laughing.

As I ride I think of him all the more keenly because we lost touch. His was always temporary accommodation. A top-up phone number that might expire. He had an email address, but his English was more spoken than written. I left university and then the country. He wanted to be a journalist or translator, but his English was not fluent enough for the latter, and he didn't have the necessary connections to make it as the former. He took some cash-in-hand cleaning jobs at a kebab restaurant or two, but was one of those people hindered rather than helped by the agility of their own mind because the world offers them nothing to put it to. Even that cash-in-hand job would have been illegal. As it still does today, UK law prohibited asylum applicants from working, condemning them to struggle against listlessness instead.

Husnu knew how to live on £30 a week, he knew how to roast a chicken one day, eat leftovers the next, and from the bones make stock and soup the day after that, so that his health and dignity remained intact. Insulting as they were, he did not let the restrictions of his life get to him. When the Home Office started giving out vouchers instead of money, ostensibly so that people like him could not spend £30 on vice, he knew not to take it to heart and probably just saw it as another ridiculous feature of an unjust world that was hardly news to him. Still Husnu went on. He walked into town. He cooked. He volunteered. He read at the library, found courses he could take. The last time I saw him was a while after the time before it, and he asked if it was possible to smell bad people, to smell evil. I said something about a bad diet and lifestyle and a bad smell perhaps going together. But he insisted he meant more that he felt he could smell morality, good or bad. After the years of struggle, his mind was perhaps losing its grip on a normalcy he'd had to work so hard to build.

In the autumn of 2022, as I was riding, protests were breaking out in Iran. Suffering under the economic hardships of US sanctions, and so too the frustrations of a vibrant society made to live with Iranian state restrictions, Iranians – as they know just how to do – took to the streets, with ardent expressions of support from across the Western world. At the same time, back in the UK, at the Manston holding facility for asylum seekers, an Iranian refugee was among those who died in the squalid conditions that led to a diphtheria outbreak. While the British public in front of their phones and newspapers and televisions professed their desire for better lives for Iranians, they allowed to die from diphtheria an Iranian who they might have helped to build a full life in Britain. As I headed east, knowing that my road would take me along the Iranian border, I thought of the double standard, wondering if people even noticed anymore, and knowing that even the injustices Husnu had faced in the UK had since then only been worsened by successive governments.

My point, I suppose, is that there is nothing more impeding of social progress than the belief that your system works if it does not. There is no gullibility more easily abused than the belief that your country is a force for good in the world if it is not. It has always been my sense that Westerners have more difficulty than most in seeing this, as if they have been minted in a need to believe not only that their states are good, but that a part of that goodness is what makes them good. This inability to call a moral corruption for what it is may not sound like a problem while it remains so far distant, while it remains the problem of Iranians under sanctions, Iraqis under war, or even the refugees of each abuse left to lead almost invisible lives in Western countries. But then they close your libraries, and then the ambulances don't arrive, and then you suffer hate crimes, and then the hate takes new forms you didn't expect it to take, and then you die cold in a house you can't afford to heat, by which time you too have also been prohibited from protesting against these rising injustices. It is, at root, the same injustice, and the injustice gets closer.

Nurdağı

From above the town of Nurdağı I descend. The crest, some fifteen kilometres above it, is no more than a truck stop, tankers pulling in and out across the gravel and the puddles that serve as sky-mirrors. Windmills spin; a restaurant and a fruit stall are all that mark the top. "Nur" means "holy light", and "dağ" means "mountain", so this mountain of holy light, facing east as it does, must receive the morning sun before those to the west of it. The motorway crosses over my own road, it cuts down at a brutal, impossible diagonal, or is carried on curved bridges that orbit valleys like the rings of Saturn. The gentle contours of mountain roads and the rigid angles of the new highways cross together as if sketched in technical drawings. Below I see in watercolour the enormous Syrian plateau, a patch-work of red earth, yellow fields, green grass and ploughed black soil, all of it smallholder agriculture, now and then dotted by the regal beauty of the Anatolian oak.

Down in the valley I ride on. Farmers selling sacks of potatoes wait with their scales. Old tractors pass: Türk Fiat, museum-grade John Deere, Yugoslav models I do not know. An old man drives by in his tractor as the road begins to ramp back up. He is dressed against the coming chill in only a jacket, has a moustache and, again, centuries of hardiness. Laughing as he *tuk-tuk-tuks* by me, he gestures to his trailer and then at me, and only after I have waved a smile and declined his offer of a ride does it seem a good idea. For centuries Turks camped in tents, travelling slowly with their animals. They are not in a hurry to return and have grown to like comfort, while I am Western enough to seek out hardship and from

237

it take meaning. Meanwhile people's amazement that I am cycling to the Armenian border, to Kars, where it will be cold, is hardly new to me, but the endless expressions of it reaffirm my worries and doubts. Negativity is always contagious. A boy rides by on a motorbike with a sidecar trailer. He comes up beside me, asks where I'm from, where I'm going. He shakes his head in a happy disbelief, he smiles at me and says, "Maşallah," before rolling his wrist over the throttle and pulling slowly away.

Fifty kilometres said the sign to Gaziantep a while ago. The sun has barely twenty degrees to sink before it falls into the horizon, where the mountains rise to welcome it even earlier. I have just gone over a pass but another is already ahead of me. Performing mental calculations, I consider how to make it to Gaziantep tonight. I look over at far hills patched with brush, and in the gaping chasm between them and me, the distances of everything out here feel enormous. The arithmetic changes. How many hours after dark will I arrive? How many kilometres until satellite cities and their street lights? Finally, acceptance. I will not make Gaziantep tonight.

Up again I roll, slowly, watching steam come off my hot torso into a chilling mountain air. I am now, at least, almost enjoying the mountain. Enjoying it, perhaps, in the fashion of a joke at my own expense, but at least I have been let in on the joke. I have given up on Gaziantep, which helps. On another long incline I see a van pulled in ahead, a man milling around it; bonnet still down, van not in trouble, odd place to stop. My brain is pedalling every bit as much as my legs. Not much cognition going on up there. On a deep level, on the same level that it knows to produce insulin and I've never once considered it, my body has decided that in the vanishingly wild and remote chance that this guy has stopped to offer me a ride, like the man on the tractor, then we're getting right in. A hundred metres becomes fifty, then twenty. He waves and, without even bothering to ask, as if he were my support car, his waving hand takes hold of the handle on the side of the van and rolls it open like the stage door and this the last act. Can I look a gift van in the mouth? The plan was to write a Turkish century, not pedal every inch. I'm through with challenges these days, I did my time, and is this man and his van not a part of the Turkish century? *Fuck it!* says my brain, we're getting in. And it looks up to see my body already on board, sitting up front, coat and hat pulled on. Ready to go.

We ride the road. Jesus, it feels so fast, on rails, the van a high top, and we rock and bounce with the undulating surface but from a towering vantage point. Mikail enjoys the company, is conversational. He smiles a lot, a man with a little moustache, middle-aged, listens intently to my thoughts in order then to talk at some length with his own views. I watch the road for both of us as he explains that Mikail followed Gibrail as the angels of Islam. I say I've never heard this name in Turkish before, and he proudly tells me it is rare as I carry on watching the road. I am not sure if my anxiety at his driving is warranted or if I'm just no longer used to such speed or someone else being in control of it. Mikail reaches for his phone, leaves one hand on the wheel, shows me his sister's lokanta, the small restaurant she works at in Norwich. My anxiety, I decide, is warranted. We cruise through the enormity of Anatolia. Gaziantep was far. It looks further than forty kilometres, and, once again, everything is just so big. The road slices down through great trenches cut through hills, half-kilometre stretches where we can't see out over the tops. "Where would you have slept?" Mikail asks. "Lots of dogs out here." And then, more importantly, "You know Norwich? Let's get Norwich on the line."

We get Norwich on the line. He talks with his sister, he puts her on. She is sorry for her English. I tell her it's good. She likes Norwich. She was a teacher in Istanbul but restaurant money in England is better. She loves reading books, but English is hard. "Olacak, olacak," I say. It will be, it will be. İnşallah. We all laugh, she tells me I must go to her restaurant in Norwich.

We drive on, dark is coming fast. Mikail tells me he lives and works between Gaziantep and the village where we began.

"Now the village is empty," he says, "everyone in the UK, everyone left."

"Really?"

"Really."

"How did they get visa?"

"Kaçak," he smiles. Smuggled.

"Really?"

"Really."

"Smuggled how? With truckers?"

"Truckers, boat. Some on planes. Few on planes, maybe two. More money."

"What do they do now? For work?"

"Restaurants. Everyone is in lokantas."

I shake my head in disbelief. Mikail explains.

"One person, £20k to the smuggler. One month in a lokanta. £2k. One year you make your money back, and you continue working."

"Everyone is safe? Everyone arrived OK?"

"Everyone."

"Smugglers are OK? Not bad men?"

"Not bad."

I look at the sparse land, at the tractors in driveways.

"How do you make £20k here? Farming?"

Mikail shakes his head from side to side. "Farming. Work. Slowly slowly, you get money."

We drive on. The lights of Gaziantep on the horizon.

"Why do you stay?" I ask.

"Me?" Mikail points to himself, smiles as he looks round. "I'm old. This is for young people."

Up ahead are skyscrapers, international hotels. Gaziantep looks big on a map but is even bigger than I expected. Perhaps it is only the feel of an illuminated highway racing towards bright columns of light, but there is something Istanbul-like about it. I write this now, remembering that energy, and knowing that by this energy Gaziantep, like all the cities the earthquake hit, will rebuild. Mikail will send me a message that week. We keep in touch. He has been bereaved, the family is in a tent. We exchange some news, I send some money to help. We keep in touch. A month later, work is restarting. "İşler yolunda," he says with optimism and I can see him smiling. Things are all right. It's on its way. He's doing OK, just wants to know if I've been to Norwich yet. But enough of this unwelcome cause for digression, let me return us to that van and that night, heading down the highway and into that city so fine.

"Gaziantep's big," I say.

"Evet." Mikail nods, matter-of-fact but proud. "Seventh city."

"Seventh?"

He counts off. "Istanbul, Izmir, Ankara, Konya, Adana, Mersin, Gaziantep."

We tail off by the end, but it sounds about right.

"Where do you want to go?" he asks.

"Centre, but where is easiest for you? I can ride my bicycle to a hotel."

"Centre is no problem," he says, waves a hand out the window. "Here are all luxury hotels."

We pass an AK Party office, bunting across the street.

"AK Party," I say to myself. "Is Gaziantep AKP?"

"Evet," Mikail answers approvingly.

Something in him is so good-natured that I think it's safe to bring up politics, and I am curious what he thinks, so I go on.

"Adana is CHP?"

"Evet." He nods happily, as if I'm doing well.

"Osmaniye?"

"MHP," we say together, and he laughs. "You know it. You know Türkiye."

"Because it's Bahçeli's memleket," I say, Bahçeli the right-wing nationalist at the head of MHP. "But I don't like this man."

Mikail brushes it off. "He's a people's man."

"Who will you vote for?" I ask.

"AKP." There is no pause. As if the three letters are all he needs in politics, but if I'm asking for answers . . . "They did so much." He looks at me. "You?"

"I don't know. They did a lot. But change is important. Democracy is important."

"Of course."

I pause. "I think Demirtaş is a good man. I like HDP."

"Pffff."

"And the environment. AKP just build roads everywhere. Industry everywhere. Construction. They cut down forests. The air is dirty. Sea. Nature is important."

Mikail laughs. "I don't like these things."

My turn to laugh. "I think AKP working with Kurds, like before, was better."

"Of course," Mikail looks round. "But HDP and PKK terrorists together."

I pause, begin to retreat. I like him and our views are going to differ. It's a sensitive week, and I don't trust the level of my Turkish. Mikail seems relaxed though.

"Urfa. Antep. These cities will be AKP." He waves a hand. "Diyarbakır, Siirt, Şırnak. They'll vote HDP that side."

I nod, thinking once again that east is a relative concept, but also that there's something conciliatory in these words. Mikail will say "terrorist", but does not seem genuinely to reject the HDP and their place in the political world. He accepts that some will vote for them, and he wants me to know there are others who think like me. Even if he is not one of them. I aim to bridge-build, talk more.

"Türkiye changed a lot in twenty years," I say, looking out the window at commuters waiting for buses in front of bright store-fronts.

"Totally changed," he says immediately. "Really super. Really super."

"Gaziantep has a new metro now, doesn't it?" I ask.

"Evet." He is emphatic. "Gaziray. Opened this month. Super!"

I smile. "I know the AKP did a lot, built a lot. I just want everyone to work together."

Mikail smiles mischievously. "Like HDP and CHP working together. Terrorist alliance!"

I roll my eyes, thinking that this interpretation spells bad news for CHP at the next election.

"I don't think it is like this. PKK is bad news for HDP, because PKK wants war but HDP wants democracy."

Mikail shakes his head. Not convinced.

"They say this," he says, "but they want to take Türkiye. They want a Kurdistan. First they have elections, but after this they make a line and take it."

He waves his hand as if he's clearing a table.

"Urfa, Antep, Diyarbakır. Gone."

Gaziantep – 18 November

In the heart of the old city I go in search of food. I walk through narrow, winding streets past old stone houses. Wooden shutters conceal windows, ornate iron bars protect others. Large oak doors, studded, hold back the night from centuries-old houses and restaurants. Inside I see a warm light. I see couples eat at tables. I see small groups of friends enjoying künefe. Outside it is cold, but men still cook on the street. Tabletops bear skewers, salads, peppers and onion for the grill. Customers pick up their chosen skewers, hand them to the maestro of the hearth. He cooks, he wafts a paddle at the coals. They glow. He places flatbreads on top of the sizzling meat, wasting neither the heat nor succulence of the escaping steam.

The food in Istanbul is marvellous, though in the countryside they joke that Istanbul is sent the bad stuff. It is far away, city folk have money, their taste is poor and they no longer know the good stuff, if ever they did. Moving east, the food gets better. It just does. The cities are closer to the fields, I suppose. The produce has spent fewer days on the road. The animals are not transported so far. The culture, too, spreads out into the streets. My skewers are handed to me on a flatbread with parsley and onion and flakes of chilli and sumac. The flatbread serves as a plate: you either wrap it around everything and bite at the parcel, or tear corners of the bread and use that to pick up your cubes of meat, working inwards. Hands take the place of cutlery.

My ayran comes in a small copper cup, with a distinctive curled handle. It is topped with the frothy cream of true, churned ayran. I remark happily, "Açık ayran!", which describes the open vat in which it sits nearby and is turned, rather than coming in a plastic cup beneath a sealed foil lid. The waiter looks at me with a mixture of surprise and pity – "What did you expect?" with a trace of "What do they serve where you're from?" At one stall, humbler than the rest, sits a giant stainless-steel pan on top of a lit gas ring, steam rising from it. The master opens the lid to reveal livers, chopped onion, pepper, garlic, all stewing in the red juice of tomato and chilli. On the way home from work, an office worker stops, puts down his briefcase, and his portion is spooned into bread. He eats. An old man, his dignity unassailable although he probably has no money and may even have no home, loiters nearby in large trousers and an ill-fitting blazer. He has heavy, dark eyebrows and a concerned expression. On seeing him, the master of the pot lavishly fills some bread with liver and vegetables and hands it over. The old man eats. Nothing has been said, and of course no money has changed hands. Eating my own meal, I watch the scene, certain that this solidarity will prevail over all the world throws at it.

After food, I find a bar, I have a beer. Then and the next morning also, I walk the winding cobbled streets with their stone houses empty, or abandoned, or for sale, but I also pass cafés and book-shops. I see students with their satchels and large, flat design portfolios as they wait outside a cultural centre. I see the metro filling, the cinema, and, for a second, I hear in my head the words of a future tour guide or Erasmus student saying, "Gaziantep is the new Istanbul," or describing it perhaps as "the Berlin of the East". In front of me run two young children, shoes skidding over wet cobbles in an alley with graffiti on its high stone walls. The girl, dressed in a red duffel coat, crouches beside a street cat, which assesses her and then darts into the shadows. The clouds scud over the hills that surround the city, where something is stirring.

Gaziantep to Nizip – 19 November

A light mist that turns into a heavy mist sits all morning over those hills before finally becoming rain. I cycle past the train station, the new metro line, and decide to keep dry by taking a look around the stations. It has wide platforms, large atriums. Futureproof.

Next door to the metro, I wait to get information about the mainline train. Two men are ahead of me in the queue. I'm not sure if both are deaf or only one is and the other is signing for him. They persevere with the ticket sales desk, a young and smiling man who has that universal energy and patience of one who loves working on railways and wants to help his passengers. When it comes to my turn, I ask where the line runs. Nizip, only Nizip. Forty kilometres east, the next town. Tickets are twenty lira – £1 for a forty-five-minute ride. Evening train. I buy a ticket, ignore my internal protestations. I've had enough of riding in and out of cities, and on a rainy day I'm happy to put this down to public transport research. I remark on the ticket inspector's job, in this quiet station. "Looks comfortable," I say with a smile, and he grins from ear to ear at the good fortune in his job. "Yes, it's like Germany."

In a café opposite the station, I spend a day drinking coffee before returning to the platform for the five o'clock departure. The train has only two carriages, both absolutely full – full, noticeably, with pushchairs and hijabs. That the passengers are three-quarters women is a conservative estimate; the only males are their young children, just as almost all the cars and trucks I pass on the road are by the same proportion male. As a whistle blows and the train pulls out through the Gaziantep suburbs, I wonder if public transport is implicitly feminist.

The rails cut through the hills above the road. Cars on homeward journeys move below us, headlights coming on. For one kilometre after another, we pass through pistachio trees. The nut that built this city. The nut that built every town around it. Gaziantep, a city of more than two million, where a statue of a pistachio appearing from its shell can be found in the city centre. This fine, green, caped crusader of a nut deserves no less. The trees stretch as far as the horizon, one hundred kilometres and more of pistachio, each tree now harvested. Now and then there is a break in the pistachio forest for a pistachio-processing factory, then the trees resume.

At Nizip, I get out and see that the train line is new. A politician smiles from a billboard. The billboard advertises free travel for young kids, students, families of martyrs. For others too. One-month travelcards offer discounted fares. It's all coming. A small town is joined to a big city, making both bigger, and at the same time more liveable.

As I roll through quiet streets, I see the silhouette of a child run towards me through the blue mist of falling rain and the white mist of evening-lit stoves. Car headlamps shine out from a side street, casting the shadow of another boy who walks alone out of a restaurant. In the mist he plays a game and howls to himself, like a werewolf. "Awoooo!" he goes. "Awooooooo!"

And I saw a werewolf with a Turkish menu in his hand, walking through the streets of Nizip in the rain.

Next morning, I ride out of Nizip along a road straight as a die. Through another fifty kilometres of pistachios I move towards Birecik, a medium-sized town on the River Fırat, as the mighty Euphrates is known in Turkish. The road travels upwards, but its path is straight, east–west, so that I can imagine the train line eventually continuing one town further. At the roadside the houses are humble. Too humble. Sad in a grey cinder block.

From the bridge in Birecik, I look down at the Euphrates, moving slowly towards Iraq. Although it is old and sleepy, the size of Birecik and its tasteful architecture point to its former significance as a place of Ottoman shipyards and naval administration of the rivers. At Birecik the slope and width of the Euphrates was more gentle and accommodating than the Tigris at nearby but higher-up Diyarbakır. The presence of Anatolian forests created a supply of wood that was missing in the drier south, in Mesopotamia, so shipbuilding thrived here. Looking out at the clear, still Euphrates, the sky reflected in its waters, the trees on its riverbanks so proud and tall, you can still imagine how grand this town once was.

And then, in the nineteenth century, upon this very riverbank at Birecik, the British put a steamship into the water, the beginning of their plan to secure the Euphrates for transit into Arabia, a function that was eventually surpassed by the Suez Canal. Before European encroachment into Ottoman lands and affairs, the Ottomans had always understood the need for Mesopotamian prosperity to ensure Ottoman legitimacy in what is now Iraq. The Euphrates was a key waterway to supply drier regions of the Empire with crops grown in Anatolia and the Balkans. When, owing to financial pressure, the Euphrates ferry was privatised in a sale to the British, Mesopotamians – way ahead of their time – protested against the British privatising publicly owned transport. The policy and reaction uphold a commonly held idea of Arabs dissatisfied with their lot as citizens of the Ottoman Empire, but not in that way normally suggested. Their frustration is not with the Empire so much as its inability, in its weakened state, to withstand the creeping tentacles of European colonialism.

Across the river is an old tunnel that cuts out a substantial hillside. I wind my way towards it, but still face a climb. As I ride up the hillside, I look out at sandstone houses and minarets, which remind me of old illustrations of what the Europeans referred to as the Holy Land. Men in keffiyehs and shirwals watch the street, looking somewhat suspiciously at me. If it seems noticeably more Arab here, then I suppose the Euphrates is responsible. The journey by river to Syria or Baghdad would have been far quicker and easier than any of those overland to the cities of Anatolia, in days when these rivers flowed as highways.

Suruç – 20 November

Since Nizip, moving south-east, I realise there has been a decrease in Turkish flags. I only notice this when I see a flag appear again with its star and crescent, and by it realise that – unusually for Türkiye – I do not recall having seen one for a while. Instinctively I like it, and feel there is something freeing in it, because the nationalism of flags will always sit uneasy with me. I prefer to think that our most important values are carried inside us, whereas one flag in one piece of earth always seems to create another flag in another. History suggests, too, that in the difference between these flags, a potential cause of conflict arises, and so it seems hard to say if the flags have solved more problems than they created.

I go slowly pedalling up one side of a huge valley with sheep, shepherds and a village at the top of it. A mosque is painted pale green. Here and there are spurts of grass where rain has fallen, where subterranean water runs out of sight. On the highway, a man passes me seated on his tractor, engine fully open, no cab or windshield, just him, keffiyeh tight round his face in lieu of any glass, exposing only his eyes and the bridge of his nose as he careers through the air. He nods at me. I nod at him. I overshoot a junction where a man stands alone, a holdall beside him, waiting on a ride, just standing there in a long coat. A story in himself, like all of us. He nods at me. I nod at him. Fifty metres on I realise it may have been my turning, and I double back. I call out to him, "Suruç?" and hear the name of the town as it carries to him on the wind and then away across the plains. He smiles warmly, the smile of someone with a hard life but happy in it. He points down the road he stands upon. "Direkt."

I leave the main highway for the first in what feels a long time. The land here is rich. Cotton appears again, families move through fields, picking peppers from their short green plants. Corn grows tall, leaves and whiskers shaken by the hand of the wind. A fine flock of sheep and goats waits with shepherds standing proud. A little further on is a man in a dusty jacket, alone with two long-haired sheep and all three of them looking like they've seen better days. The bumps and ruts of the road surface have a positive effect on me; now that there are limiting factors beyond only the rider, I grow more at ease with the slower pace. The traffic evaporates, people in the town walk to where they are going, gone is the screaming hurtle of the car on the highway, inciting me to go faster. A calm comes over everything. There are more men in flowing pantaloons, keffiyehs too, chequered black and white and red and white.

Watching their herd of goats, a few boys run up to the road and wave at me. Otherwise the children and their families seem apprehensive in that way of villagers who prefer to keep to them-selves and not trouble the outside world or invite trouble from it. I see a family in a harvested cornfield, three generations moving through with sacks, gathering any last cob that has been missed by the mechanised teeth of the tractor.

Cycling through streets with missing or broken paving stones here and there, I arrive in Suruç. The place I am looking for is hard to find, for it was renamed after the event for which I know this town. Outside a bakery I ask a man the way to the Amara Cultural Centre. He speaks Turkish in a strong accent, points left. His son, still a boy, interjects, and gives the same directions in a clearer accent that probably reveals a generation attending school. His father returns, beckons me over. He points to a water tower. "Under that."

Outside it I pull to a halt. It is a youth centre. Which fits. In a garden, at picnic benches, teenagers sit. In all my riding I have never had any aspiration to court trouble. I have cycled in places that might have been deemed unwise to ride, or dangerous, or unusual for a touring cyclist; but I never went looking for drama. I just want the world, honest as it comes. The bicycle and distance expose me quite enough as it is, and I am not in Suruç to investigate, merely to pay respects in a place that was done injury.

At the gate are two men wearing red-black vests that read *Özel Güvenlik*. Special Security. A misleading name, for such guys sit outside almost everything in Türkiye, making them far from special, and, slouched here in front of me with cigarettes, they offer questionable security. Now I stand here, the question I want to ask is politically sensitive and also somehow indelicate, even were my tongue charming and fluent in Turkish. In truth, I don't know what I expected. Epiphany? Revelation? I look around for a memorial to guide me, but I don't expect to see one and do not. And so I ask security:

"Excuse me, did this use to be Amara Cultural Centre?"

He glares lazily over his cigarette; the name irritates him and so do I.

"Evet."

That went well. Now what, I wonder.

"A bomb exploded here?"

"Evet." He looks at me. Of course the answer's yes.

The guy is the least enthusiastic conversationalist in all Türkiye, exposing my reliance on people's willingness to talk, to chat. I have few questions in me, and normally they are more than enough to get people to speak their mind. But not here. News of my showing up, a foreigner, on a bicycle, curious and asking questions, will also probably not take long to reach busybodies who are more interested in what I want in Suruç. I may just leave it.

I try a final question. "It was Daesh?" He grunts a yes and looks at me, like he's telling me to go, so that it doesn't escalate beyond irritation for him and disappointment for me. Hanging in the air and his glare at me are two questions – *Who are you? What are you?* – as I stand there in shorts and knee warmers. I leave it.

Across the street I sit down at a new café with a coffee machine where I can get an espresso – a rare thing since I left the coastal cities. I can see the trees of the Amara from where I sit, and this will have to be enough for me.

Let me bring you up to speed. In 2015, when Daesh was at its peak, Suruç was bombed by the terrorist group. The target was the Amara, the date 20 July, and thirty-one people died in the attack. Thirty-one lives, gathered from across Türkiye. They were predominantly young and predominantly socialist, assembling at the last major Turkish town before the border, which they planned to cross to plant trees and construct a small library in the Syrian town of Kobani. Then the bomb went off and thirty-one of them were dead. Of all the Daesh attacks it is the one that hits me the hardest, because what better intentions could there be than to plant trees and build a library, and because the morning it happened, almost by accident, because I never watch these things, in my room in London I saw a video of it. They were singing and a banner was waving as they prepared to begin work. Then came a crash unbearably sudden and the screen went black.

That it was a state failure on the part of Türkiye does not need saying. When thirty-one of your citizens die in a terrorist attack you fail to prevent, it is the definition of state failure, and you must figure out how to prevent it in future. This is the responsibility of a state. It was only in the following year, after Daesh attacked Atatürk Airport, Istiklal and Sultanahmet, outside Aya Sofya, that the gravity of the threat became impossible to ignore. By then though there had been more deaths. Daesh bombed a rally of workers and HDP at Ankara railway station, killing 109; the suicide bomber a member of the same family as the Suruç coward. The PKK immediately struck back against the state for these security failings, killing gendarmes in the south-east, then bombing Ankara themselves in 2016. And so, in addition to those who died at Amara, and at all the other attacks, so too did the peace process between the Turkish state and its most longstanding terrorist threat. In that death, there closed the peace process known as the Kürt Açılımı, or Opening, and with it what was arguably one of the most crucial, fruitful periods in our Turkish century. The word "açılım" is important, for the restoration of dialogue between the Turkish state and Kurdish groups remains a national imperative, though one too seldom acknowledged by any political party.

And so, minuscule as I am, I sit and drink a coffee in Suruç, the town on my route that caused most confusion when I told people I planned to go there. Somehow, it feels good. I enjoy my coffee, the first in days. But so too do I enjoy my Suruç café. The walls are painted a rich green, nicely chosen. Furniture in metal and dark hardwood. Steps up to the bathroom, a house plant on each step. The coffee machine shines proud next to a cabinet of cakes. It all has a gentrified feel that is hard to love until it is enacted in those places that know what it is to have gone a little unloved. In the corner, in a cardboard box, a puppy has been brought in off the street and placed beside a heater. A few pieces of sucuk have been given to it, and the girl who made my coffee is now fussing at the adorable ball of fluff. Friends of the café owner arrive, sit beside me, as if my arrival is news. We talk, all of the normal business. I introduce myself as a foreigner, and then one guy slowly asks, the elephant in the province:

"Why did you come to Suruç?"

I look at him. Some stubble, hair cut neat and short. He wears a dark jacket, unbuttoned. I think about how to say it, without sounding like a ghoul or a voyeur, but there's no way to avoid it.

"I knew about the bomb that exploded. I wanted to come."

There's a pause as if he didn't expect an answer to the question, and certainly not *that* answer. He gives a short laugh, a *Would you look at that* laugh.

"You knew?"

"Evet. Before it was the Amara Centre, wasn't it?"

He smiles, sort of slow, for another time. "Evet. Amara."

We look at each other, another guy is at the table too, with a straggly beard and a few spots and a denim jacket. He has a soft face, looks like he can't have been that old when it happened. They smile at me. I would not attach any high meaning to my going there, but on a very simple level I feel like it means something to them that I have. It means something that people want to see their town, that people outside it also hurt at what their town suffered.

"Is there a memorial?" I ask.

"Memorial?"

"Evet. A memorial."

"No." Flatly.

"Why not?"

"These things happened a lot in Türkiye. In that time. In the past."

It is true. I don't want to push my dislocated, distant and small grief on them, even if inside me is a determination that Türkiye will make it so that such things can never be considered normal again. This resilience that accepts it with such dignity will be put to better tasks.

"I know that. But I think a memorial is good. One day."

They shrug, as if it's a nice idea. Why not, I suppose? We smile. We move to other subjects. All of the subjects. The guy doing most of the talking tells me of his work, was with an organisation helping refugees when the Syrian war was at its peak. The project finished. Now he volunteers in child protection. He has a work permit that will get him to Germany, one day soon he'll go. He has family in the UK, not close family, but in Liverpool – a good city. I agree. He points to the other guy, the young guy in denim who leaves in a week for Germany, to drive airport service trolleys at Frankfurt airport. They need the workers. The money is great. I ask if he's worked at a Turkish airport before, perhaps Diyarbakır? He shakes his head, he trained here, at a centre. I ask if he speaks German. He says he'll learn, and there are Turks there already.

The older guy looks up, realises he didn't ask.

"What's your job?"

"Writer," I answer. "I write books."

"Politics? Culture?"

"Evet. Like this."

"You know about Turkish politics?"

I shrug, then say by way of an answer, "I guess here is HDP?"

"Evet. Well, we elected HDP. But now we have a kayyum."

"Kayyum, kayyum." I know the word but it escapes me. "Like a man from the state?"

"Evet. Like a man from the state."

I sigh at how selectively democracy is used, its virtues extolled by those who backtrack the moment it returns answers they dislike. I think of the fate of meaningful opposition back in the UK, including his family's city in Liverpool, but refrain from mentioning it. It's good to leave some illusions intact, enough innocence was already broken in Suruç.

"You are writing a book about Türkiye?" he asks.

I nod.

"I love books," he says.

I look at him and feel duty-bound to him, as I do to so many. As I do every time I write a book and, perhaps, without which you cannot or should not write a book anyway. He looks up suddenly, as I am realising he has a habit of doing, a lively mind that flits to a new thought as it occurs to him.

"Have you read Tolstoy, *What Men Live By*?"

I smile but shake my head. I have not read *What Men Live By*, by Tolstoy.

"It's really good," he smiles. "Read it."

For too long I stay talking, finally prepare to hit the road in a hurry. Four hours till dark but I've a solid five hours' riding. I go with my wallet to the café owner, happy to be giving custom to his new business. "Ikram," he says with a smile. It's on me. I try to insist, but he just smiles again and shakes his head, and to insist more than twice feels rude. I smile, I wish him luck.

From Suruç I ride south, the thoughts turning in my head. So much has happened in so many lives here. In the centre of the town are concrete barricades around the police station. In a village on the edge of the town is a military checkpoint, soldier in full body armour, rifle held across his torso. The light is still good, is beautiful even, lending these scenes a serenity they do not merit. Kissed by golden light, they appear so soft against the hardness of their purpose, as if in a dream we wait to wake from. A part of me condemns Türkiye for inflicting this on itself. Another part of me is conscious that the Syrian border is only a few kilometres away, and there the US government supports a militant group overtly committed to a pointless fight against the Turkish state, one which drains from its community an energy that could be better spent.

During the height of Daesh, and Syria's collapse, conscious of the Kurdish Regional Government in northern Iraq, conscious that Kurdish separatists held a swathe of northern Syria containing most of that country's few resources, I remember thinking that perhaps some enlarged Kurdish statelet might emerge after all. I wondered what that might look like, and if I was starting to mull this over, you can be sure the Turkish state was thinking harder still about the prospect and what it meant. The US is arming separatists on your border, they control territory, they are committed to fighting you. States don't take chances with militias simply because the United States have decided that the people they're arming are useful. Because the colonial imagination of the region demands one state for each ethnic group. Because Western audiences seated at an office desk and doing nothing more remarkable than paying down the mortgage like the idea that someone else, somewhere in a distant desert or mountain range, is fighting for some unexamined version of "freedom".

Again I think of the bar in Istanbul, the man from Hatay: comfortable in both his Kurdishness and Turkishness, wants to work remotely, be closer to his family. I think of an Afghan friend, her colleague in Kabul a young Turkish-Kurdish man employed with the Red Crescent: a good job, the chance to travel, do some good in this world – nothing but disdain for the idea that he must be simply a Kurd. None of this is good enough for Westerners, including many Kurds now in the West, with a low-stakes engagement and their lives elsewhere. To the colonial mind, what these men need is not a job but a rifle, a Kalashnikov. For them the IT department is not enough. They must go to the mountains. In those countries that fall even partially under the umbrella of "the Middle East", only a fight to the death is good enough; work-life balance is too mundane for this land, where useful fools seek out or glorify vicarious thrills they would never for a second entertain at home. This is not to argue against solidarity, but to wish that people might temper their enthusiasm with a little knowledge, and consider on whose behalf they speak.

Akçakale

In the soft twilight, with the road snaking up and over the hills, Syria almost visible from the tops of them, it is astonishing that things could have gone so wrong in so serene a place. I see a man in an old black jacket walking through a field of picked cotton, the black of his coat against the brown-red of the harvested plant. As I get closer I hear a crackling that is somehow loud, or, rather, the sound emanates invisibly from a wide area. The snapping of stalks continues as I realise the man is a shepherd, and he is walking his sheep through the field in this first stage of breaking down the chaff. On a hilltop, glowing, a sandstone house, perfectly square, stands alone. A woman pumps a well handle. Two men get out of a car at a village turning where the asphalt becomes a mud track. In sandals and keffiyehs and the smart blazer so many wear, they walk the last of the road towards their own destination. They wave at me. Life moves slow, peace abounds.

The light lasts longer where the earth turns flat, as if night is shyer than it was in the mountains. A horizon returns to the sky, and it waits for the sun to meet with it. Children run after the tractor, jump on to ride the harrow. I hear shouts, laughter. Their large shadows move and refract in the dust, like reflections in moving water. In a village that consists of shacks and earth, animals stand either side of the road, and a fibre optic cable is being laid under the road. The internet will come. Now and then I have to leave the road and cycle on a track, through mud and pampas grass, because the next stage of the modern road is still being built. You can feel the determination of the Turkish state to connect everything, to combat isolation. The village will be connected to the road, the road will connect it to the next village, the two villages will be connected to the nation. The dusk is soft. Children wave. A stray is too intrepid at the edge of the village, a man picks up a rock, tosses it after it. Not far from here is the presence of conflict, but again you feel the commitment of the state to building conditions of consent: where loyalty becomes a more appealing choice than exit. To help us navigate between these two binaries, voices are needed to speak across divides.

With Syria only a few fields distant, it is impossible not to think of the Arab Spring and what happened just across the border. I know a few touring cyclists who, before the war, crossed this border here. The bicycle I first cycled to Istanbul in a university holiday I sold to another London courier who then rode it to Syria. Just how, if times were different, I would like to follow it there. Türkiye now spreads across the frontier. Its electricity cables run into the last stronghold of the Syrian revolution, protecting the population from the power cuts of the Syrian grid. The Turkish Postal Service delivers letters. The Turkish lira circulates alongside and in preference to the Syrian pound, a currency destroyed many times over by US sanctions, corruption, catastrophe. Along the M5 highway, Turkish troops and hardware guard against the brutal advance of the Damascus regime and Russia, who without that military cordon it is presumed would advance and send yet more refugees towards Türkiye. The remains of the Syrian revolution exist in north-west Syria, under Turkish protection and the infrastructure of the Turkish state. In colonial minds perhaps the territory could just be annexed, but it is a small stretch of land in the Idlib region, filled with refugees, division, problems. There is little there that would make it viable as its own state or attractive to the Turkish one. Had Syria's resistance prevailed in the commercial hub of Aleppo, then perhaps it would have been different, but now this is only fantasy.

As I leave I feel a sadness in the air, even if it is only my own mood. The air is only air. Back in Istanbul, a friend once explained to me how it started. Tunisia had thrown out Ben Ali. Egypt rebelled and threw out Mubarak. In the small, south Syrian town of Daraa, children tagged in graffiti, "You're next, doctor," Bashar al-Assad having trained as an eye doctor. The secret police found the boys, disappeared them. Parents went to the police station, demanded their children back. The police replied that they should send their wives, and they would give them more children.

Rebellion broke out. When rebellion could neither succeed nor be put down, civil war followed. Türkiye backed the rebels, full-blooded backing. The AKP, for all their faults, know exactly what the fake-secular political dynasties such as the Assads are all about. Bashar al-Assad, son of Hafez al-Assad, educated in London. He wears a suit, speaks French too, don't you know. His wife Asma is British, born in Acton, West London. Studied French Literature, the pair of them perfect guests at the Élysée Palace or a coronation. Another Western client, poster child, "Reformist!" they cry . . . until it all goes wrong. Türkiye wanted a quick end to the regime. Backed all the opposition, backed Syrian Kurds, in the hope that the international community would replace the Assads in Damascus and help make a Syrian state where its Kurdish population could also be meaningful stakeholders. This – as with Kurdish Iraqis taking places in government after Saddam Hussein – was always the truest path to reducing the allure of separatism along Turkish borders. Some five years after war broke out, think tanks were hypothesising how the country could be renamed the Syrian Republic, more inclusive than the Syrian Arab Republic. At the time that felt like a fantastically small return on so many millions dead or displaced. Now it feels fantastically ambitious.

Life is complex but the simplicity of pedalling at dusk lends clarity to my thoughts. If you wanted the Syrian and Egyptian revolutions to win through, if you wanted to welcome their refugees or their exiles, then you had a Turkish foreign policy. If you wanted the attempt at a Libyan democracy rather than a warlord to take hold after the West's disastrous intervention, you had a Turkish foreign policy. If you supported the Tunisian revolution and its decade of democracy, you had a Turkish foreign policy. If you supported the Palestinians and their struggle for their homes and their democracy, you had a Turkish foreign policy. While the Saudis and UAE were paying for the coup in Cairo, Erdoğan in 2018 asked rhetorically of the UAE Foreign Minister Abdullah bin Zayed: "What spoiled this man? He was spoiled by oil, by the money he has."

Of course none of it was perfect, but equally clear is that it was the better of two options. The problem was that while Western populations have been conditioned not to see that the Turkish preference is for greater democracy among its neighbours, each regional tyrant understood only too well that these were Turkish preferences, and that therefore these preferences were a threat.

Perhaps the truth and trustworthiness of my words can be best evidenced by the fact that they are no longer exactly current or convenient to the Turkish state. At the time of writing, a great mending of fences is underway; those who opposed one another now shake hands. If I were a partisan, I would just hold my tongue, but I cannot be swayed from the conviction that truth works in ways we cannot always control, and because eventually the truth outs itself and achieves good, it is incumbent upon us to plant seeds of it.

Ten years after these revolutions, I try hard to see the optimism. It is true that expectations of freedom and revolution were implanted in people, and the value of this cannot be downplayed. The fear of revolution was instilled in tyrants, and the value of this, too, cannot be downplayed. It was one of those periods where history enters a state of flux, and for brief moments it becomes possible to envisage and seize an opportunity to make change. With four million refugees now sheltered in Türkiye, its troops protecting the last of the revolution in Syria, and Türkiye having supported every single democratic movement until it fell because nobody else would, if somewhere there sits a higher power, judging good and ill, keeping count, then Türkiye ends this decade in credit. Whatever its faults, of this I feel sure.

*

The sun is gone, as I knew it would be. The last daylit sign said twenty kilometres to the next town, meaning an hour's riding if the going is good. Farmers work late, their tractor headlights moving over fields. Under floodlights, the work continues in illuminated hangars. Cotton. Wheat. A fox, I think, runs across the road, tail flat behind it, into the high stalks of the crop. Now and then I share the road with tractors and men still at work, welcome company in a darkness that feels deep and penetrating. I think of war close at hand, of crimes darker than war. The night is marked by it. Dogs do not help, at every village they bark at me as I approach. Many are tethered. Some are not, but are contained behind fences. The fear is in my head, until in one village the dog is out, out in the road, and the fear that perhaps started in my head becomes the dog itself, gnashing right there beside my leg.

Apprehensively I continue, head down, riding with no thought of distance. Just pedalling. Often the best way. In the end a long line of lights appears, perhaps the wall with Syria. Street lighting begins. It's been a while since I've stopped to check the map, preferring to remain a moving rather than stationary target. I am reluctant to stop and knock on the door of a house for directions, to test how the dog has been trained to treat approaching strangers after dark. For all I know, I may have missed a turn and ridden half an hour in the wrong direction. The glow of the street lights spreads. Is this it, the border town? By way of an answer a large military truck, a wagon with a heavy, camouflaged canvas top, crunches over gravel, then bumps down off the road. Its lights illuminate plumes of dust and in their beams I see the blue sign with the town's name in white lettering: Akçakale.

The only hotel in the town. A street away is the new border gate to Syria. A heavy-duty affair of red railings and watchtowers, a crossing for cargo and military movements. Over the wall, between the two frontiers, is a parking lot full of ambulances. I watch from my window, curtain-twitching meeting geopolitics. The old border

263

gate I will see in daylight the next morning: it is quaint, smaller. A yellow concrete arch with Atatürk's face in the centre. The arch now with bullet pockmarks. Right in the heart of town, perfect for hopping back and forth. *Güle güle Türkiye*, says the border. Translated: Goodbye, Türkiye. Literally: Leave happy. We are optimists.

An Arab-Turkish family run the hotel, if we are to specify ethnicities. Khalil behind the desk smiles a lot, has a crop of thick and curly hair. He is in his teens, wants to practise his English, insists on carrying my bags upstairs. I shower and head out, passing Khalil and his friends around a dining table. They encourage me to sit and eat with them, but I decline, say I want to see the town. As I leave, I wonder at what point hotel owners switch from sharing their own food with guests to instead trying to sell it to them.

Walking the streets into Akçakale, I remember a thought long ago, that in planning this route and book I would visit a refugee camp. It's not like there is any shortage of the things. I'd go, I'd report some stories. Now I'm on this border, I just can't: it seems so pointless, when the object is simply to record. Haven't we seen enough? How many stories and what level of evidence are required? I'll tell you what happened, the story that made them all.

The US with British help invaded Iraq, they blew it up. That's the story. The Iraqi state and its army disintegrated but did not disappear. Along with many of the Iraqi population, significant numbers of these men are murdered and tortured by the violent US sadists who run Abu Ghraib and Camp Bucca. Electric cables attach car batteries to genitals. Attack dogs are set on naked men. Photos of US fools grinning, thumbs-up, with dead bodies. That they photograph it at all says everything of who these people are, *what* these people are. Top to bottom the US military and its full chain of command enable it, they protect the perpetrators.

When war breaks out in Syria, the remnant of that broken Iraqi army helps to take a great swathe of territory across both countries. They work together with locals who have only known life under corrupt dictators, and with Western and foreign recruits who have fallen for the romance of war. That Daesh execute Western hostages having first dressed them in the same orange jumpsuits as those men still to this day incarcerated by the US in Guantanamo Bay might have carried – were it not for the bulletproof sense of their own innocence a useful message to Western audiences concerning what set this horror in motion. Sadly it was not to be, and so now the war festers. The refugees are in Türkiye, or Germany, or scattered through Europe, if not left to drown in the Mediterranean, the Meriç, the English Channel. The US places Syria under those same sanctions it already does Iran. The US cannot help itself. For good measure, it sanctions Afghanistan too. Afghanistan faces starvation. Syria fares little better, and under sanctions the country becomes a narco state. A new drug, a methamphetamine known as captagon floods out of it into the region, across borders. It breaks young brains, makes addicts, US-style. The lobbyists and think tanks are all so high on their salaries and self-importance that they perceive this to be an argument *for* more sanctions on Syria, when it is quite clearly, to any sane person, an argument against them.

What more is there to say? Sure, everyone has agency. But all said and done, the US, the biggest power in world and region, it did it all and now exacerbates it all. Sanctions torture those it has not already killed. It starves them, it denies life's basics, it ensures the existence of a black-market economy to bypass sanctions because you will always find someone poor enough, someone wronged by the world, who will take a bribe. With that black market in place, the state corrupts and rots further, and then, when the people are reduced to desperation and a shadow of their former selves, all the West need do is send in its media and its photographers. Let the world observe how low they have been brought, how hopeless or helpless or perhaps sinister these people are. That all this happens on the border of Europe, that this chaos altered the entire direction of European politics, may be seen as a warning that the European Union, like Türkiye, should maybe take more interest in its autonomy, but this new body that fronts an old continent is not there yet.

That's the story, and it may not have started out as a Turkish story but it became one with the refugees that crossed the border. As some endure this fate to have their lives destroyed or dictated from outside, Westerners, meanwhile, for now at least, have only to put an X in the correct box every five years. To face down the inevitable smears of so-called polite society when, once in a generation, a good woman or man comes along with words like peace, or justice, and offers the opportunity to vote for them. I cannot bring myself to visit a refugee camp, to tell the story of someone else's heartbreak, to ask them to tell that story again, if it will achieve nothing in those societies where the stories are to be read, and from which the bombs and sanctions are controlled.

But all this is abstract, all this is nothing. This is only so-called *geostrategy*, a word that at least confirms it is deliberate. If such strategy is the language of death, then in Akçakale that night was the language of life: defiant and joyful and indefatigable. People find life, in spite of what is done to them, because the human spirit is the mightiest of things.

A few streets from my hotel, music begins to drift softly my way and grow steadily louder. Its foundation sounds recorded, played from a speaker, but on top of it the unmistakable ringing of instruments played live. The thump of the big drum, the dancing woodwind song of the zurna. I follow it, down to a street closed off by a crowd dancing and clapping. Boys form in a line before me, holding hands. Other boys hold hands in a circle. The stereo system and musicians play loud over the top of them, their sounds crashing in waves to leave such joy on every face. A man, short and round and dressed in a sequin waistcoat, sings in Arabic, sings so proud and with such feeling into the microphone, interrupting himself only to lift another glass of çay from the silver tray which a circling waiter returns to offer. He sings, he sips, he sings, he sips, and the boys in the line they dance and they beam. A short man beats the large white drum, its skin as full and glowing as the moon, the drum doubling the size of the not unimpressive round belly that it rests upon. From the pavement the women watch, dressed in sequins and hijabs and burkas of different lengths and degrees of cover. Every generation is out. An old woman sits in a wheelchair and smokes a cigarette under her hijab, her face showing a pleasing mix of happiness and disinterest, as if she herself has seen so many of these weddings in her life, but can still while having a smoke raise a smile at the enjoyment of youth. The girls watch the boys watch the girls, and over to one side a large man in jeans and a T-shirt, surrounded by a crowd of kids, points a silver handgun into the air and with the barrel firing tiny pyramids of pale orange against the black sky, he shoots – *crack, crack, crack* – into the night. Younger boys hold at his legs, his waist, in thrall to this father or uncle who commands such awesome power. And all the time the music lifts and the man sings, and the girls watch the boys as they dance for them, and the girls and the boys they watch one another. Some are so young that they are interested only in the party. Some are so old that they are interested only in the party. And then some have reached that age between the two where a look in their eye – something between self-conscious and curious – betrays that they are imagining what this party might be like if it were for them, and which of the dancing boys, and which of the watching girls, would perhaps stand beside them on such a night?

As I take my leave of this fantastic sight and walk on, I lift my camera for a single photo. I can see this is conspicuous behaviour, for nobody in all this gathering of perhaps a hundred is taking pictures, which – though I normally reject ethnic generalisations – is a clear sign that these are not Turks. I lift the lens and I capture, reframe a second, and again capture. An old man looks round at me with a gentle scowl on the lip that holds his lifted moustache. He doesn't say a word, but his eyes fix on me and asks the question: Why would you do that? Why would you do that to us?

Shamed by my own impertinence, I give a nod and lower the

offending object. I watch a little longer, then retreat, the sound of music and gunfire fading behind me as I walk into town to find some food, some skewers.

Outside the restaurant the guy manning the coals is Arab, the guy running the place Turkish. "Öz Urfalı," he says, when I return to him his question of where I am from. Original Urfa. Not for the first time, I consider the value of that strength in Turkish regional identities, the cities and provinces that people love and hold as part of themselves, transcending the distractions of ethnicity and even nation that too often preoccupy and divide.

"Öz Urfalı?" I smile as I repeat him.

He nods gently but looks at me intently.

"Urfalı."

"It must have changed a lot since the war."

"A lot."

I look at him. He sits uninvited with me at my table but with a far stare, one arm out over a chair and one hand holding his side of the table. The boy looks so distant. Were this the US I'd guess he was medicated. Here, I don't know, there are any number of sober reasons for that depth of stare. I can't tell if I'm seeing resentment in his eyes that I can just leave, or the guilt inside me that I can. Or perhaps the look is fixed on me but is for something else altogether. After a while I stop returning the increasingly brief points of conversation. As I walk back to the hotel, a young boy walks down the lane ahead of me, and I hear him quietly whisper goodnight to each of the street dogs. "Iyi geceler," I hear him say a final time as he turns into his own home. And then he too is gone.

Syrian Border – 21 November

In the early hours when I can't tell if the sky is blue or if it is just the border floodlights, I awake to what I think is an explosion and then realise must have been because the dogs are barking frantically. I feel the bed and pillow, remind myself I am not camping, am behind brick and door. Next day I learn that Turkish planes bombed Kobani, a few kilometres from where I had coffee in Suruç, retaliation for last week's bomb in Istanbul. Once again, this level of politics feels like an accident in my route. Some they love it, call themselves *journalists* or *war reporters*, but really the market is just to visit the thrill and scenery of war and turn it into exoticised sentences for safe people back home. Someone else always dies for those sentences, while after a point those guys they take their passports and they leave. The guy from the Suruç café sends a message to ask if I found a place to sleep and am OK. I tell him apart from the dog chases I'm fine.

Next morning I walk the old border, towards downtown. Near the hotel I talk to some bored customs officials; the story of my ride is the most interesting thing to happen for a while. They fetch çay. There must be about ten of them, gathering in green shirts. They talk over the different borders they've known, one guy five years at Ipsala, on the Greek frontier. "I've been there," I say, and we bond over Ipsala. He asks if I am married, laughs wearily when I say it must be hard for him to have a family as a customs official, if he was then in Ipsala and now Akçakale. We discuss my route, borders, terrorism. We talk about Kurds and Arabs, they are amused that I know about the different groups and the dialects of Kurdish. Zaza, Sorani, Kurmanji. They point to one another.

"He's Zaza, he's Kurmanji, he's Sorani."

Inside I laugh to myself. In the West and within the diaspora people talk only of the grievances of the Kurdish people in Türkiye, while down here they man the border wearing the uniform of the state, laughing at who's Zaza, Kurmanji, Sorani.

A block away from an empty stretch of train tracks, sleepers and the railway graveyard of an abandoned station, a large man sits in a folding chair. He is facing south, facing Syria, facing the sun and soaking it in. I walk past him, then turn back. "Beautiful morning," I say. He looks up, happily surprised that anyone has spoken to him. "Allah razı olsun," he replies. God bless.

Picking my way through the rubble and craters of old shelling, I walk down to the border wall and its perimeter, until dogs in the no man's land start to bark. One either lives this side of the fence or knows its way through and comes barking at me. I pick up some rocks and back away, through an old, crumbling station platform where the dog does not follow. An old lady walks with a small flock of sheep, holding a shepherd's crook, her head down.

It is Sunday and Akçakale is starting its day. The tobacconist with scales and bags of tobacco, the butcher, the man selling walnuts, the baker; all life and commerce are out on the street. An office building hosts posters for its two main tenants, both political parties. The front of the building is a lawyer's office, and I think of what it might mean to those who come here to have political parties compete for their vote, to be told their view is worth something in this state, that they can speak their minds on the street, there exists legal redress, when across the border, in the country they have left, the spoiled child of a political dynasty will pull down everything rather than accept he isn't wanted.

Across the street from the clocktower, a Syrian man from the other side of the wall, from the town of Tel Abad, is attempting to start a café. He has a coffee machine, will make me an Americano. It arrives thick and viscous and strong, a true Syrian coffee, an entire mug of it. We talk a little. He got out. Escaped Daesh. He places his wrists together, as if in handcuffs, to demonstrate how serious it was. He got a boat to Greece. Was successfully trafficked to Germany. Just a small town. The police found him. Sent him back to Türkiye. Family from Tel Abad. But everyone is here now. Istanbul, Urfa, Akçakale. People in the UK have sent him money, they help. Good people. You miss Syria? Of course. And it is hard here. Money is hard. Inflation. Business only two months old. The man is dressed in a smart tan leather jacket, neat goatee, ankle boots, a strong pleat in the trousers. His voice is soft, sad. He shows me a photo of his children, the third but a few months old. He smiles with such warmth, but throughout the conversation I feel he's a breath from tears. He leaves me be, goes to the kitchen.

At least, I think, I can provide his business with decent custom on a slow morning. He makes me a sandwich. Such a sandwich. Sucuk, cheese, tomatoes, green peppers, puréed red pepper. All of it pressed under a flat iron and toasted. I ask if he has orange juice. "If you want orange juice I can go get oranges." I want orange juice, I want a second coffee, would have a third but it's so strong my brain would bounce. He sits in a corner as I eat and write. When he's not serving, he plays a video game on his phone. And from it I hear such a vivid sound of gunfire that it begs the question of how a man can lose the life he had to war, find refuge in an upside-down world, then play war games on his phone. Still, who am I to judge, whatever works for him. At least this is a war he gets to control.

Time passes, it's time to leave. I walk towards him with a smile, half-apologetic I can't spend more. I ask to pay, a smile flickers briefly, then he shakes his head as if not comprehending what I've said. I ask for the bill, he shakes his head again. "It's from me." I shake my head. Please. He begins to seem hurt. It's free. Ikram! I'm not going to insist, like that might break the barrage holding back the sadness. Let the man give, allow him that power, Emre. I wonder if this is just him, just his humanity. Or if there is some spirituality at play, and the lira I will pay are worth less than the value of a good deed that will see the business and his life blessed. Who knows? I feel guilt at overthinking it, along with the guilt that, in effect, I just sent him to buy oranges for me. To go and spend his money on oranges, for me. I thank him, try to express in a look the strength of my wishes for him, that I wish the world for him.

Walking back through town, I think of an Afghan teenager who squeezed an orange juice for me on the Karaköy dock a few months ago in Istanbul. He told me that life in Türkiye was hard. But in Afghanistan, impossible. The orange juice was fifteen lira. I handed him twenty. I was just back from the US and their little guilt complex, their *tips*, their pocket money for the unpaid workers, and so I said not to worry about the five-lira change. He seemed a little hurt. Protested. In retrospect I regret insisting. Tipping is the death of dignity in work and the upending of the first rule of the labour market. Walking through Akçakale I think of the two moments, and that these men from Afghanistan and Syria, two country names now used in the West as bywords for disaster, have little money but maintain the priceless quantity that is their dignity, while the US service worker has anyway been mostly stripped of the concept of dignity, has given up on wages from their boss, and so may as well go after the money. There in a place so wealthy I am made to feel guilt for not paying more than my bill, and here, in a place so poor, for trying to pay my bill at all.

Back at the hotel, Khalil is on the desk. He looks somehow different. There is none of the pleased recognition that passed between the two of us when we met a second time yesterday evening and were happy to have remembered one another's names. More sternly than I'd expect, he reminds me of checkout times, and also of breakfast in the building opposite. You don't want anything? Not even soup? I accept, I never need to be offered soup twice.

I cross the small courtyard to the building opposite with its vats of soup. I take a seat on a divan out front while possibly-Khalil fetches me a bowl. From round the corner Khalil appears with a familiar broad smile, and I realise, of course, that it's a family business and they are brothers. From inside a man beckons. I go in towards him, but sit with my soup and for a moment can think of nothing else as I drink it. Oooff, but that soup. How is it always so good?

They are older men. One in a red and white keffiyeh tied in a perfect braid around his head, with a smart navy blazer over his thobe. Syrian. The second is the father of Khalil, Abdulkarim, and the owner of the hotel. A large grey and wiry beard grows from his chin, the hair on his head is cut short. He wears a long off-white thobe. A Turk, but clearly he's spent long enough near the border to speak Arabic and have Arab friends, and two guys this Muslim aren't about to differentiate Turk from Arab. One nation under God, and I wonder if any religion will ever be so uninterested in race. Malik el-Shabazz knew as much when he dropped his Malcolm X. Both shuffle tespih – prayer beads. Abdulkarim quizzes me on my journey. His Syrian friend does not speak Turkish but looks keenly at me, nodding ardently now and then as if he wants to be involved. He reaches over with a small vial of perfume, something to contribute. "Ah! Ah! Iyi kokuyor!" he exclaims, pressing the bottle on me. Smells good! The Syrian takes my hand, and on the back of it he pours a drop of some citrus scent. He inhales sharply through his nose, gestures that I should do likewise. I sniff my hand. Not bad. Abdulkarim goes on talking, then shows me a video on his phone from wartime. "I took it myself," he says, as I look at smoke rising from the shelling on the main street I just walked. His friend keeps on looking intently at me, a part of the conversation even if he has little to say. Abdulkarim scrolls on, shows the phone again, him and the beautiful Dome of the Rock.

"I went to Israel."

"Filistin," I correct.

"Evet." He smiles at my correction. "Filistin. Al Aqsa."

I point. "I went there too. So beautiful."

He nods, he smiles. I'm not sure we've much more conversation here, and I've finished my soup. The Syrian man reaches into a pocket, brings out a small pouch of cloves. Asks for my hand and taps out a few. "Ah!" Abdulkarim makes a sound of approval. "Good for toothache! Good for your heart," he says as his friend mimes the same, touching his chest. I take the cloves, I put them in my pocket. They look at me for a moment before getting down to business, ready to broach that most important subject. They ask:

"You're a Muslim?"

I smile. This one again. "A little."

"A little?"

Abdulkarim leads, but his Syrian friend nods earnestly in backup.

"I like Islam. Evet. I like the Ummah." That global family of Muslims, which I extend to mean everyone.

My man smiles. As if to say, this is positive, we will go to the next stage.

"Do you pray?"

I pause, shake my head.

"Come," he says, "we go to the mosque. Together."

His friend smiles encouragement, I laugh at their enthusiasm.

"I have to cycle to Urfa."

"No problem," he doesn't bat an eyelid, "we'll get the car. We can drive you to Urfa after."

I laugh again, both at the simplicity of their solution and at how it exposes the oddness of choosing to cycle, to make life harder. The Syrian smiles, reaches over and taps more cloves in front of me, like a bribe from Allah. I smile back, the most enthusiastic I've known anyone about anything in a while.

"Thank you," I say, "but I want to go with a bicycle."

They elect not to press, are after all on a mission from God and there are other ways.

"You know the saying?" Abdulkarim asks, eyes sparkling. I know what's coming, that phrase by which, simply in saying it and bearing witness to Allah and Mohammed as his prophet, one is apparently made a Muslim, and as a result many will delight in helping you repeat it. "Eshedu en la . . ." he begins, then looks at me. "Say it!"

he says with a warm smile, going back to the start. "Eshedu en la ilahe . . ."

And he waits for me.

"Eshedu en la ilahe," we go together, "ve eshedu enne Muhammeden abduhu ve resuluh."

Ah! What beauty! They're both delighted. Not even noon and they've converted an infidel. How I come to speak Turkish or am so well-disposed towards Islam is not important. Mere details. The key thing is I'm in the bag.

"Allah büyük!" Abdulkarim says happily.

"Allah büyük," I agree.

"Allah büyük," Abdulkarim concurs again. Allah is great. "All the universe," he goes on, lost in wonder, "every galaxy. All is Allah."

He shakes his head happily, as if it's too much to consider. Still blows his mind. He has a point here, for when I think of Christianity, much like William Blake, I never escape the words *Thou Shalt Not*. Islam somehow always managed to hold more of the universe in it.

"Allah en büyük," he continues. Allah is the biggest. His friend nods from across the table, a warm smile above his small white beard. He puts a finger in the air.

"We are small," he goes on, "so small."

"Like ants," I add, entering into the spirit of it.

"Evet!" Abdulkarim looks at me, startled, as if I'm really getting it, might be good at this. "Like ants! Every day, for Allah."

He pauses a moment, closes his eyes a little, then opens his chest, begins to, my God . . . He's sounding the call to prayer.

Allahu Akbar! Allahu Akbar! Allahu Akbar! Allahu Akbar!
Ashhadu an la ilaha illa Allah. Ashhadu an la ilaha illa Allah.
Ashadu anna Muhammadan Rasool Allah. Ashadu anna
　　Muhammadan Rasool Allah.

"Very good," I say in the pause, cock my thumb at him while looking at his friend, who has his finger in the air in delight.

"He's good," I say to the friend. "What do you—"

Hayya 'ala-s-Salah. Hayya 'ala-s-Salah.

He's doing the whole thing. We're getting verse two . . .

Hayya 'ala-l-Falah. Hayya 'ala-l-Falah.
Allahu Akbar! Allahu Akbar!
La ilaha illa Allah.

Damn, I think to myself. How could anyone love anything this much? They both sit back and smile. But you need some of these guys around in a revolution, to overthrow a tyrant or an occupier, because not everyone's coming home alive and in a spot like that, well, paradise helps. All us frauds who did public policy at Berkeley or studied International Relations, we'll only get stage fright, we'll leave you in the lurch, decide we enjoyed life too much after all.

He finishes, chest empties of air, he comes back down from the call, the song. I want to clap but it seems disrespectful. He gathers himself. Picks up his phone again. Means business.

"Have you been to Mecca? Hajj?"

That escalated fast.

"No," I say. Abdulkarim is already scrolling through his phone, turns it to show a picture of himself at the Kabaa. He smiles proudly.

"You must go. So beautiful," he says. "If you have the money, all Muslims must go."

I have always liked this practical caveat, religious devotion that takes pains not to shame the poor. Still, I make a face, uneasy.

"I don't like Saudi Arabia, though. They say they're with Palestine, but they work with Israel."

His eyes are wide again, happily amazed, like I'm a natural at all this.

"This is Mecca!" he says. "Mecca isn't Saudi! Saudi will pass.

Everyone is the same. Hitler, your Queen Elizabeth," I adore that these two people come out of his mind together, "we all die. From Allah we come. To Allah we return. Mecca is Mecca!"

In Abdulkarim's mind this is quite clearly reality, not religion. If this is representative of how he spends his days, then visiting the Kabaa and walking it, well . . . that must be one hell of a high. The Syrian smiles on, like he's been enchanted by a lifetime of his friend's sermonising. Then he starts a little, realises a question he knows how to ask, and that I didn't introduce myself.

"What's your name?"

"Julian."

"Julian?!" He makes a face, Abdulkarim follows suit. They don't like my name, but luckily I have a second. I laugh, give it to them.

"Emre."

The faces disapprove less, but still we're not quite there.

"It's small," says Abdulkarim.

Very forthright.

"But you said we were small! Like ants, remember?"

The Syrian straightens, suddenly bold. "Emrullah!"

I make a face. I always liked Emre.

"Emrullah." Abdulkarim snaps his fingers, they say it loudly together, "Emrullah! Emrullah."

A half-hour later, still laughing inside, smiling from it all, I load my bags onto my bike. Khalil and his brothers come out to see me off.

"Your dad!" I laugh, still happily disbelieving.

Khalil half smiles but wearily shakes his head like he knows, he knows.

I nod, looking for the words. "He's a *big* Muslim!"

The boys fall about laughing. "Don't listen to him!" says Khalil's brother, like he learned how not to.

We all laugh and smile together, then for a moment we talk road, the distance to Urfa. Suddenly I remember important business.

"Say, that lentil soup? Breakfast. It was just lentils?"

"Just lentils," Khalil's brother says seriously.

"No chicken stock?" I ask, equally serious.

He shakes his head. "No. Seasonal vegetables . . ." He considers what else. "Onions. Some carrots. Not much carrot."

I nod, visibly impressed. He smiles.

"Mum made it."

As always, I take a moment to relish the importance of cooking, appreciated even by a teenage lad. With this last vital piece of business addressed, alongside paradise and salvation, once again, I am gone.

Akçakale to Şanlıurfa

At a tyre stop I pull over. A crowd is gathered, one kid covered in dust from sanding down the primer, preparing to do a paint job on a car. A man stands in keffiyeh and shawl, looking boss-like. Warmly I suggest to the child, nose and mouth and brow all in white dust, that he should be wearing a mask. I ask those standing around if they have an air line. I am met with confused expressions, as if they are convinced that my being here is a mistake, but a young boy gets to his feet, proud to be the only one to understand. "Hava!" he repeats, striding over to the compressor to get its hose and an adapter. He returns to my side, stooping down as we locate the wheel's valve. He applies the hose, air rattles. He is careful not to overinflate. "Enough," I say. Yeter. He steps away, stays in his squat and scampers, knees up, round to the front wheel. Air rattles. Tyre firms in my squeezing thumb-finger. He stops. A little more. Air rattles. Yeter.

Riding into Urfa from the south, because I have heard it is there, I take a left and climb slowly up narrow backstreets to the hill in which you find the cave where the prophet Abraham is said to have been born. At every second corner is the catacomb of the old city. I stop to ask the way. A child sees me and tugs at the black cloth of his mother's burka, pointing at the odd man on a bicycle. At head height, she carries on one shoulder a large steel pan filled with charred, roasted red peppers and minced lamb. I smile at the child, and then a different expression, maybe more covetous than intended, comes over my face as I see the lamb and the peppers. She responds to it as a mother, tearing away some pepper and scooping up some mince, handing it to me in this black-red parcel so delicious. As I eat and smile, she directs me through the maze of old stone passageways – left, then right, then left again – and with her shawl behind her and the steel pan shining, they round a stone corner and are gone.

At the mosque in front of the cave a small crowd has gathered for the evening. Children play, an old man, perhaps on the edge of homelessness, feeds a large flock of pigeons who peck grains of wheat from the floor of the courtyard. It must be nice, down at that end of things, to still be useful to somebody, if only the birds.

The cliff that houses the cave hangs over us, and the high minarets of the mosque perfectly catch the evening sun, their sandstone glowing against deep blue sky. My bicycle stands outside the cave entrance. Some are here to pray, some just to look, and others have the fervour, recognisable, of being in a truly holy place. I am reminded of Jews, nodding in the reverence of prayer, beside the shallow waters of the Sea of Galilee in Palestine, and I consider how Jews, Christians and Muslims all – in essence – fall under the story of Abraham, a boy once from this cave.

Loosening the ratchets with a zipping sound, I remove my cycling shoes and place them on the mat in front of the entrance, where they stand out against the regular footwear of a city. I make my way into the stone room with its thick carpets. There is a spring with a tap, and small bowls of hammered copper, with handles, to drink from. On the other side of a small glass partition is a pool of water, and a shadowy doorway inside the rock leads into the cave itself. I drink a little water from a copper bowl and wait to see which thoughts come first to my mind. I take these thoughts as a sort of prayer, and with them I leave.

Through the empty, winding passages of the old city I make my way into Urfa. Abraham always makes me think of Caravaggio and his painting of Abraham, blade held high, ready to prove his devotion to God through the sacrifice of his son Ishmael, though Christians differ from Muslims in believing it was the son Isaac who was to be killed. It is a story – the sacrifice of a child – that makes it hard for me to accept the wisdom of any holy book, though I was told that the Mandaean sect of Iraq also part company from the bible for this very reason. At the last minute, the angel comes down to take hold of Abraham's raised arm and stay the knife, and Caravaggio's gift is to capture in Abraham's face and brow the intensity of the foul act to be done, the hurt at it, and the first hint of relief that the angel's arrival brings. My thoughts turn again to John Berger, though this time in his capacity as art critic. Of the mood and feeling that Caravaggio was somehow able to instil and convey in his works, Berger wrote:

"The past grows gradually around one, like a placenta for dying with."

Often as I travel, riding through the past and the present of Türkiye, that line comes back to me. I think of the past; the actual history of a country and everything that happens in it. Then comes the recorded history of a country, from which states pick and choose, in order to make histories of convenience and utility. A healthy society requires a recorded history that is able to process the tensions of its actual history. I imagine this placenta of history, carrying us, comforting us – nourishing us where the history is good, leaving us sickly where it is weak – as we make our way through this life.

How does the individual sit within this construction of history? The elite are often taught to believe that they make history, but this is just the delusion used to flatter them into servicing it. Those who make history tend to be those raised with the sense that it would be audacious even to try; that history is above them, but they must nevertheless alter the intolerable failings of the world rather than endure them. John Berger, Stendhal, Shakespeare, Caravaggio. Such names and a belief in the necessity of art are mostly taken as the markings of the bourgeoisie and not the working class, but great art is most essential when you find yourself beneath the bourgeoisie. When you are not born into comfort or prestige, it is the higher meaning, passion and the rendering of the world afforded by art that help you make sense of the fire that is in you, a fire lit to help you process all that is wrong around you, and to help free you of it.

The social function of the arts is to keep your soul safe until your reality is safe. It is the elite who most often mistake the arts for amulets, because amulets are all they need, to such an extent they cannot begin to fathom that for others the arts are not trinkets but talismans and even lifebelts. The lessons of Stendhal are in fact as fundamental to life as knowing to look before crossing a road. They may touch greatness, but they are in fact just practical instruction.

Part 4
Şanlıurfa to Kars

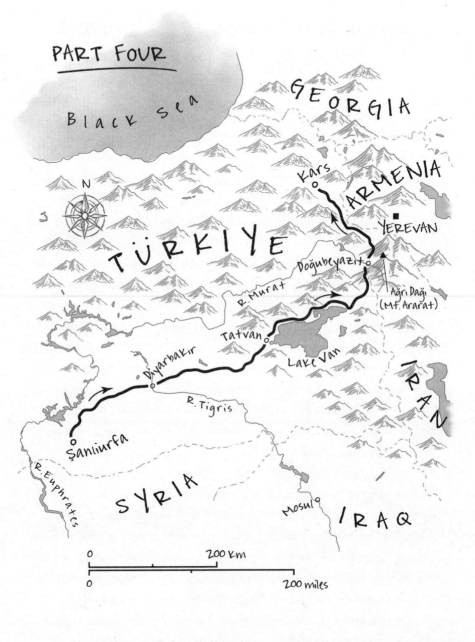

PART FOUR

Black Sea

GEORGIA

TÜRKIYE

ARMENIA

Kars

YEREVAN

Doğubeyazit

Ağrı Dağı
(Mt. Ararat)

R. Murat

Tatvan

Lake Van

IRAN

Diyarbakır

R. Tigris

Şanlıurfa

R. Euphrates

SYRIA

Mosul

IRAQ

N

0   200 km

0   200 miles

Şanlıurfa to Siverek – 23 November

A headwind blows down from the mountains. A first mountaintop under snow comes into view. A man waits at the roadside, a van eventually stops. This is his ride to the next town. This is his transport. At road signs I smile at the beginning of the Kurdish alphabet, the Xs and Qs in the place names, characters famously banned in the 1920s romanisation of the Ottoman alphabet into the modern Turkish script. Part of me has some sympathy for that early Turkish state; there is little recognition that this was not some petty bigotry of theirs, nobody just woke up overnight possessed by some desire to repress. Ottomanism was pulled apart by European powers making insincere appeals to ethnic distinction within an empire far more cosmopolitan than their own. And so the Turkish state was founded out of a tragic lesson that difference was dangerous, or could be exploited, and so it insisted on sameness. In these Qs and Ws and Xs, alongside the Turkish, I see our future, and it will be a happy one.

The further I go, the harder the country becomes. In the hills into and out of Siverek the climbs are all long and slow. The roadside is nothing but scrub and the same loose stones and boulders that lined the last hundred kilometres. I see men in newly turned fields, pulling large rocks from under the earth where their plough blade has struck. The rock is taken to the edge of the field, the closest place to set it down, and this inadvertently marks the limits of each field, so that over the centuries an agricultural grid has taken shape. This is one of the only signs of human life, certainly of human construction. Higher up the hills I sometimes see semicircles of stone, walls of some height. They look like ruins, ancient, but occasionally they are still in use, and in them shepherds shelter out of the wind while their flock looks for grass or plants. Sometimes a small square has been constructed, large enough for a shepherd and an entire flock. Elsewhere the grass and plants thin out altogether, leaving only earth or rock.

Nearby is the site of Göbeklitepe, now the oldest example of Neolithic architecture on earth. "Discovered" recently, it upended archaeologists' understanding of human history. All around I see smooth and large round stones placed atop small hills, resembling the historic site to which tourists now begin to arrive. At an Oxford dinner table last year, a British scholar enthused to me that Göbeklitepe changed everything they'd thought they'd known. At an Istanbul dinner table last year, a friend said he'd visited Urfa ten years earlier, and a local man had taken him to Göbeklitepe and grilled him chicken for lunch. Charged fifty lira.

As I ride, shepherds are my only company. Most of them are as silent as the hills. They seem simply to watch me. From under an Armco barrier, though, one appears with a wave and smile. There is a famous old photo of a shepherd on Ağrı, and he wears on his back a frame of wood, with an animal hide over it, so that he may anywhere be able to sit with his back to the wind and enjoy a little shelter from this contraption. This man at my roadside wears the same structure, only the hide has been replaced with the material from a heavy plastic sack, which presumably is easier to use than a hide, even if his agnosticism about materials jars with my recollection of the image and the romance of that earlier version.

In time, the plants have stopped growing and the sheep are the only thing that continue to move beside me. They are possessed of that innate animalistic awareness of mortality that drives them to keep searching, seeking a way to avoid death, while the plants finally call it quits or wait on a wind or flood or animal fleece to move their seed somewhere more favourable.

Wild animals also keep the company of the road. Slick black, shining like ink but bursting with the red of a fresh death, is the uncoiled form of a snake. It still looks live enough to shock me into a jolt when it suddenly appears in my peripheral vision. I often see these snakes, but a moment later, as I come closer, they reveal themselves to be a curl of spent rubber from a tyre wall, or the worn material of a windscreen wiper. Rare is it that the snake remains a snake on closer examination. In this particular casualty, I think I see what happened; the snake was out on the tarmac, because winter is coming, so the sun is weak and less easy to come by. The road retained the warmth of the morning sun, so there the snake was lured, despite the warning of the vibrating traffic that eventually did for it.

Further on, tossed at the roadside, a trio of rams. Horns locked against the rock where they were left, at least one with an abdomen split open through its wool, so this must have been livestock road-kill and not just dumped animals that never made it from their transport to slaughter. In the fields, especially on the edges of town, are small groups of wild dogs, but they too have been tamed by the weather. Many are thin, sometimes I see them canter nimbly through the rocky ground, knees high as they pick their way with precision and elegance between the stones. They look at me as if I were merely another of them, another animal out here that either poses threat or poses none, and that's the only decision they need make. They do not waste energy on the chase. Life out here has calmed them. Over time, as the days and kilometres go by, I notice there are other rules too. If a dog's tail is down, it will not chase. If a tail wags, it may, but palpably in play. And then there is a grey area, where I cannot explain what is happening until the chase begins.

Most of the sheepdogs are the same breed, or a close mongrel of it. It is sand-coloured, so that often I will wonder if the smoothed orb upon the field edge is a dog lying down or yet another large stone. "Rock or dog?" becomes an unwanted game in my mind. If the human brain has been trained to see faces – in car headlamps and radiators, or seeing the two windows of a house as eyes and a door as a mouth – then my brain has now undone this learning and the dog has established its primacy. Sometimes in Rock or Dog the stone will move in answer, other times I never know. Perhaps a rock, perhaps only a more tranquil dog. In their own way, the dogs make me think of weapons, which to an extent they are, but more than that I begin to see them in terms of an arms race and arms control. Wolves exist, so a dog is necessary to protect a village, humans, animals. Of those dogs, some are unused, or escape, and they make their way into the wild, where they join the wolves as part of the problem rather than its solution. As the number of wolves and feral dogs increases, you are more likely to need a dog to protect against them, until eventually dogs are everywhere, and the existence of dogs has become the defining logic.

Of the dogs, there is a breed I trust more than all the rest, and perhaps a book of Türkiye is incomplete without its introduction. The kangal, to give it its proper name, is the shepherd dog of Anatolia. It is a dog, but in stature, speed and power, the animal more closely resembles a lion. Here in their native Anatolia, they fend off wolves from the flocks they guard, and their effectiveness in this means they have since been exported to sub-Saharan Africa, where they guard livestock just as well from leopards and cheetahs. This has been fortuitous for local cheetah populations, since cheetahs – wisely – avoid confrontations with kangal and their flock, meaning farmers now have no reason to shoot dead the cheetah. The quality of the kangal, however, is as much in its gentleness as its strength. In Anatolia they are raised from puppies with the sheep and goats they will protect, so that they grow as one with that group, bound as family to the flock. It is only when necessary that they reveal or resort to the fierce animal that lives inside them, and otherwise they live among herbivores, their strength placed at the service of the group. In my mind, the kangal exists both as an individual and in a group, demonstrating that perfect social maxim: *From each according to their ability, to each according to their need.*

Moving east, I watch them watching me. Assessing. The kangal's head turns with my wheels, but correctly concludes there is no threat. Naturally intelligent, they can be trained to be aggressive. Years ago I was chased by a kangal, and of that moment, luckily in full descent, I have no wish for a repeat. Even when they are barking, their teeth thrashing, you suspect they are too smart to attack unless they need to, but it takes a good deal of faith to believe that at the time.

As I come over the crest of a hill, a flock of sheep scale a steep cliff, a white seam in the grey ridges. Bringing up the rear is a shepherd in keffiyeh, his kangal beside him, climbing the rockface, almost human. Its front paws serve as arms, pulling it up, its hind quarters push, a long back stretches. From head to toe it is as long as an average human is tall. On another hillside I see a flock left mostly to its own devices. At the crest of the hill is one of the stone-built nooks where a group of shepherds lie out of the wind, smoke rising from the fire beneath the kettle, their kangal lying calmly with them. Its tail is up, as if it is one of the shepherds, waiting for its own çay.

For the traffic alone they are no match, though they might destroy a car, if not a truck, should they be hit by one. I see a dead kangal, dressed in a collar of sharpened spikes, something I once dismissed as needless aggression, but here – maybe turning more primitive myself, my own instincts sharpened – I realise it is to guard the dog's neck and jugular from any wolf that comes for it. I ride by the body, maybe only a few days dead, the spectre of collar and carcass too unsettling for me to stop, as if more dark things may pass here if I linger. Another evening brings a sight of purest sorrow, as a kangal newly dead and still intact lies slouched on the hard shoulder. On the brow of a small bank above the road a second kangal has appeared, still working, but transfixed by the sight of its dead kin. It stands there motionless, assessing this sight too. For a moment, its charges are not under control: its guard is down. The sheep wander towards the road, and a young girl, working an adjacent field, runs down to the flock. Silhouetted in the dusk, waving her arms, she momentarily becomes the shepherd dog, and chases the rogue sheep back up off the road.

Diyarbakır – 24 November

The city comes closer. The land feels high already, and despite seeming to move higher, is also somehow flat. One of those invisible climbs that happens across days. Plateau, I suppose. Now and then some grass grows, bright green. Over one pass, trees return, though nothing of any size. What looks like a watering hole was either dug or formed naturally. Trees have been planted and short fences put up around it, presumably in the hope that they will take root and shade the water in the blistering heat of summer, keeping the pool from evaporating. Such weather is unimaginable today. The sky is white cloud. The wind gnaws. Radio masts rust overhead. The call to prayer comes suddenly and, since I can see no mosque, surprisingly loud, so the minaret must be upwind of me, the ezan being blown straight to my ears.

What I guess to be a few hours before the city, at a near-empty village, I stop outside a small concrete building with a drinks refrigerator and, I hope, a shop. If visitors and their currency are welcome and needed all across the south-east, this is even more the case in a layby just beyond the village of Tosunlu than in Diyarbakır itself, so I elect to buy my next packet of biscuits and a drink here. Inside the building are a few old boxes of confectionery, watermelon seeds, packs of biscuits. A man wearing a grey blazer over a purple sweater sits at a desk with a calculator, a heater and two plastic chairs in front of him. He looks at me as if I must be lost, my biscuit and soda water purchases doing little to change his mind. The warmth of the heater touches my bare legs, invitingly, and so, unusually for me, I opt to sit inside. The man looks at me from across his desk.

His hair is purest black, face and skin the brown of many years' hard work in these lands. Eyes watch me softly. He asks in Turkish if I speak Kurmanji. I shake my head regretfully and smile at the universal assumption of the village, that all who go there must have some idea how to communicate in the local language, for why else go there? I say that I am from England, but my father from Izmir. He puts the lid back purposefully on his pen.

"How is England? How is life there?"

I frown, eat my biscuits. "It's OK."

"Which is better? England or Türkiye?"

Again I smile at the question, one which normally would make me bristle, because here it is rooted in raw practicality rather than nationalism: where makes for an easier life? I can see him weighing the options no doubt presented to him by smugglers who offered him the same service that emptied other villages. The calculation: is it worth it?

"If you have money, if you have a job," I say, "then I think Türkiye is better."

He processes this. My answer doesn't cover the circumstance of having a job but still no money.

"Hmm. I know Kurds who are there. In restaurants. Working. They say it is good."

"Maybe," I say uneasily. I spare him my opinion that those who migrate to rich countries are often not eager to admit that they are still just picking lettuce from the plughole of the sink at the end of a long shift for little money, working to pay their landlord. It is preferable to be thought of back home as a king.

"Which is bigger?" he asks flatly. "England or Türkiye?"

"How do you mean?" I lean in, enjoy the warmth of the heater.

"Bigger. More powerful."

The diplomatic circle and its priorities meet the village.

"England is richer. The rich in England are richer than the rich in Türkiye."

"Hmm." He thinks about this.

"But in England," I say, "many people are poor. There are more people living on the streets in England. In England there are more children without food. I don't think Türkiye is like this."

He shakes his head. "It isn't."

"The weather?" His census and survey continue. "It rains a lot, doesn't it?"

I weigh it up, cradle my chin. "It's always cloudy. Lots of cloud." I look out the door at the flat Anatolian plain meeting flat white sky. "Like this. But every day."

He pauses, strokes the side of his head. He waits, searches for the words, a little awkward at the intimate nature of his next question. He looks at me solemnly.

"How is it with women?"

I lean in, crunching a biscuit, thoughtful. Not sure I follow, old chap.

"How do you mean? I don't understand."

"Do wives leave you? People say in England couples separate. Marry and then go."

"Ah. Sometimes they separate. If they are not happy, they separate. If they are happy, they stay together."

He moves a little easier, relaxes into his chair, relieved, almost as if the departure of his wife might have been something that happened automatically at the border.

"The most important thing," I say, "is freedom to choose."

The man nods thoughtfully, as if this is reasonable, and his own marriage can clear this bar. So long as separation is not mandatory. He fixes another hard look at me.

"You have animals in England?"

"Not like here. No street cats, street dogs. Animals are in the house."

He looks confused, and I realise that this too is another practicality. He is figuring out what he might do if he moves. He tries again.

"But the villages, you have animals in the villages?"

"Ah, yes. Animals in the villages. Sheep. Cows. Hens for eggs. I have friends in a village, they have some animals."

I think of an unproductive but loved smallholding in Devon and I smile. Damn but this man would knock that land into shape. After a short silence I get to my feet, prepare to leave. His serious face warms as we shake hands and he smiles gratefully. He thanks me for the information, as if I've been a real help.

Head down I ride, hungry for the city and willing the kilometres to pass. As always, from the Kazakh steppe to middle Anatolia, anywhere on earth, in fact, when I want to break long, tiring distances into smaller, more manageable parcels, my basic unit of measurement is Leicester-and-back. That was the twenty-mile round trip of my teenage training rides from home. Flat out, head down and full with dreams of becoming a professional cyclist. From this wind-beaten hillside to Diyarbakır is now only Leicester-and-back, and there are at least two more daylight hours. This time I will be fine.

As the wind howls through the empty expanse, as a man considers leaving home because of the want of opportunity, I feel the likeness extend beyond the distances. I think of those Midlands towns that had so little in them back then. Passing a tractor ploughing, not knowing the vibrancy of the city up ahead, I wonder if I am perhaps cycling through the Badlands of Türkiye, which summons the music of my youth. Out here on the wind I hear Springsteen: "Poor man wanna be rich, rich man wanna be king . . ."

Bruce is perhaps right about the glory and beating heart of the Badlands, that despite the work being hard, in it you have to create your own triumph. But he is also wrong, or at least he is in Türkiye, because the poor man in Anatolia – unlike his US counterpart – does not often want to be rich, simply less poor. Although money is important in a country that also knows the absence of it, Turkish culture does not covet wealth. That dignity exists outside of wealth, and that wealth can often corrupt but never buy dignity, are moral safeguards deeply embedded. In my head the song plays on, and

Springsteen demands that the Badlands be built up, that we can't rest until "these badlands start treating us good".

Here is the core of the issue: the Badlands cannot simply be left. Diyarbakır and Mardin province cannot decamp to Marmara, to Berlin. They remain home both to all who leave and to all who do not leave. Social mobility is no substitute for universal betterment. With social mobility, by its very nature and definition, come those who are not mobile, and so there comes the left behind.

Sometimes for just a moment I allow myself to think that I understand Turkish people better than many of my Turkish friends, who tend to come from the top of society. They are Anglophone, Western-educated. They are hardly the elite, and they are committed to what is best for their country, but most are comfortably bourgeois. Unlike them, I grew up knowing what it was to be, statistically speaking, quite normal: a family worrying about holding it together, worrying about money, in ways they mostly did not have to. My experience growing up was therefore more typical of the average Turkish household than theirs, because an average household the world over is just that: an average household. The Diyarbakır plumber understands the daily concerns of a Manchester plumber – how to get that wrench on that washer behind the cistern – better than he does those of an Istanbul banker, who works for the same bank as his London counterpart. Class is a universal language.

As the city builds around me, a child steps forward with a wooden tray held on a strap over his shoulder. In it are lighters, confectionery, packets of tissue paper for sale. He wears a smart shirt, hanging loose on his small body that cannot yet fill it. He stands there, full with his responsibility. We half lock eyes as I roll by. Aged six in Izmir, my father did this job. Selling oddments to tourists taking west coast bus journeys. I look at the boy, he looks at me.

My father as a boy sold oddments to Westerners on bus journeys, and now I sell my description of this boy to Westerners. Is this progress? And what would my father think? It is a question I often ask myself. It is justifiable if my account advances the lot of the boy with the tray of goods, so he need do it no more. Or so he can do it out of choice, not hardship. My father worked every day of his life from the age of six. He was gifted, he read a lot. My mother's father, a Midlands factory man, joked that my father spoke English better than he did. My parents separated. A childhood friend of my mother remarked on learning this that he had heard Turkish men could be conservative. My mother, a woman from Coventry who had to leave it, who fell in love first with, and then in, Istanbul, corrected his hearsay: "It was Cemal who first got me to read about feminism."

I had wonderful parents, but that is all I will say of that. In a world that creates fewer stories, a marketplace for stories is created instead. The immigrant, the minority, the mixed-heritage, sometimes even the working class, they provide their stories for that marketplace: the storied give themselves to the unstoried. And it can be nice to have your story listened to, but be careful what you give, for the emotion of their human story is often what marks people as unfit to pull the levers in the emotionless world of power. Up there the ranks are filled by those who, having mostly been born into it, are unmarked by the efforts of the climb to the top, and what is in truth only their inexperience of the real world manifests as a shimmering glow.

Dicle – 24 November

On I ride into the wind and drizzle, the sky lowering flat and white upon me. I move slowly over hills and ridges in the earth. A tiny, advancing black dot. I give a wave to two teenage boys surrounded by pomegranates for sale in a rudimentary wooden roadside stall. Their first excited words as I near: "Kürt müsünüz? Kürt müsünüz?" Are you Kurdish?

Dear reader, if only it were all so simple. I confess that I have not told you the full truth of this issue as it develops. As I go, I operate under a strict assumption that I should not always tell you everything right away, for I do not immediately want to report every outsized, hare-brained boast from each passing man, in case the person saying it happens to be an idiot.

Once is coincidence. A second time may be chance. But the third time I must accept that there is something to report, or I would be misinforming you.

In a Diyarbakır wine bar the barmaid rolls her eyes as the man courting her sits beside me at the bar and says, steadfast, when I return his question of my origin, that he is a Kurd. Only a Kurd. I ask what he means. I say that I can be both British and Turkish, and, most of all, be simply *me*.

"Evet. It is like this!" the woman at the bar replies with enthusiasm.

She smiles as she says it, as if she's heard enough of the conversation we're about to have to last many lifetimes. Deadpan, however, he shakes his head. To him this mixed heritage is apparently not possible. He could not be anything but a Kurd, and most certainly not a Turk and a Kurd. Unfortunate though it may be, I cannot begrudge him this, and though we are about the same age, history heals slowly and some things that were done should never have been.

He turns the conversation to British politics. Do we have another new prime minister? Credit to the guy, Kurdish politics is sufficiently full with tribalism and feuds that he is adept at keeping pace with rotations at the top of the Tory clan.

"A new prime minister? Evet," I reply.

"Johnson, Truss . . . Sunak?" he checks his understanding.

I nod, laughing.

"From Pakistan?" he asks.

"No, Indian. Well, his family was Indian. British."

"Then Indian," he says.

I blink. "Huh?"

"He thinks like an Indian, not a British."

I blink again at this characterisation of multimillionaire Rishi Sunak, alumnus of Winchester College, of Oxford, of Stanford, of Goldman Sachs. I assure this man that for all that I dislike Rishi Sunak, he thinks like a British person. I am tempted to add that Rishi Sunak thinks worryingly like a Californian. But not an Indian. How to summarise this? I decide to keep it simple. I stick to class.

"In fact," I clarify, "he thinks like a banker."

The man accepts this beguiling new piece of information, if only – I think – because it is new and has a conspiratorial ring to it he quite likes. But still, he insists, Sunak will remain an Indian banker. I contradict him again. British. He shakes his head, the woman behind the bar shakes her head, as if not sure why she keeps this idiot around, but times are hard and he is at least persistent.

"İmkansız," he says. Impossible.

Another time. Seated in that restaurant, finishing my rice and beans, and the owner comes down to me. A large, laughing and eccentric man with a wide smile and high-pitched boom.

"Where are you from?"

"England. Where are you from?"

"Here! Kurdistan!"

And as I finish my meal he returns and slaps down a glass and saucer. "Kurdish çay!" he laughs.

"What's the difference?" I ask, sincerely, but he only repeats, "Kurdish çay!" before barrelling on through his restaurant, leaving me to think quietly, in the safety of my own head, "You, sir, are an idiot."

Most confronting of all, riding into the square of a small town where two boys run up to me, barely double figures in age. First words out of their young mouths, in chorus: "Kürt müsünüz?!" – "Are you Kurdish?!"

Taken aback, confused, I shake my head. Concerned that this can matter so much to children so young.

"A mix," I say, hesitantly.

"Mixed?! But Kurdish?"

"No." Hesitant again. "British-Turkish."

An adult, maybe a father, comes over, laughing at the children performing this interrogation.

"A human," I say. "This is the important thing."

Over and over I return to that encounter with the children, in particular. It confirms that the twentieth-century policy of trying to suppress a culture has unintended consequences: it is only likely to push back stronger, perhaps acquire the national dimensions that were the very thing you wanted to avoid. It confirms too that crude nationalism – nationalism without critical thinking, without civic responsibilities – is merely a drumstick. Some may beat out the rhythm you wished for and play the tune of the Turkish state. But be careful, because others will learn in time that same stick they were given can also beat a different drum and in a different tune. If you attempt to ban that tune, then be doubly warned, for it is the tendency of prohibition to make everything more alluring.

But what of the Kurdish community, who are not without agency in all this? What does it mean if the question children most want to ask strangers arriving by bicycle in their town is whether they are part of the same tribe? And then what? Their sub-tribe? When Kurds sub-divide again into Kurmanji and Sorani and Zaza, not to mention their disaffection towards Arabs or Turkmens in the areas so simplistically declared "Kurdish Regions", whatever that means; as if the rocks whisper Kurmanji. Northern Iraq shows the potential for Kurdish statehood; two decades of Western arms, of the ability to sell half of all Iraqi oil as if it were their own. And what is there to show for it? What was built there other than the fortunes and overseas property portfolios held in the names of two clans known to all: Barzani, Talabani. This is not to say that a Kurdish villager should suffer any more than she has to for the failings of her elites, but it might give outsiders pause for thought concerning the political visions they sign her up to.

Türkiye, for all its failures in some moments and its clumsiness in others, has a plan in which all can participate as equals: economic development moves east, populations move back and forth, and with investment in people and infrastructure the difference in opportunity between the two can anyway come down. This approach, that it is all Türkiye, has left Istanbul with a Kurdish population far larger than that of Diyarbakır, and a country where millions of Turks and Kurds now not only live and work together, but also love, marry and start families, building lives that form evidence against the imposition that they are fundamentally different. The language and ideas of separatism begin to diverge ever more from the realities of life in Türkiye.

For a final time in this journey, I delve into the diaries of Sabiha Sertel. The year is 1921, war is raging across Thrace and Anatolia. Like many of the elite, she has left the country on a scholarship, is in the United States – Detroit, motor city – but her heart is always at the service of Türkiye. In Michigan she helps mobilise the Kurdish and Turkish diasporas labouring there in the pit of US industry.

She works to build awareness of the war back in Anatolia, the need for them to unionise, but – no different from the Gastarbeiter a half-century later in Germany – workers talk of being blacklisted if they unionise in the US. She says the Kurdish majority in Michigan take more convincing of the self-harm of strike-breaking than the Turkish one in New York. With a delegation from Türkiye, she tours the US, building awareness of the war and solidarity of Turks and Kurds.

Sabiha arrives in Manhattan, is due to address a fundraising event for the war effort. An argument ensues over whether she will receive the hospitality of Turks or Kurds. She considers staying at a hotel but is talked out of the idea on the basis it risks offending everyone. Eventually she stays with Kurds who are in better-paid jobs at the Ford factory, so are likely to donate more. Together with a representative from Türkiye, Sabiha tells of the hardship inflicted on Türkiye by the war.

> Brothers, I know what happened yesterday. I appeal to your conscience. Our brethren in Anatolia are being massacred. 90,000 orphans are languishing in the streets. They are hungry and have no roof over their heads. In such a crisis, we can't be discussing with whom I'll be staying.

The war effort back home is relayed in detail. She describes grown men crying in response to stories of the hardship war has inflicted on Kurds, Turks ... simply everyone back home. Men remember the soil of their villages, and the tour sees hundreds of thousands of dollars donated. Decades of savings from Detroit and New York, jewellery, gold. It is all to be sent back to Türkiye in a collective solidarity that pulled down difference and together helped build victory. Sabiha's account concludes: "All they asked in return was for their photos to be hung at the orphanages and hospitals that would be built back in the homeland."

*

From the castle walls of Diyarbakır I look out on the Tigris valley below, known in Turkish as Dicle. Some of the towers and battlements, all in black basalt, are nibbled at by weather, pulled at by age, but for the most part stand proud and strong. On some sections, restoration works are taking place. On others the stone is pressed bluntly inwards from the face of the wall, as if still nursing the strike of the last catapult or trebuchet. From the cracks and crevices of sheer grey rock, there grows a fig tree with its familiar smell and broad leaves, that most resilient of all the fruit trees, which like a word of truth can spring from any hard stone or scrub and yet still produce the most delicate of fruits.

A boy rides a horse with an embroidered saddle and harness; blues and greens show beneath his jeans as he gallops below the rampart. A young couple cuddle and caress on a grassy bank in the shade of a tree; she lies on her back, head in her hijab resting on his lap. They kiss, he says something. They laugh. She reaches up and slaps his face. All along the hillside bloom yellow courgette flowers from the thick, fleshy green stems of the spreading plant, the courgettes all picked.

On the paved terracing below the city walls are picnic benches. Friends and families sit, drink çay. In the valley, I watch autumn coming. Farmers plough fields. A shallow tributary winds its way across the land, as do columns of smoke from brush being cleared. Silver birch, a tree that dominates the landscape, its leaves turning yellow, is farmed and harvested. From this elevation, it looks almost no different from the wheat. In a distant field stands a digger, and near it I see a birch felled: peeled gently off the horizon, from tip to trunk. The wind blows east, carrying the sound in the opposite direction, so I hear nothing, and I feel nothing, despite the fact that a high tree crashed to earth. I watch it, and the impact as it falls, and the consequences are nothing to me. This, I think to myself, must be how Westerners watch that place they call the Middle East.

Diyarbakır to Silvan – 25 November

I come down from the city walls and cross the Tigris. Its waters run low and wait on rain. Clouds reflect in still blue shallows, trees move green to red or are already bare. A small island in the middle of the river, which must often be submerged, grows bright with grass. After the river valley I climb, moving again to a high plateau. The ridges of mountains appear in the distance.

Open your mouth and the air comes in. It is like drinking water that is too cold, ice cubes set through your teeth. A down jacket, no matter how packed full with feathers, is no help; the cold picks through them like a fox among chickens.

In a field that spans three ridges on the high plateau, a tractor ploughs. I smell the earth and its turned soil. A farmer stands alone and surveys his land, his image little more than a crown of white hair and a long black coat. Hands on hips, and then with one hand holding a wrist behind his back, he strides away from me. His heavy coat pulls behind him in the wind. And there stood a man.

At the roadside are pale yellow grasses and vast fields, as far as the eye can see, hill after hill. Tractors drive along the highway, make up half of the traffic. Many have steel rollers or metal chains for harrowing. They ring out metallically against the asphalt, which cannot be good for its surface, but is apparently just the way it is. I begin to pass road signs that show Türkiye's distant, easternmost city of Van. I can't believe that I am closing on the city of Van, that Diyarbakır is now to the west of me. Mostly I take it for granted, but there are still moments when the irrepressible magic of it hits me anew: I just cycled across a country. I did it again. As with some books, I am simultaneously excited to be close to completion and sad to be reaching the end. The pages of the country are diminishing, and part of me wills myself to read more slowly, while another longs for the finish, and respite from the logistics of journeying.

The road dampens my spirits. There are mountains ahead and days are short, but the sight of the military is more miserable than dusk, drizzle or gradient. In Diyarbakır they were parked on corners here and there in armoured jeeps with gun turrets. The one justification for it is the story of a tour guide friend who told me of the time she led a group through Diyarbakır's central mosque, about twenty years ago. Out in the street, they were suddenly surrounded, encircled by gendarmes in response to the apparent threat of an attack against the tourist group. The PKK laboured to ensure the Turkish state could not bring tourism to eastern Anatolia, and it is only with the weakening of the group that there is the same prospect for its development in the east of the country as there has been in the west.

Out on the farming plateau, the military presence is more discreet, though perhaps only because the landscape is bigger. Radio masts and other basic infrastructure sometimes have a small hut at their base: a terrace of vines for summer shade hangs over sandbags. And this – guarding infrastructure – is I suppose the cost of a lack of consent. Consent is always the finest security, the strongest and the least visible. Gendarmeries are defended like fortresses with concrete walls. A slalom of oil barrels, placed on alternating sides of the approach road, denies anyone a clear run at the armoured gate, which has slits for rifles to shoot through. At one village, the military press right up to the roadside. Sections of concrete barrier are painted with the Turkish flag and the silhouettes of soldiers, tanks and attack helicopters. How I hate it all. A couple of guard dogs wander freely; hideous and barking they come for me, teeth exposed. They are called back by a soldier they ignore, but somewhere in them, subconscious, I think I can feel the wiring of their training, the invisible leashes in their minds. They can feel as well as I that they are commanding this situation, there is a line I have not crossed and so they have no need to come for me. And how I hate it all.

On the highway I am caught, then overtaken, by the thump of an engine. As it passes I see a black armoured jeep with what looks like a heavy-duty gun turret; on each side of it are sturdy, three-pronged antennae that must be for the radio but look like tridents or pitchforks, so give the vehicle a demonic appearance.

Mikail, who drove me into Gaziantep, wanted my number. He messages every so often to ask where I am and how it's going. I send photos. I say the military presence is bad. He says the safety of the soldiers is the most important thing. I tell him people only want peace. He tells me there are terrorists. I tell him people only want peace. Two weeks later on a road near here a car bomb goes off as a van transporting police drives by. It is an amateur attack for which none claim responsibility, indicating one vague militant group or another. There are no fatalities, unless, that is, you include my argument.

I pull in at a petrol station. I am out of water, there's nothing left of my biscuits but crumbs, and the highways feel like huge funiculars that are missing the counterweight carriage to pull me over them. I do not want to find there are forty uphill kilometres until the next source of water. On the forecourt the owner watches his empty road, a little despondent. He wears a black sweater and quilted body warmer. The wind is chill. He follows me inside, takes his seat behind his desk, hands folded on top of it, then counts, takes my money, gives me change for my biscuits and water. I smile thanks, he looks back, a little apathetic about everything, but a half-smile appears between his thick black stubble and strong, neat moustache.

Back outside I rest my biscuits on a pannier and wolf a few. I rub warmth into my arms, lift my feet to keep the muscles remembering movement. The man from the petrol station comes out. He asks about my journey and I ask if he's the owner here, what business is like on this empty road. He grimaces.

"Difficult. There's not much. Petrol twenty-three lira a litre now. It's expensive."

"How much is for you?"

He lifts one finger. "Bir lira. Maybe. The rest is tax."

In the man is the energy of one who thinks there must be a better way to make a living but has yet to figure it out. Then he straightens, as if he's forgetting himself.

"You cold?" he asks. "Çay?"

Inside I sit on a small divan with red cushions embroidered in golds and greens. Mehmet brings me çay, places it in its saucer on the wooden arm of the divan. We make small talk, and then a friend arrives and they talk petrol. In the end both shrug, as if there is nothing to be done. I sip my tea, then decide to ask.

"You're speaking Kurmanji?"

He looks up with a smile in his eye. "Evet! You know Kurmanji?"

I smile, shake my head.

"But you know Kurds?" he asks. "You like Kurds?"

"Evet!" I laugh, and he looks at me keenly. There is a tentativeness to our exchange. Two people are about to step outside the realm of small talk into more meaningful conversation, but don't yet know whether they can trust one another.

What Mehmet is really asking me is, "Are you aware?" I imagine it is similar to the exchange within Black America that gave rise to the word "woke", as in, *have you been wakened from slumber to an awareness of structural injustice and racism?* A term of subtlety and metaphor until white people got hold of it and turned it to a performance of either their own pseudo-morality or outright racist disparagement, and then by incessant bickering ruined the term for everyone. But so it goes.

Mehmet gives another small smile, happiness and curiosity now lighting in his eyes at this strange stranger on a bicycle. He gives a quick shake of his head, like a "Now let's talk". His friend smiles and gestures that he must go, waves as he leaves.

"Where are you from?" Mehmet asks curiously, and the time it has taken him to ask it means that again I do not bristle at the question. It is possible, too, that the further I travel, the less I bristle. When it is asked in the west, sometimes I think I feel, loaded into the question, a desire to ascertain how eastern you are; a snobbery so barely veiled it may as well not be. With the kilometres moving behind me, "east" is liberated from any value judgment, for now it is simply our location.

"From England," I say.

Mehmet smiles. "England!"

"But my father is Turkish."

"Turkish?!" He is delighted. "From where?"

"Izmir," I say, and this too is important, for as we now know, Izmir is both one of Türkiye's most socially liberal cities, but also a hotbed of Kemalist thought that knows just how to produce a nationalism that is anything but. My Turkish line is technically from Izmir, but Mehmet as a Kurd from Diyarbakır is integral to it also, and I do not want a Türkiye that does not acknowledge fully his place and culture within it.

"From Izmir?" He loves it. "But you understand Kurds? Turks always say we aren't Kurds. That we're Turks." He throws up his hands. "But I'm a Kurd!" He points to his tongue. "Allah gave me this language!"

The Allah in this answer also points again to how the pious AKP and the pious Kurds were the electoral alliance that first brought Erdoğan to power. For all we must strive to end for good the struggle between Turkish and Kurdish nationalists, this political shift gave the country a significant forward step that was achieved, in truth, through religion.

"I like seeing the road signs here," I say, "the villages with X and Q in their names."

"Ah! Biliyorsun! Biliyorsun!" He points at me. "You know! You know!"

"It got better, didn't it?" I ask, willing it so.

"Az," he says, as enthusiastic as he was about the profits at his petrol station. "A little."

"They say Syria is Arab, Turks are here," he shrugs, "then where are the Kurds? They say we are PKK terrorists. All I want is peace."

"But some PKK don't want peace, do they? They like fighting."

"Then they can go too!" Mehmet exclaims. "We don't want this."

I echo him. "Peace is necessary. I think we're stronger together. Like one big family. I am Turkish and British. Both. It's simple."

"Doğru! Correct!" He points at me. "Turkish, British, Kurdish, German, French. Not important." He pauses, sticks out a single finger as he says clearly and definitively, "Bir insan!"

One human.

I smile. I never know what causes it, but there is a magic in the fact that the owner of a petrol station will announce at ten in the morning that there is just one human, that humanity is indivisible. I wonder if it is Islam, the recency of Ottoman cosmopolitanism, or the tragic loss of that cosmopolitanism, which showed clearly the awfulness that can ensue when conflict replaces insistence on humanity.

"We want people to come here," Mehmet continues. "Foreigners. Tourism. There are beautiful places here. The east. History! They love other places: Istanbul, Marmaris. But they won't come here if they think there is war!"

I shake my head, realise that I am an outlier for now, though hope to be an outrider: an early adopter of east Anatolia.

"And we love it when people come." He points at my çay glass, possibly the best of all icons for Turkish hospitality. "In Izmir, Istanbul, Kayseri . . . people give you tea and they ask for money." He throws up his hands like a man innocent of capitalism. "Here it is just tea!"

I smile. "I think the government has the same idea. They know we can make tourism here also. Like Göbeklitepe," I suggest.

"Ah! Göbeklitepe." He lifts a finger. "Urfa!"

"Evet!" I say, excited, eager to reassure him that it's going to happen. "In Istanbul now there are many adverts for Göbeklitepe. People know about the Doğu Ekspresi, they are taking the train from Istanbul to Kars. Tourists are coming. We need the border open with Armenia. That will be good for trade and transport to the eastern cities. To Kars, to Erzurum. Tourists will come. Cappadocia is in the middle of Anatolia but now tourists go there. We need to build it, but people will come. The economy will come."

Mehmet nods, happy with my prognosis. "After war, it will all come."

"I think the state understands this," I say, "they know it is bad to have fighting inside Türkiye. They don't want this."

"All we want is peace," Mehmet repeats, as if I'm a messenger, an emissary who is to report his words back to the capital.

"I think HDP is important for this," I say. "We need Selahattin Demirtaş to be free."

"Of course." He smiles happily. "You know HDP?"

"Of course." I laugh and nod. "My mum is English, but she loves Türkiye. She speaks Turkish very well. She has a house in Muğla, in Datça. In 2015, at the election, she was campaigning in Muğla for HDP, knocking on doors for them."

Mehmet's face lights up warm as a stove in winter. He smiles and says, "You give your mother many selams from me. Annene çok selam söyle."

Silvan – 26 November

I stay the night in Silvan, but the morning rain falls so heavy that I cannot bring myself to leave. Once it has eased to a drizzle, I walk the town, which is of some size but with the rural feel of most of the towns ahead. Two men walk down a street, one of them with a hen held under his arm inside his jacket. The thing clucks a bit, red neck wobbling, as if it knows what's coming and isn't sure about it but realises making a fuss right now won't help matters. A man chops wood outside his bakery. Tailors and cobblers and watchmakers line a street where incomes are low and everything is repaired. I am reminded of the friend who relayed an old news story about the man out east who'd hotwired his local electricity line and connected it to a metal bedframe in the roof of his house to provide heating. It's different out here.

On the edge of the main street is a garrisoned police station with an armoured jeep out front. Above the door, a large metal sign with a faded star and crescent commemorates the seventy-fifth anniversary of the Republic. Time passes. A man in plain clothes asks me what I'm photographing. I remark on the sign, and that it will soon be a full century compared with the faded seventy-five. He gets out his wallet, shows me ID. A cop. I explain again that it's twenty-five years since the sign went up, and next year will be the centenary. He smiles as if he likes the small poetry of my observation.

Around the corner a beautiful old stone house is being rebuilt, a new wood-panelled balcony installed. It is covered with scaffolding, but I venture in, knowing that this was, as with my Selanik starting point, Atatürk's house for a time. From inside comes the scratch of trowels and pointing of mortar. I ask a stonemason if I may come in all the same, and he hesitates, then nods. Two of them work, a tree stands in the courtyard. We talk. The work will finish soon. The house has been restored before. Atatürk was here in maybe 1915, for maybe six months.

"Battle of Bitlis?" I ask. "Against Russia?"

"Yes. Against Russia."

I wander through briefly, admiring the house. I am sure that this and other local historic renovations – a fine mosque, a bridge of which Mehmet spoke – will help to attract tourists: Turks, who, as at Selanik, will want to see an Atatürk house, international visitors wanting to see more of the east. I take heart at the thought, for if such people come, the police station will disappear as part of the renovation, or at least have its fortified exterior taken down. There is a further dimension to tourism, beyond and perhaps more important than the lira it brings in. The process of a place attracting visitors also has the permanent benefit of telling those who live there that it is somewhere worth visiting.

In a lokanta close to Atatürk's house, I look at the counter and consider lunch; should it be aubergine or chickpeas? I ask the young chef what we have today. He begins the list: "Aubergine, chickpea, köfte, bulgur . . ." An older chef sees that there is a customer, comes downstairs and interrupts the young man.

"Aubergine, köfte, chickpea, bulgur," says the older chef, the list unchanged but for the preferable sound of his own voice.

I feel so tired of all these meaningless hierarchies, invisible until that moment they are triggered, and each in its own small way a riposte against the qualities of democracy. By the time the young man is no longer young, he will have been interrupted so many times that he'll be damned if he's not going to grab someone else's airtime himself.

"I know," I say, "your friend told me."

The chef looks hurt, his self-importance gone. Deflated. I feel bad. The meaningless hierarchy meant something to somebody after all, and perhaps it was not only pointless but also harmless, so that now I am the aggressor.

As I eat my aubergine and rice, the older man joins me, brushing crumbs from his chef's tunic. He lights a cigarette and blows smoke courteously out the open door. Middle-aged, tired-looking, balding. Just a man. A man at work.

"Başbakan şeker," he says to me.

It is one of those many moments I have in Turkish where I understand each word perfectly but together they make no sense to me. The president is sweet?

"Erdoğan şeker?" I clarify.

"Evet." He exhales.

"Şeker? Bal gibi? Çay gibi?" Like honey? Like tea?

"Evet." The man is happy to be understood; that I do not actually understand is irrelevant.

On the restaurant wall is some Quranic script, photographs of some solidly Muslim men. Good beards.

"Müslüman?" I ask.

"Müslüman," he says, happily.

"You're AKP?"

He gives a thumbs-up.

"I thought here, this region, was HDP?"

He likes that I know HDP. Gives them a thumbs-up too. "Evet. This region."

"HDP and AKP together?" I ask.

Also gets a thumb-up. We talk about the town, why I'm here. I'm travelling. I mention the Atatürk house. Can't help but ask if he also likes Atatürk. Another thumbs-up. This man approves of the Muslim, of the secular-nationalist, and of the pro-Kurdish leftist currents of the Turkish political spectrum. That is a lot of approval. We talk life, which is hard with inflation. Is England the same? I nod, say that mostly it is. He goes quiet, as if he had wanted to believe that it wasn't like this everywhere. I pause.

"Her şey çok güzel olacak," I say. Because it is an apt sentiment but also the heart-warming campaign slogan of Istanbul CHP mayor, Ekrem Imamoğlu, and I am curious to learn if it has made it as far as Silvan. "Everything will be OK."

He smiles at my words, but without recognition, and responds logically.

"Ne zaman?" he asks. When?

I shrug, smile. "Yakında." Soon.

"Soon?"

"Evet. İnşallah."

We talk life, where I learned Turkish. Mostly in Istanbul. He lived there too. He's from Diyarbakır but life is easier in Silvan. Less expensive. Where was I in Istanbul? I can't bring myself to say Cihangir, it's too embarrassingly loaded with class connotations, so I go with Taksim. He was Esenler. Near the bus station? Evet. Where the people from the bomb last week lived.

"You saw?" he asks.

"Evet," I say, "maalesef." Unfortunately.

"When did you go to Istanbul?" I ask.

"At fifteen."

"With your family?"

He shakes his head, puts up one finger. "Yalnız." Alone.

"You sent money back?"

"Yes. Every month. Twenty years there."

I point to the restaurant we sit in. "Are you the owner here?"

He shakes his head. "İşçi." Worker.

"The owner is a good man?"

"Evet. A good man."

He looks at me with his smiling, tired eyes. With his smiling teeth yellowed by the smoking I wish he and everyone would quit. He is happy just to sit and talk, the national pastime of Türkiye. On the street an armoured vehicle goes by.

"There are more police here. On this side of the country," I say, "more than in Istanbul. Lots of gendarmes on the road."

"Evet," he says, casting an arm wide across the land. "Karakol." Police station.

"How is it?" I ask.

He looks glum, despondent. A sort of awkward fact of life, and he makes a pained expression like he isn't one to complain but, well . . .

"It's difficult. Feels uncomfortable."

We pause. And I think anew of how we must resolve this. For this man, loyal to the current government, the Turkish state and the political party that seeks to resolve Kurdish political problems within the parameters of the Turkish state. We are quiet, but the man's humility is such that I feel I should say something, because on the larger questions of life he will not, as if he defers to my interviewing and my views.

"Geçecek," I say. It will pass. I say it partly because I believe it, and partly because how else but by willing it do we make it so?

"Geçecek?" he says, looking at me as if to say this sounds nice. "When?"

I don't have the heart to pronounce too confidently on a matter so outside my control and on which his daily life is so reliant, so I add, guiltily, "Inşallah."

He nods. "Inşallah," he replies.

I am reminded of a Libyan-Irish friend whose mother would always demand to know when her daughter said it if she meant inşallah in the Libyan or in the Irish sense. The Libyan or Arab use of inşallah often carries almost an acceptance that something won't be done, but we will be at peace with it regardless. The Irish, I suppose to her mother at least, left open the possibility that the inşallah would be acted upon. I think of this as I say it to him, and so find myself saying "inşallah" one last time, as if to let him know I mean it, that I mean inşallah in the Irish sense.

Silvan to Bitlis – 27 November

Today will be a day of labour in the pedals, a climb to altitude, into Alpine terrain. The rain has cleared, the colours return slowly through the grey. The burnt oranges and reds of autumn. Trees glow like lanterns in new sun. Fruit stands, beehives. I see a man in full protective garb, the net hanging down from his hat as he lifts out honeycomb on a metal hook. Beside him, not looking in good shape, his colleague in the same protective overalls is stung, lying face down, waiting for the pain and shock to pass. Nobody pays this too much notice, I don't think it's his first time. On a hillside I stop for fruit where two boys wait with their stall. "Kürt müsünüz? Kürt müsünüz?" they call out as soon as I appear. The Kurdish national project has never felt more like hot air.

A road is being constructed through the valley. The old one has been reduced by the weather to rubble. My road winds patiently on as viaducts and tunnels take shape. Now and then we join with the new surface, then leave it again for the old while the next section is constructed. Rollers move under large tents that shield the new highway from snowfall, fresh asphalt the only warmth around. I pass a large restaurant in the hills, boarded up, glass windows broken, the building measuring about a hundred metres from end to end: a large place, as if an entire food dynasty was planned but is now fading back into nature. The new road must also have been its enemy: fewer breakdowns, a three-hour drive turned to a one-hour drive, a rest at either end, no need of food in the middle.

A wedding party drives by, red ribbon trailing down the white metal of the van and some of the following cars. I sneer at it, detest

314

this sight. The ribbon represents the red band that some brides wear around their waist, to symbolise the blood that is supposed to present when on her wedding night she loses her virginity. Is this tradition or is this backwardness? It would be wrong to assume that this is merely proof of male control; I'm sure many women also subscribe to and derive a sense of honour from this code. What is for sure is that it is the bride's problem if – depending on the levels of idiocy involved – she does not bleed on her wedding night, as amateur gynaecologists decide that this represents evidence of something, or simply a disappointment. Perhaps it is a disappointment for her too, because she expected that manifestation, and she alone knows the truth.

At the roadside I see a sign for Hasankeyf, an old village of Kurdish heritage now submerged beneath the waters of the reservoir that rose as the Ilisu Dam was built, holding back the water that now drives the turbines. In Western media and the Kurdish diaspora, this was broadly represented as an attack on Kurdish culture, and while it surely leaves questions to answer, in the east of Türkiye, the dam represents cheaper, cleaner and more reliable electricity for millions of people who – again, if ethnicity must be invoked – are often Kurdish. There is no right, no wrong, only complexity and hard decisions.

The road to Tatvan recalls a friend who once told me about her father, when he was undergoing teacher training sometime in the nineties. He took a minibus with other trainees from the Black Sea region down to Tatvan. It was in the worst days of the fighting between the state and the PKK, when the PKK had been known to execute teachers as state actors. To do so was to assert their own authority, and obstruct the teaching of the Turkish curriculum and language. The policy served only to make the PKK more hated by Turks, by Kurds comfortable as Turkish citizens, and by those who wanted the conflict to end. It also served to deprive all children from the southeast, Kurdish or not, of opportunities for literacy, development and better integration within Türkiye. That day, as they drove through these mountains, their minibus was stopped by PKK militants. The trainee teachers were taken off the bus, pushed about a little, scared a lot. My friend's father told of how he thought he was going to die, but after a while they were put back on the bus and sent on their way alive. He decided not to become a teacher, went into business instead. I can't help but think he would have been a good teacher, while he was a terrible businessman. The wasted potential, the forced decisions, are once again, as with the broad fear it engenders, casualties arising from terrorism. This is why, if you're going to pursue it, you have to be sure your cause is worth your terrorism. And you should be sure your terrorism will not destroy your cause. Across the region, crony businesses thrived instead, as the main criterion for opening was that organisations be loyal to the PKK and willing to pay protection money in exchange for the licence to operate undisturbed. The PKK ran this racket profitably enough, so that in time the Turkish state cut investment in the east, knowing that a percentage of it was going direct to the PKK. In this the PKK furthered the conditions for the underdevelopment of eastern Anatolia, an underdevelopment that in turn benefited PKK recruitment while disadvantaging the wider population they professed to serve.

I pass a turning on the right. Were I to take it, with a half-day's pedalling, I would reach Iraq. The road leads south to Siirt, to the border town of Cizre. A little way across the border, the first major conurbation on the Iraqi side is the beautiful city of Mosul, with its special place in Turkish history.

"Yurtta sulh, cihanda sulh" was a saying of Atatürk's, one of many still at the heart of the Turkish nation. Peace in the home, peace in the world. Turkish centrality to so many places, the disaster of World War I, and something more special than mere logic have left a country that despite, or maybe because of, its internal struggles, has a strong history of multilateralism and seeking good relations with everybody. The people of the country are natural traders and natural hosts, neither of which is a mentality of needless war.

Atatürk in particular, ahead of his time, was ready for multipolarity.

He was conscious that good relations were more important than territory, and even superseded the need for it. If you have good relations, you have access to territory anyway. The loss of Selanik, his home town, must have predisposed him to this. His beloved Balkans, beloved city of his birth, were never to fall inside his beloved Türkiye. Even if the country always retained the military strength to take them, why bother? Why seek to make a majority Greek city your own, and in the process diminish the good relations by which you would never have needed to. On a deeper level too, for Atatürk the loss of Selanik must have imparted a sense that something you know intimately, and that is part of you, sits outside the borders of the country that is yours. And that's OK. This is the emotional essence of multipolarity: an awareness of the whole world, of loving something outside of your own borders, and so realising that the people there will love it too.

If that was the Ottoman west, here in the Ottoman east a similar choice was made with Mosul. Before the Western powers created Iraq as a Türkiye–Iran buffer, Mosul remained throughout World War I under solid control of the Ottoman army. Even with the world's oil economy taking off, and an inkling of what was in the earth of northern Iraq, Türkiye ceded the Mosul region to Britain in an effort to build good relations there.

Is this now a cause for regret? In the country there certainly endures a memory and idea of Mosul inside Türkiye. I imagine that the oil of the province would have made for a useful trust fund, but by the same token it would have – as oil always does – induced corruption, or corroded the Turkish ability to support itself using its labour, minds, and capacity to organise. Sometimes I think that a Turkish state founded with more Arabs inside it might have made society more diverse in its inception: maybe lessening the potential for friction between Turks and Kurds, lessening prejudice against Arabs. Other times I consider that there are anyway many millions of Arab-Turks to have helped achieve these goals, if indeed it could have been a solution.

A century later and Mosul and Hatay in my mind appear side by side. I feel it is sad Mosul was given up only for the same reason I am glad Hatay was incorporated from Syria into Türkiye in 1939. That many millions of Mesopotamians and Moslawis would have been safe when the US and UK waged war against the Iraqi state they had only recently created. Mosul Central Library would not have had to be rebuilt, nor the Great Mosque of al-Nuri blown up, after Daesh eventually took Mosul in the footprint of that war. It is nice to imagine that the Moslawis could have avoided all of that, to think they could have remained ours, and we theirs.

In time the rain is too much, I am too wet, and even the distractions of my historical musings cannot keep me going. I pull in at a village, head straight to the shelter outside the çay evi. Men stand and smoke, greet me with looks of surprise and the first questions of an interrogation. I am cold in my wet clothes and I make a beeline for the warmth of the stove and çay. I peel off a couple of layers and my gloves, place them over the backs of chairs and nearer to the heat so they might dry. The man running the show brings me the first of what will be many glasses of çay. The room is lined with men in long coats and moustaches, all sitting on stools around the walls, around the stove, around the card tables, around one another and the gossip of the village. They raise their çay glasses to me in a small gesture of welcome, then continue with the conversations that have been going on uninterrupted in this place for all eternity.

I get to my feet and in my cycling shoes clip across the tiles and round to the bathroom. I run warm water to wash my face. I take a few sheets of paper towel to dry my hair a little. I return to the main room, see the man who serves tea now carrying an armful of small logs, loading them one by one into the blazing stove, its lid lifted like a hungry mouth. He is a large man with a serious face that, on seeing me, breaks into a smile of reassurance and a thumbs-up to suggest that this will do the trick, he will see to my warmth. I smile, go back outside to my bicycle, grab my down jacket, call its feathers back into service and pull it on, zipped right to my chin. I walk back inside to the çay evi. I see the çaycı, having stoked the stove, now busying himself with my clothes, placing a glove on a chair arm, rearranging my sodden jacket over the back of the chair so that it catches more of the warmth of the stove. He sees me watching him and smiles, gives me another thumbs-up. In this man is a heart of gold, a tenderness, that warms as much as his fire.

In a break in the rain I return to the road. Mist presses over the hills. The dogs on the edge of town, a pack of a dozen mongrels of many colours and breeds, pick their way down through the wet air and onto the road. They stand silently to attention and watch me pedal by, all of them on full alert but clearly distracted by something other than me, taking this break in the rain to do something I know not what. A little further on I see one mutt alone with a bin bag, its fur mangy and patches of pink showing through, the animal neither part of the pack nor able to fend for itself.

On the road ahead a sheep, then a dozen sheep, then a score of sheep, then a hundred sheep and more. I see soldiers with rifles and body armour, and shepherds with staffs. The soldiers escort the shepherds who escort the sheep. The shepherds laugh when I ask the soldiers if they are shepherds. The soldiers do not see the funny side. A couple of large dogs pad dutifully and calmly among the flock. On one the fur either side of its head is stained red with blood where its ears have been lopped off, a modification that stops wolves and wild dogs from seizing hold of them in a scrap.

The sheep flood down the roadside and along a narrow bridge where they cross the valley and absorb the road, winding up into the opposite hill, a stream of wool babbling around rocks.

A little while later I stop at a small checkpoint, want to ride through but a combination of police and soldier boredom, and a desire for conversation, a break in routine, results in my being stopped. We talk of my journey, they say that I am like an explorer, like Evliya Çelebi, and laugh. I take the compliment. They bring out çay for me. We talk about the road, about work, about life up here. They are two police and one soldier with a rifle, he a Kurd from Iraq and now, since the Gulf War and becoming a refugee, a Turk. A happy one, he says.

Tatvan to Erciş – 28 November

I accelerate, not riding faster, but spending more hours on the bike. The writing and riding of days begin to blur together. My pen pedals, my feet inscribe. It was always going to happen this way. An end point comes into view and brings with it some mix of impatience and focus.

Lake Van takes an enormous bite from the horizon, so that water and sky blend together and hang there like some giant blue lantern, glowing with the sun. I skirt water. I crest hills. I ride under sheer cliffs, and on the edge of the Armco barrier I sit and eat what will probably be a last pomegranate of the year. The ruby seeds glisten as a few missed opportunities fall at my feet. A shepherd in a scarlet turban rides a mule slowly up a large and impossibly steep slope, ahead of his flock and above the lake. The mule is slow, but it does not falter. As the road straightens and lures drivers into acts of complacent stupidity, a small lorry has crashed with its cargo of fruit. Pomegranates and oranges are juiced, the lorry upside down, the window smashed and cab also pressed like a fruit onto the asphalt.

I return again to pedalling, to lake, to mountains. I see the blue of the lake. I see the mountains a second time in the mirror of the lake. Yet all I can think of is that in 2020 there were sixty-one refugees who drowned here when their boat sank in this water. The east of Lake Van sits close to Iran and its border, but on its west you are comfortably inside Türkiye, so that it became for a time a useful crossing point.

It is the punishing cold that gets me. Everywhere is so cold here, or set with the nearness of cold, creeping up my sleeves or down my neck, that I cannot bear to think of their last moments in that water. Predominantly Afghan, the refugees had fled the US war against their home country and found a home in Iran. Then, as the US set to destroying Iran by sanctions, prohibiting any financial interaction with it, conditions for a million Afghan refugees inside the country had predictably worsened faster than for most, causing them to flee. And as they fled that second time, in a boat unfit for passage, they drowned in this lake in eastern Anatolia.

As I ride I think of the great Irish cyclist and writer, Dervla Murphy, who cycled to Afghanistan in days when you could. Before the US first started arming the mujahideen that became the Taliban, because they worried that in the streets and universities of Kabul a Soviet influence might develop, bringing with it the prospect of socialism that the US has never stopped at anything to destroy. Credit where it is due; none could say that the US policy to root out socialism in Afghanistan was not a resounding success. The US did its work, and now I can no longer begin to imagine being able to cycle in Afghanistan, as Dervla once did, alone with her bicycle.

Such a basic thing – can I still travel by bicycle there? – is a good test of whether something has grown better or worse. I remember the first time I planned to cycle around the world, and Afghanistan, then destroyed by the US, seemed out of the question but Pakistan, except for a small stretch at Quetta, did not. Later, Pakistan seemed out of the question, but Iran did not, and many friends had ridden there. As the United States set about its efforts to destroy the Iranian state and its relations with the West, riding through Iran also began to seem unwise. Iraq was impossible because of the US invasion, but that evil destruction had not yet spilled into Syria, so that a few friends had ridden through it, before Syria too became – for now – an impossibility.

Place by place, the United States has destroyed so much, with Westerners encouraged to believe that it is just the way it has to be, the way it always was, or that perhaps each of these states did something to deserve it. It is a problem of polite society that people often prefer to say things that are novel and sophisticated than those that are plain and true, and as a result some of the truest things are never said, or are said too quietly. The US engineered the conditions that led directly to sixty-one deaths in the perishing waters of Lake Van, and sadly it is as simple as that.

From a European perspective, it is impossible not to also notice that what the US destroys is getting closer. Its trail of unmitigated disaster moves from Afghanistan, to Iran, then to Lake Van. Some make it to Samos and some beyond that. It is an uninviting prospect to imagine that the US must destroy itself before it irrevocably damages still more that is good, but it grows no less difficult to imagine a country so pathological changing itself. Afghanistan provided a degree of acceleration here perhaps, for the military hardware that was withdrawn from Central Asia has to be put somewhere, and so US police forces now find themselves armed with the same tools and second-hand vehicles that fought insurgents in Kandahar. Now those giant military vehicles are deployed to police the streets of Missouri or Portland, where people begin to see that, eventually and inevitably, the war always comes home.

The light is fading and on the forecourt the three of us stand: the father, his boy, me. Across from us is Süphan, the second highest mountain in Türkiye. It dominates the horizon under it, shrinking everything around. The mountain is covered with snow, the deep blue sky streaked with pink. I pull on a jacket as an intrepid cow wanders up the bank towards us. The young boy sees and in alarm runs over to it, arms up, to shoo it away. Next to me, Dad shakes his head, rolls his eyes. "Cows," he mutters, as if they're always doing that.

In the difference between the voices of father and son, I hear a few decades of smoking and age, but also the accents of the Turkish east and west coming closer together. The father smiles warmly. His boy is bright-eyed, beautiful. I hope school goes well for him, that his Turkish helps him access whatever education and job he wishes, or to be happy right here tending the cows beneath Süphan. I hope the Turkish state develops correct policies for a multilingual country, and that in this village and at their table, the family speak Kurmanji and none shall ever interfere with that again.

The father follows me into his shop, no more than a room with a few shelves. I take down some bars of cake that feel dense and like the sort of calories I need. I eat one as I go to a fridge to get a drink.

"War in Iran," he says, and I jump, fearing I've missed vital news, then taking stock.

"Protesters?" I clarify.

"Evet."

I decide to seek his opinion. "Türkiye is like this?"

"No! Not like this," he replies.

"Here we have peace?"

"Evet. Here is peace."

"Here are fewer gendarmes than south, near Bitlis, Diyarbakır."

"Round here was always mixed," he says, "lots of Armenian, Iranian, Kurd, Turk."

"Everyone is here," I laugh, and he smiles, but then looks seriously at me, raising one indivisible finger. Again the same vital words:

"Sadece bir insan."

Only one human.

At the counter the boy is sitting, waiting for me with his calculator. I go towards him, look forward to paying, to supporting father and son. The boy tots up everything on the calculator. Twenty-eight lira. Less than two pounds towards the fuel bill for them, towards next week's shopping. Damn.

Father and son follow me back outside and I add layers. Long sleeves come out. I pull on the shell of my rain jacket over the feather jacket, a statement of my intent to keep warm. The boy stands beside me as I unload and load panniers. He plays with my bike, the handlebars, the brakes. He has a lean face to his father's very round one.

"Your son?" I ask dad.

"Evet." Proudly.

"A beautiful boy," I say, meaning it, for he is a mixture of shyness and curiosity about everything. I smile, and I wish the world for this boy, wish for it to give him all he needs, all he desires. I need to strengthen and support Türkiye, for that is how I will best help him.

"You have a bike?" I ask as he holds my handlebars.

He shakes his head.

"You like bikes?"

He nods in earnest. "Çok!" Very much.

The three of us stand together as dusk approaches. The father, his boy, me. The sky glows a brighter pink against the great mountain under snow.

"Forty kilometres to Erciş," says the father, which sounds about right, and I know that it will be head-down riding. Even where we stand, the cold is racing over the cusp of the horizon and coming at us.

"Go fast," says the father, "it will be cold."

I ride. It is cold. I am apprehensive, and then realise that the first hours of darkness are not much different from the dusk. It is the sun alone that brings any warmth, and it left some time before dark. Not for a while will night temperature come. Animals are another matter. At a work camp for highway construction, silhouetted against the lake, I see dogs, the kind kept by scraps from the camp. I look, then realise they are playfighting together on the shore, jumping up, tails high, running in circles, a dance so innocent. Beautiful. But now they've seen me. Shit. They're coming. I hate them. I've a good head of speed. I press harder. Three of them up. The bank from shore to road is high and steep but recent experience has shown me the vast power difference of four legs. They breeze up it, run behind me on the tarmac, but these things are sprinters and I have gears. The barking fades until the next village, where it starts up again. My habitual question: is the barking moving? Or tethered? Moving.

And then under the lights of a house I see the shape of a dog flash through a distant field. It comes fast, I keep going. Barking fades. In the quiet of the darkness between villages I stop, dismount, and turn off my rear light. That soft red glow, even in the distant darkness, but with my spinning limbs on top of it, is clearly the finest dog toy ever to hit the roads of Van province. My panniers have reflective patches for car headlights, and for now I'll take the risk of a dumb driver over the certainty of the dogs.

I keep on, keep on looking for Erciş. Villages are visible, wrapped around the lake, but nothing of the size I had expected to see. The road rises ahead, I see lights climbing high, diagonal. On the road cars are ascending, up towards space, where the stars are out and a new crescent is lifting. I'm not sure I've the energy for a whole pass but what choice do I have? A truck races by, a trail of sparks follows under it: orange flashes as a broken exhaust drags along the road. I wonder if the driver even knows? A few kilometres up the highway I see the truck pulled in: he certainly knows now, is lying on his belly and looking under the chassis as a friend stoops beside him. A burning smell hangs over the road. There's some smoke, then more, and then the loudest bang you've ever heard rips the night and they roll out and away from the explosion, somehow laughing with all the heart of the world's working class, for whom life was never supposed to be easy.

Up the rise I ride. Everything is shut under a cold darkness, the only warmth the light of the moon on the rock, but still no sign of Erciş. I climb out of the saddle as the lip of the hill comes into sight. And suddenly there it is. And it looks so pretty, with so much light, that unmistakable orange, glowing against the night, so that Erciş becomes at once the most magnificent metropolis I've ever seen. Under the mountain like that, and with just two main streets way below it, but with light so bright, so magnetic, it may as well be Los Angeles. Hollywood Boulevard is right there and all aglow. Only I'm not home yet. In those glowing shadows, dogs pace under the large billboard on a metal column that announces the first consumer offers of the coming city. Tails up, a whole pack, barking and running for the road. They are only a few metres from me, no distance at all to cover to get close, there'll be no escape. There they are, atop the mound of earth that lines the road. I've a split second to size it up, but no, no need. This is a good pack, just marking territory, like a troop of failed actors who hang out above the bright lights of Erciş and share stories of how they nearly made it that time. They assemble on the ridge and bark at me, a howling guard of honour.

Street lights begin. Signs of life. The magic of electricity, of light in the dark. A man rides an old town bicycle the opposite way down the road, is maybe taken aback at the inexplicable enthusiasm of my smile and wave for our transport solidarity, which to him is obviously just the easiest way to get about, and to me the least easy but best way to cross a country. I pull in at a petrol station for only the thrill of its floodlit forecourt and people milling about. I pull on an extra jacket and walk to one side, beside a large puddle of water, to see that a trailer has been dropped off. It is loaded high with a root vegetable I've seen all day: delivered to factories, piled at roadsides, accidentally spilled from a trailer and crushed to pulp on a hard shoulder. I'm curious, and after the dogs and the dark, conversation feels almost as pleasant as street lighting.

"Brother," I ask a man milling about, "what vegetable is that?"

He doesn't hear, replies something about the petrol station.

"No. The vegetable there. What vegetable?"

"Ah! Pancar!" Beets.

"Pancar everywhere," I say, delighted to talk. "For sugar?"

"Evet, for sugar!"

He smiles wide and warm at this strange encounter and this man so curious for sugar beet. I smile back, delighted to talk and be back in the norms of society rather than on the edges of the animal kingdom.

"We have the same in England," I say, "beets for sugar."

"Really?"

"Evet." And I nod happily with a thought of Norfolk before changing the conversation, looking for some human empathy, some understanding of what I've just been through. I exhale deeply and point over my shoulder.

"Lots of dogs." I point back to the mountains. "Out there."

"Evet! Lots of dogs!" And he laughs when I explain how they love the red light. He asks where I'm staying, I say a hotel rather than a tent tonight.

"That way?" I ask, pointing.

"Evet, evet. That way. You're close!"

Erciş to Doğubeyazıt – 29 November

The road winds into higher hills. Sacks of coal begin to appear at the ends of driveways, delivered by the state for the coming winter. The sacks are plain white with a red crescent and the instruction that the coal is not for resale. Poplar and birch grow near houses, offering the home some mixture of firewood and protection from the elements. A group of young men sit on rocks in a small clearing filled with sheep, a couple of kangal at their feet. Repeatedly they gesture to me to come sit with them, they look like they have a fire and probably a kettle going too. Although it is only noon, it already feels somehow as if dusk is nearing, and the small difference between noon and its half past is the same as that between five and darkness. I can't afford that half-hour and so just wave back, at which they gesticulate with more enthusiasm, as if I haven't understood, and then I am gone.

Finally, by mid-afternoon, the road opens onto a flat plain. A shepherd with his flock, high plateau, mountains so near at hand their peaks seem barely higher than we are. I watch him watching the sheep and the mountains, hands resting on the staff he holds in front of him and – passé as it may be – I am struck by the nobility of this ancient way of life. The decision not to leave your village, to shepherd sheep, raise them and earn a modest living. To ask no more. I don't advocate it, could never do it myself, but just as I find it hard to imagine contentment, so I find this hard not to admire.

Into Çaldıran I arrive, down the main street. As always I am sweating from the climbing, and as soon as I stop I am frozen. Wet layers stick so horribly to me. I get off the bike and dive straight into the first lokanta. The place is bustling, well-staffed and well-stocked. Skewers of minced lamb are stacked in front of the hearth, where the chef wafts a paddle over embers and a young boy watches and learns. To one side are pots and oven trays: roasted vegetables, köfte, chicken thighs. All I want is rice and beans in tomato sauce. I want the instant feeling of home that comes from plain rice with a little salt, and the rich warmth of beans. Then I remember soup, and order that too, before taking a seat at a low wooden table. Lentil soup arrives soon after me, in a shallow metal bowl. I squeeze a lemon into it, scatter the red of chilli flakes. It is too hot but does not quite scald, so I drink it down. I do not want the soup to cool in the open air, I want the soup to cool in me: want every bit of its warmth inside me. I feel it moving down my throat, slightly too hot, as if melting over ice, and in that respect wonderful.

The food arrives and from the opposite table a man begins to talk to me. He asks what I'm doing, here in Çaldıran. Not an unreasonable question. He is a social worker, speaks some English, and we switch between languages for a while as I talk about my trip. He excuses himself from the friend he has sat with, asks if he can join me. Be my guest. I apologise also to his friend, now alone. The social worker slides down onto the divan opposite. He is quite tall, with some beard and a large and very sensible coat of the sort that someone ought to own if they work in Çaldıran. He has a soft but serious expression, tells me that people cannot easily access state services here. He is from Van, but up in the villages he translates Kurdish languages to Turkish, so that people can access services, especially health services. "I think life is probably difficult here," I say, in what may be the understatement of the journey. He tells me that people are very poor here. There is violence. Problems with it. I grimace. "In the home?" He nods. And many disabled children. Why? Often people marry within the same families. Cousins. We need education about this, and to support the disabled children.

Inside me is a grim smile at how quickly reality responds to my romanticism of village life, if not wholly negating the romance also.

The man has a calm sense of purpose: it is difficult work but it will be done, and he will do what he can. He asks if I am Muslim, is pleasantly surprised when I describe myself as borderline. We talk a little more, he tells me that I should be careful on the coming pass. Many animals. Really? Yes. Bears. Wolves, many wolves. Be careful with the wolves. I wonder if there is ever a point at which the advice to be careful with wolves is preferable to simply not knowing there are wolves. The wolves are near the road? Yes, when it is cloudy it is very dangerous. I lean to one side, look over his shoulder and out at the cloudy street. I smile to myself. His friend at the next table shuffles in his seat, and finally my guest excuses himself and must leave. A short while later I make to do the same, find that he – a humble social worker in Van province – has paid my bill. I leave for the staff most of the sum owed, hoping that the small but constant outward ripples of thought for others are enough to build a nation.

Back on the road I climb towards the higher mountains, the pass with the wolves and the bears. Iran is over my shoulder, nestled behind the mountains under snow. On the grassy plateau a herd of cows grazes. The concrete shell of a house, abandoned or unbuilt, it is hard to tell. A pool of water reflects the white sky and so looks like ice. The beginning of the mist. A rusty old water tank is leaning broken and punctured to one side; in yellow paint are daubed on it the words "sıcak su". Hot water. A lie. Up above the hills, I know a wall now stands, cutting us off from our Iranian neighbours, built to stop the train of Afghan refugees that made their way in ever greater numbers towards Türkiye.

For the hundredth time in this journey I consider refugees and what happened. Türkiye welcomes millions of Syrians, just as it supported their revolution, out of a belief in Arab democracy, and because of the association between Muslim and Ottoman kin. It mostly welcomed Afghans too, albeit with more difficulty, before finally building this wall. It saw the humanity of those across a frontier that for most Westerners was insurmountable. And so Türkiye let them in, believing that the country, poor as much of it is, had enough to share and enough in common that the welcome was a formality, while the suffering that would pile up beyond a closed border was an impossibility.

As I ride, in a cold that feels prophetic, I fear for the future. I fear that at the end of these years, with so many millions of refugees, Turks and non-Turks struggling inside Türkiye, the country will not be able to repeat the welcome if the US embarks on a new destruction. Already, in my own lifetime, I have watched Syrians beg on Istiklal with their passport out in front of them: such was its value as a display of their need and Turkish understanding of it. And now, down by the Karaköy dock, you can see their children take black bags of – albeit clean – food, and tear them open and sit on the street making as if to eat from bins, hoping that this will move passers-by to give. I have deep faith in the humanity of Türkiye, but I fear the world and see the danger of complacency. I fear Turks will come to think of themselves before the humanity of the refugee, and allow monstrosities to be committed, or learn to look away as monstrosities are committed, which is – in truth – all that is needed for monstrosities to be committed. Maybe this is the point at which Türkiye, finally, will have become a European country.

In my coat of cold sweat I ride into the sky. Food is digesting. My body is slow. Ahead I see a ring of mountains. A high ring of mountains, set dark. Often with such a sight you see the way down. Somewhere you can see a low point in the ridge and can assume that the road will veer towards it and, even if there is some work to get there, from that point gravity will take over and do its work. There is no low point. The only way out is over the top. My mood falls. In front of me lie hours of elevation, snow and suspected wolves, then a descent of huge proportions that will have to be done in the dark. At the roadside are two young men with their sheep, they see me and wave, hands high. Something in it is bright and cheerful and so very welcome, and I wave back. The kangal at their feet sees their raised arm, and my raised arm, and is up, after me like a shot.

"Dur! Dur!" they shout out after the dog. Stop! Stop! I shout too, not that it will make any difference. As the dog makes a dash for my legs I whimper that we were just waving, we were just waving. I accelerate as best I can. The dog is barking mad, teeth flashing right beside me. We look into one another's eyes and I see that its collar is flashing too. The blades of the wolf collar are back, and I am struck by the realisation that this collar, though the dog itself is the size of a lion, is for its own protection.

A village stands up ahead. Nothing much, but I make a decision. I'm not doing this again, not tonight. Not in the dark with an unknown number of hours riding ahead. Doğubeyazıt is forty kilometres, perhaps I can do it. Of course I can do it, the point is I don't want to. I never love myself so much as in those moments when I decide to avoid needless discomfort or forgo a meaningless target. My truest acts of self-love.

At the roadside two men get out from a minibus that looks like a dolmuş. Could it be a late afternoon service to Doğubeyazıt? Nope. No such thing in Soğuksu, a village whose name translates, believably, as Cold Water. One man takes more interest in me than the other. He is holding a thin staff, has a friendly smile and a gleam in his eye. He cuts to the chase. Give me money and we'll take you. At least that's sorted. The option exists. I ask how much, they ask how much. I have no idea, say a hundred. They say four hundred. It seems high. We leave it there. They go through a gate and stand in the garden of a house. I watch the road. I weigh up the situation. I offer three hundred. They talk Kurdish to one another, stand firm. I return to the road. I go back to agree to four hundred. The quieter of the two men, scruffy hair and small eyes, denim jacket, the one who will drive, suddenly says five hundred. I say no and walk back to the road. The man with the gleam in his eye hits his friend with the back of his hand, as if to say he shouldn't be unreasonable. The man calls me over. Four fifty. We do four fifty. He slides open the door. I climb in. The driver with the scruffy hair waits until the bags are in. Five hundred. No! I'll unload it all, will sleep in Soğuksu. His friend hits him again, speaks in Kurdish, sounds like he's telling him not to be an ass. He turns back to me.

"Four fifty is fine."

His friend wants to see the colour of my money, wants it handed over now, when we haven't budged an inch and are still in Soğuksu and his pricing seems so fluid. No way! You take me to Doğubeyazıt. It's OK, says my man with his smile and friendly eyes. "Biz polisiz!" We're police! You can trust us. I laugh, both at the idea of trusting the police and also, since he carries a shepherd's staff, at his claim to be a police officer. I call him a joker and he contradicts me, gets out his wallet and shows me his official identity. Not exactly police, but security, and I have a feeling that I've just met the köy korucuları, the village guards: Kurdish villagers who, content to be in the Turkish state, worked with it to keep order and to counteract the militant presence in the villages of the south-east. The guards have not always behaved well, and have been targeted and killed in the hundreds and thousands by militants.

"You're with the state?"

"Evet!"

We drive back the way I've come, wind off the highway and make our way down a bumpy village track – I'm unsure why. Our negotiator steps out, goes into a house, comes back holding an empty gas canister he loads into the back. It turns out they make the Soğuksu–Doğubeyazıt journey no more than fortnightly; the cost of the petrol and the mountain ascent are both high. I pay for this journey, and from it will be extracted every bit of use. The family propane canisters will be refilled on me.

My man with the smile climbs back up front with the two of us, and I ask about his role as korucu.

"So," I say, "everything is peaceful here now?"

From his coat pocket he pulls out a shining handgun, slides in a new clip of ammo, slaps it locked with the base of his palm, then pulls back the barrel so it is loaded. He leans forward in his seat, shepherd's staff between his legs, slides the weapon down the back of his jeans.

"Evet!" He smiles warmly. "Now there is peace."

As we drive, we talk about the different Turkish words for rifles, handguns, Kalashnikovs. Why do they need the gun? "PKK". I thought they were all in Syria and Iraq now? He points to the hills. "PKK." I suppose that just as a cyclist is an easy target for a wolf or dog, so too is an unmarked van known to be driven by köy korucuları an easy target for a militant. Anything in these mountains is an easy target. Perhaps small arms will be around here for a little while yet; remote mountains are hard places to build consent: the tension between humans and nature, between borders, between countries under sanctions and those not, all create frictions, opportunities, and so, in turn, potential conflicts.

In a field I see a kangal sit up and look at us as if he sees me but is disappointed by my decision to take the lift, is puzzled where my bicycle is, was ready for the chase. Watching the road from the front seat, everything slides by slowly, that regular transition that happens when moving from the bicycle to the frame of the windshield. The immediacy of the world dulls, a road slips by as images in a reel of film. The setting is cinematic. We climb into white snow on a black mountain, snow against stone, flakes falling on rolling hilltops and ridges topped with concrete watchtowers. My friend points to lights on a ridge to our right: Iran. He points to an unmarked mountaintop: PKK. Smugglers. They point to lights on a ridge to the left: Turkish army.

"Difficult life," I say.

"Evet."

"PKK too. Must be cold up there. Poor guys."

He laughs. Evet.

"Türkiye and Iran, we're friends?" I ask.

"Evet," they both say, then the driver adds, "Akraba. Aile." Family.

"And Türkiye and PKK? Inside Türkiye, Türkiye and Kurds . . . everything is better now? Better than twenty years ago?"

"Yes, yes. Much. Everything is good now. Much better."

The engine heaves over the pass, the road snakes down. Snow falls. A few faster cars overtake us and the road looks ready to fall off the mountainside. The negotiator points to a crumbling track of asphalt collapsing into the mountain.

"That's the old road. Before it was hours to Doğubeyazıt."

"The AKP built a lot of roads," I say.

"Evet. A lot of roads. But the new road is dangerous, people died this year after it opened. It's more dangerous because they can drive faster."

The road heads down, the furthest buildings of a town begin to appear. Having agreed the price, the driver starts haggling for his costs instead, bargaining for where he'll drop me. We agree the edge of Doğubeyazıt is fine, the petrol station where they'll refill the propane. He needn't drive the last ten kilometres to the centre. The negotiator and I have struck a kind of rapport; he has more energy for life, is curious, jokes a lot, while the driver grumbles more and finds endless causes for complaint. Absent-mindedly the negotiator, handgun now tucked away, picks at a logo peeling back from the lycra of my knee warmers, and I laugh at this presumptuous intimacy, slap his thigh. We talk families; the driver has six kids, the negotiator five. Kurdish families are like this. We talk life in Türkiye, life in Britain, I tell them Turkish people are warmer, the food is better, and yes, the pound sterling is a stronger currency but everything is more expensive in the UK. I return to politics.

"So you're zabıta?" I say, provocatively, but with plausible deni-ability, because there's no reason I'd know this was a lower and ridiculed police rank.

"Evet," says the negotiator, comfortable in his own skin.

"Jandarma," grumbles the driver, promoting himself.

"And you are Kurdish, so HDP?" I ask, presuming not, but it seems a good starting point. My friend leans in, like there's something I need to understand.

"Biz polisiz," he says, smiling like it's obvious. "Biz AKP."

I make a wide-eyed expression, genuinely concerned at his ease. I place my two fingers next to one another to illustrate this troubling closeness of the executive branch and police of the country.

"AKP and police together!" I say. "Brother, but this isn't good!"

He nods, raises a hand as if he can see how that could be a problem, begins to retrace.

"We're police. We just want peace."

The driver interjects. "We don't have a side."

And I savour for a moment that, even if this quixotic ride of mine achieves nothing more, here for this instant in Van province I have quickly brought about the total depoliticisation of the Turkish police.

"Evet," says my friend. "Not AKP, not CHP, not HDP. No politics. No side."

And then they turn the spotlight on me. Both look at me.

"Which party do you like?" asks my friend. "You like Erdoğan?"

I pause, picking my words, go for safe ground. "I think the AKP did a lot of things. They built a lot of roads."

Broad nodding in the cab. They did build a lot of roads.

"But I think democracy is important. I think HDP is important. I think Demirtaş is a good man. He needs to be released."

They chuckle. "PKK."

"He isn't PKK," I protest. "Demirtaş wants democracy. PKK want to fight. PKK don't like Demirtaş. He is a good man. HDP and AKP working together would be better."

Surprisingly fast, they accept my logic.

"A good man, but he is a poor man. No money."

"Evet." I smile sadly. "Often the good man has no money."

They nod. Turks always so naturally receptive to socialist thinking.

"And the bad man has money," my friend finishes the equation.

"What do you think about CHP?" I ask.

The driver gives a scowl formed by the twentieth century and what the CHP did, fully aware of who was originally responsible for the Turkish treatment of Kurds; that disdainful and bigoted divide based on a sense of cultural superiority and an urbanite's indifference to the village. He mutters something inaudible. My friend translates, laughs as he leans in, puts it real simple.

"We don't like CHP."

"But they changed, didn't they?"

In a soft grumble from the driver comes perhaps the most revealing of all the words I hear in these weeks of travel and discussion.

"Değişemez."

They can't change.

"But with Kılıçdaroğlu? He's different. He's . . ." I search for a word, go for "hafif." Something like gentle or soft.

My friend laughs, turns to the driver. "You hear? He said Kılıçdaroğlu is hafif."

The driver nods, laughing too. "Evet. He is hafif."

Something tells me that hafif is not what these guys, with wolves in the mountains and a handgun down their jeans, are looking for in a leader. The mountain is easing. Lights are coming through the mist. Doğubeyazıt just about appearing in the belly of the hills. I track back a bit, address my friend with some finality.

"So you are Kurds, and Turks? Both?"

With certainty he says, "Both."

Not for the first time I consider how it is that self-identifying liberal Westerners, believing in plural identities, would demand these guys be one or other ethnic group, while a generally right-wing proto cop like this is more than capable of handling what is, in truth, a remarkably simple duality. The driver pulls from the road and into the forecourt of a petrol station, where all the propane canisters of Soğuksu will be refilled.

"And things are better than before? It's not like war now?"

"Evet," he says.

The driver turns the key and cuts the engine. My friend opens the door and shuffles out. As he steps down, his shepherd's staff falls out with him, clattering on the tarmac. I smile at this hybrid man of sheep and handgun.

"And you are shepherd and policeman?" I ask. "Both?"

"Both," he says, as certain in this as in the dual identity of his citizenship. He smiles, we shake hands and say our goodbyes. A second later, the obvious and most important question occurs to me.

"Which job do you like more?" I ask as I pull down my bicycle and reattach the panniers. "Police or shepherd?"

He smiles, warm as ever. "Shepherd."

Ishak Paşa Sarayı – 30 November

Atop the wall of the mountain, the palace has been hewn from a rich red rock, the domes and balustrade a warm orange against dark cloud and cliff. A higher dramatic crag of mountains sits above. These are young mountains, jagged, unsmoothed by age and weather. Under them is a small mosque, its minaret barely visible through the mist. The setting is as perfect as the architecture: man-made places built serenely into what was there.

I walk through the palace, down through basement grain bins and enormous storerooms that once held the food that kept guests fed through winters as hard as this one just beginning. The stone on one wall of the kitchen is stained black, from its time as an Ottoman barracks where function for a time clearly took precedence over sublime form. Above a small fountain a quotation is written in Ottoman script. Its translation reads: *As long as both sun and moon shine in the sky, may Allah make this state and stove eternal.*

The centrality of food to state was a spirit that the Ottomans extended without regard to borders. When the British began starving the Irish in the 1840s, appropriating their potato crop as a means to suppress the population, Sultan Abdulmecid sent three ships of grain from Istanbul, skirting the blockade of Dublin ports, and sailing inland on the River Boyne. I walk through to a court-room, but the words stay with me. In another chamber in the palace, the walls have Western-style rococo frescoes. There are Byzantine columns, a Selçuk dome over the mosques – and I consider how perfection of aesthetic and faith seems to exist best of all in hybrids.

A central court has walls of alternating black and white stone, and I imagine dancing and banqueting here. I sit alone a while in the palace mosque. The red carpet is plush, the softest thing I've touched for a long time. To sit even a moment on it eases the miles in my legs. From a narrow window, I look through the thick wall and see the edge of the mountain below. It is so quiet I could almost pray. No, it is so *silent* I could almost pray. One of those moments where Allah is everything, where Allah is the name for the mist and the mountain and the settling silence. The silence inhabits, as if I and everything else here are now deep inside the mountain. I imagine the centuries of travellers who saw this place as they came out of the mountains and instantly took comfort. I imagine the centuries of travellers who on leaving this place and moving into the mountains quickly felt a longing for its walls and hearth. I once cycled through Urumchi, Kyzylorda, Shymkent, Almaty – the Uyghur and Kazakh cities of the Silk Road. I remember that road, and imagine it in the days when the commercial and political centre of the world was to be found in Eurasia. In Doğubeyazıt and Ishak Paşa Sarayı, I realise, are that same road's western reaches.

On a forecourt in front of the palace, two men pace about in large coats, cold hands stuffed into pockets. They watch over empty café tables and an unvisited stall that sells fridge magnets, key rings, small pieces of rock from the vast sides of Ağrı. A barrel holds a small fire, and the younger of the men takes a hatchet to a large stump of yellowing wood. He manages to hew some sizeable chunks and throw them into the fire. The older man comes over, takes matters into his own hands, and drops the entire stump into the barrel. I laugh, he says it is kavak, poplar, and it will burn just fine. When I order a çay, the youth brings it over and together we warm by the fire. He gestures to the older man, stout with a long coat and neat moustache, a fetching red neck scarf. Dashing. The boy, laughing, tells me Mehmet here has three wives. Fifteen children. Five with each. Mehmet looks at me nonchalant, neither confirming nor denying, but surely proud of the figures given. There is a certain happy arrogance to him, clearly content with his appearance. His bearing asks: a face like this, what did you expect? I ask if that's even legal and Mehmet clarifies that they are not exactly his wives, rolling his eyes as if I'm an idiot for even asking. I say instead that fifteen children sounds expensive. Mehmet rolls his eyes again; I'm definitely an idiot.

"They all work," he tells me

"Ah, so like a pension then? Insurance?"

He makes a sound of affirmation, as if now I'm getting it. He asks after life in England. He says Doğubeyazıt is hard. East is hard. It is hard because of terrorism. We had Daesh, PKK. A rarity that they are named together, ideologically different as they are. Into his mouth there rises a disdain for both. Once the contempt is formed, he spits it into the barrel of the fire with its smouldering poplar.

"Eşit," he says firmly. The same.

Doğubeyazıt to Iğdır

The black mountains of the old volcano merge with the black sky. The drizzle fuses the two into one dark layer. Everything is darkness, as if the mountain were a wolf, as if the mountain itself might bite. Ağrı, Mount Ararat, has disappeared into cloud. The ground is littered with large black rocks: the basalt and ash from millennia as an active volcano. Now and then golden scrub grows between it, but under this sky that too has turned a monochrome grey. On the edge of a village, I see a dark black rabbit hop around the edge of a dark black stone. I see the results here of millennia of evolution. The lighter rabbit was seen by the wolf, by the dog, but the black rabbit hid against the rock, then bred, and in time all the rabbits turned this same jet black. Three dark black donkeys stand against a dark black wall of stone, their coats slicked wet, seed pods stuck to their sides and long faces. When dogs and cats have proven to be no use or have left, it is the donkey that is most trusty, or most stubborn.

A half-dozen goats graze near the road. A kid sneezes, its long coat covered in droplets, and then runs to its mother when it sees me so near. At a distance is a small flock. A shepherd holds an umbrella and runs after a goat that has wandered free. Out here it writes itself, all you have to do is watch. A shepherd raises his staff, I raise my hand. These men stand here in the rain with their animals, generation upon generation of hardship in them, and here I am out of choice, dripping wet and frozen through, with one eye on the dusk and the other on the dogs. Three hundred or so more kilometres to go. "Why are we doing this?" asks my body. My brain doesn't have the gall any longer to say it's for the Republic, not in this cold and this wet, immersed in this exercise of apparent futility. Sometimes I allow myself to think that the endeavour is needed to vest the words with sufficient meaning, to gouge it in and impregnate them with purpose. But not right now, not when I am riding, only when I am dry, when I am warm.

All around is hardship, hardship and a sense of loss. Concrete carcasses of failed houses, places where people resolved they could not live after all. Places where the project did not come good. The old stone houses, with gaps between each basalt rock, have been abandoned in preference for concrete, and that grass now grows out of the old roofs is a rare success story. Elsewhere roofs have collapsed, tiles are scattered. A few small mounds of roadkill come into view. A live dog eats from the carcass of a dead dog, the remains hollowed out and a gaping space in its side where it has been emptied of its guts. At the rear, the thin tissue of an asshole has long ago rotted away. Reluctantly I stop to take a piss, having held off a while because each minute of light is precious, and to stop is to feel cold. As I step from the road, my foot dislodges a rock and disturbs an eagle, which takes flight from an old rock wall but with a majesty that seems out of place here. After a time, another village produces a few attempts at roadside cafés. The çay evi, tea house, is always the enterprise of choice, because a samovar and tea leaves and heat – and if people will come then a promise of community – must be the lowest of barriers to business entry. Still, in most cases, the people did not come, and the attempt has failed. The outdoor toilets, they too have failed, their doors fallen off, the "WC" daubed in large letters distorted by holes in the brickwork and failing plaster. A motorbike is parked outside, like a getaway vehicle leaning on its prop stand.

As I pass through, I think of Ceren, from the Maths Village in Şirince, who was originally from this place. She gave the Kurdish name for Ağrı, but when I asked what made her feel insecure in Türkiye today, it was being a woman and not being Muslim. Although she spoke right away of Kurdish language, it was not from a need to be recognised as a Kurd. I look at the hard lands here and think of Şirince in autumn. I wonder what we might do so that one need not leave here to build a life, and how we might bring the energy of the Maths Village here.

I consider, too, those who have explained this country to me – Ceren and Ayşe and Berika and more besides – and how, as I have moved east, women have become less a part of my roadside, and less a part of my information gathering, even though Western media laud these places as the stronghold of Turkish feminism. This is not to say that many millions of empowered Turkish women do not exist inside their homes while their men work upon the roads, but it is a cautionary tale against Western propaganda and the use it makes of women.

Over the skirts of the mountains I go, orbiting Ağrı. I ride through a small depression, like a mountain gutter, where the mountains took all the earth when the plates pushed together and then rose up and up and up. It is one of those days when the sight of an ascent brings relief, because pedalling uphill is sure to warm you. The scale here is enormous. I feel that if the mountains were accidentally to crush me, nobody would ever know. That you could be lost or die out here a thousand times and still never be found. Through the cloud and the rain I ride, head down, with no thought of the future, for I cannot imagine anything beyond the cold and wet of the present. I crest a ridge the rain has hidden from me, after which an ease comes to my wheels and I am suddenly in the flood of descent. And I fly from here.

Iğdır to Kars – 1 December

Iğdır is not at first a compelling sight. There is rubbish on the edge of town. Coal smoke blankets the city, the smog is the price of warmth. It has rained, and there is a grey film to the slicked streets, as if construction dust has mixed with coal dust has mixed with the black basalt rock of Ağrı that darkens the earth. I find a hotel. That the water in its pipes be hot has long ago become my only criterion for staying in a place. In the lift, the boy who carries my bags checks his reflection constantly as the lift takes us up through the floors. He brushes his fringe to stand upwards, but it won't. He says disdainfully there is not much in Iğdır, and I ask if this is his home town.

"Noo!" he protests, offended. "I'm from Doğubeyazıt."

I laugh, can't help myself. "Isn't Doğubeyazıt only fifty kilometres away?"

"Evet. But it's different."

I say that Doğubeyazıt has more life in it, which is what he wants to hear. Inwardly I think that it is raining in Iğdır and wasn't in Doğubeyazıt, but he doesn't need to know this part of my thought process. He tells me that ten years ago everything was good here, Iğdır was a boomtown, but the AKP spent all the money. I am not sure that the information stacks up, but for him it is a truth, and that's all that matters. Sometimes perception is all you're up against.

Wearing dry clothes, my wet garments draped across a radiator and pipes, I head out to find food. A water processing facility is being built with Turkish and EU funds. A mosque and pedestrian square

are under construction. I look around and see a poster watching me from above the main square. Erdoğan is shaking hands with the local mayor. The AKP have built a number of schools here. Half the schools have solar energy facilities on them. They have built the new sports club I cycled past on the way into the city. To be honest, the buildings aside, merely setting foot here counts for something. You cannot fault Erdoğan for the amount of shoe rubber he has put down on the streets of Türkiye. There is not a sports club he wouldn't visit, not a mayor's hand he wouldn't want to shake. In its way, this is its own kind of nation-building, a sign stronger than ever before that the Turkish state covers all corners of the country.

Near the new development by the mosque is a bright restaurant, warmly lit. I go in, decide to order a pizza. I sit and write, but impatience gnaws at me. I want to be where I will be at this time tomorrow, and tomorrow and tomorrow. My thoughts can't stop flitting back to the map and seeing where I am on it, the mountain passes to come, as if by looking hard enough at them I will complete the gradient. I want daylight and morning to come, so that I can start riding again, even if I have little enthusiasm right now for the riding itself. To ride is both the last and only thing I want to do.

Walking back to the hotel I pass a künefe salon. *Gaziantep* is stamped above the establishment, and the name of Gaziantep is to künefe what hallmarks are to silver. In I go and see a man place five white discs of thinly rolled pastry on a wooden surface as he makes katmer, a twin of künefe. I watch as the white discs turn a speckled green from the crushed pistachio sprinkled over them. I order my künefe and take a seat in a booth by a window, but I look back through this empty restaurant and watch the chef making katmer, throwing down the pistachios with an unmistakable purpose and pride. The words from Ishak Paşa Sarayı come back to me: *As long as both sun and moon shine in the sky, may Allah make this state and stove eternal.*

That relationship between a kitchen and a state is another of the many invisibilities of a household that quietly sustain a country. The kitchen is seldom found in either speeches or statistics, but *You are what you eat* describes a body politic every bit as much as it does a body. That first surface on which food is prepared, and then the second at which it is eaten, make up the bedrock of a country, and in Türkiye it is a strong one. Some of the most celebrated of cuisine is in Türkiye what is known simply as *a meal*, and if the Turkish can at times accept too much in politics, then the table maybe has some guilt in their placation. The food of both the wealthy and the working class is the smell of mackerel grilling for the sandwich. It is rice and chickpeas, haricots in tomato sauce, lentil soup. It is every meal that begins in its cooking with the smell of onions sautéing. It is vine leaves soaked before they wrap the rice and turn it into dolma. It is the cabbage leaves that do likewise and are less famed but – though I would hate ever to have to choose – perhaps more delicious. Beside all of that, most reliably of all, yoghurt, always yoghurt, the word itself originating in the Turkish "yoğunlaşmak", meaning "to thicken". Credit to the Greeks: they beat us on the marketing of that one. It is watching these things done when we are children, and then realising as adults that we know how to do it, so in turn can provide for ourselves, nourish others.

After five minutes my künefe arrives beside a small plate of fruit. Sliced apple, segments of orange, a stalk of grapes on the last of their vine, and then, of course, most blessed of all, ruby red, the pomegranate seeds. In the small city of Iğdır, where life is no doubt not easy, still this plate stands triumphant. What is wealth without künefe? What are riches if nobody ever places a small pile of pomegranate seeds beside your künefe?

A final sleep comes and goes. An early start in blue light. The river valley runs north, easing me into the gorge beside me, its walls vast and deep and spectacular. Unfortunately, I must climb out of it. I look across at the Armenian watchtowers on the far ridge of this border so misunderstood. History here is as dense as the rock. As we move from Greece through Türkiye, and alongside Syria, Iraq,

Iran and Armenia, every mile is loaded. Please give me some easy miles; in this, the last tenth of the journey, must I really tell you of our story with Armenia?

I am weary, but it is important. High above my roadside is a Turkish watchtower: a sentry has his binoculars trained on me. I raise a tired arm in salutation, he raises one back. And I continue on my way. I look up at the hard black stone above. There is so much climbing to be done that perhaps I shall take leave of the exhausted cyclist awhile, leave him pedalling these switchbacks as I take up the story of Türkiye and Armenia.

A first thing to know is that this border has been open in recent history. When Armenia became independent during the dissolution of the Soviet Union in 1991, Türkiye was among the first countries to recognise it. Open borders, full relations. With all my strength, I want this border open and Armenia integrated with its neighbours, with the long-lost family in Anatolia and Türkiye to which it was once integral. This border, for now, is closed because of a dispute between Armenia and Azerbaijan, after Armenia invaded Azerbaijani territory in 1992 and seized the enclave of Nagorno-Karabakh following the demise of the Soviet Union. Armenian forces massacred Azeris when the Armenian army invaded, but both countries committed atrocities, no doubt. In solidarity with Azeri Turks, hundreds of thousands of them displaced by the Armenian invasion, Ankara broke off relations with Yerevan and closed the border. With Azerbaijan having retaken Nagorno-Karabakh in its 2020 war with Armenia, and peace talks beginning, Türkiye and Armenia are seeking to restore relations and this border will soon open, in the first instance, to nationals of third countries. The notion of a Turkish–Armenian border open to everyone except Turks and Armenians, I take as an absurd but positive first step.

That poor relations between Türkiye and Armenia are a result of a conflict between Azerbaijan and Armenia is, perhaps, not what you expected, but the history of Türkiye and Armenia has been set inside a frame as deep and rigid as the gorge from which I ascend. The future here is held hostage by a perspective of the past, and the maps of history can be gerrymandered every bit as easily as an electoral boundary.

The Armenian diaspora has worked with some success to attach one word to a culture, people and country from which they are by now quite remote. That word has nothing to do with the reason for this closed border, and that single word is *genocide*. It does not help matters that much of this diaspora is concentrated inside France with its ready prejudice against Turks, nor that the diaspora's single largest community is in Los Angeles, where the sprawl of consumerism, concrete and highways leaves an absence of meaning in the present that leads many a diaspora there to take with greater fervour to its past. This fixation on genocide works well for those who hold vilifying Türkiye as a foreign policy or pastime all of its own. Just as Nietzsche wrote that had God not created humans then humans would need to create god, likewise if a demon were not incarnate in the Turkish Republic pulled from the Ottoman Empire in 1923, then it would be a Western imperative to create one.

In a union of these goals – the diaspora seeking memory and the lobbyist seeking villainy – the word *genocide* has been laid down by those outside of it almost as if the one defining feature of Armenia. That Yerevan and Ankara seek determinedly to reopen their border, that Azerbaijan is the remaining obstacle to that, that an entire Armenian rescue team picked through the Adıyaman rubble of the 2023 earthquake to find survivors and show the neighbourliness that waits: none of this is of interest to the lobbyist and the fanatic. They see only genocide. I refuse the association, not to deny atrocities, but because with Armenia I would sooner think of the magnificent old ruins of this border, the deliciousness of Armenian cognac, the verdant hills of Dilijan, the smiles of my friends and the shared future we will build. As with so much along the road I have ridden, there is an obsession, almost tantamount to bigotry, that demands these lands be lived in terms of their history rather than their present and future. This fetish becomes in its own way a death sentence levelled against that future.

Lobbyists have rigged the terms of this debate so that they and I know exactly what I am to be called for taking this approach. Even though I deny nothing and defend nothing, to them I must be a *denialist*. I am an *apologist*. It makes no difference that I would refute any denial of Ottoman state crimes every bit as forcefully; I am to be a denialist simply because I insist that the word "genocide" is political. The word is not neutral space, it is deliberately unsuited to building peace because those who fixate on it do not care for peace.

There is an Armenian phrase that sets a path. Meds Yeghern. Great Catastrophe. Just as Shoah for Jews translates as Catastrophe and Nakba for Palestinians translates as Catastrophe, human cultural-linguistics settle again for Armenians on that same word: Catastrophe. Meds Yeghern I will use, for unlike the plasticity of "genocide", which hypocrites deploy or withhold at will, Meds Yeghern means something, it has depth, it belongs to Armenians, and even the Turkish state is able to use it because it is a word spoken to and with our Armenian brothers and sisters, and not at the behest of Western double standards.

If we must rake through history, then know that the brutalities which caused so much Armenian suffering and death began not in eastern Anatolia but in the Balkans where we began our journey. There, at the onset of World War I, the Ottoman state has, within living memory and on roads you and I have now travelled, seen half of its territory and almost all of its European territory wiped out. This is in addition to the banishment or destruction of the Turkish population. It is done with the moral and military cover of the colonial powers, principally Britain and Russia.

Enver Paşa, a hero still to many of the most dislikeable Turkish nationalists, and the architect of much of the tragic removal of Ottoman Armenians, grows up in the Balkans in the years after those horrors of the 1870s, which do not feature in Western or

European histories, so these people may as well not have existed. Turkic villages are emptied of their civilians, death-marched towards Istanbul if they are not killed in their homes or en route. And after that, the Balkans are gone. The memories of the losses are etched into the state and the population.

A few decades later, when Armenian nationalists, again supported by Britain and Russia, begin similar massacres in eastern Anatolia, preparing to claim their own state from a collapsing Ottoman one, the Ottomans have no appetite for a repeat of the Balkans. Nor is this just some strange bloodlust with which the Turks just woke up one morning: it is World War I, death and killing is abroad all across Europe and Anatolia and the world. An Armenian population in a village, majority or otherwise, proclaim Armenian territory and, with foreign support, massacres begin. In response, merciless, the Ottomans set about rounding up Armenians – who have lived for centuries with everyone throughout the Empire – and they are driven from the country.

Finally the Armenians of Ottoman lands are marched towards the deserts of Syria, down the Euphrates and in particular to the town of Deir ez-Zor. With the state collapsing and supplies scarce even for those inside it, few if any provisions are made for their survival of the deportation. The procession is attacked on its way. Countless perish or are killed, a number I have no wish to venture because I have no wish to take my place among all those who ghoulishly try to overstate or understate it. That Turks too were massacred in the violence leading up to it, that Kurds also carried out much of the killing, that some localities and sections of the Armenian route towards Syria witnessed more death or survival than others – this is erased from the record. That Ottoman troops are few in number and cannot or do not wish to guard the departing Armenians against a local population that has also suffered greatly, often at Russian and Armenian hands, is deemed uninteresting. Atatürk put it succinctly: "When a Turk was killed, nobody raised an eyebrow, but when a Turk killed someone, they raised a ruckus."

351

Much suggests chaos and breathtaking brutality during a world war and collapsing state. Far less substantiates the accusation of planned extermination. But it does not matter, all that matters a century and more later is that countless died and all who are human should grieve. It was a great catastrophe of humanity. It was Meds Yeghern.

There is no hierarchy of which was worse – Balkans and Turks, or eastern Anatolia and Armenians – and I have no desire to propose one. If Armenians, diaspora or no, cannot forgive what happened to their ancestors – I mourn but understand this human intransigence. If Turks feel aggrieved that their suffering in the ends of the Ottoman Empire is erased from history – I understand this grievance too, but would counsel against being defined by it, or in it foregoing the virtue that is human compassion.

What I would like to know is why a Western perspective blessed with not having had to suffer directly this miserable affair is so determined to dictate its own conclusion by cropping the history of the collapse of an empire during war with one event in the east, while ignoring that done by Europeans in the west. Two events that cannot be separated, and a first that clearly informed the decisions of the second.

These differences will be settled not by abstract arguments but through an open border. Abstract arguments can hit against one another for all eternity, but quickly melt away before the richness of experience. When all is said and done, there is no better way to settle difference and build understanding than to meet people. To talk about history, to discuss shared pain, guilt and loss, and in all this gain that closure needed for the most important thing in all of it: a future together. I want Turkish farmers to sell their harvest at Yerevan wholesalers. I want Yerevanites to come and climb in their long weekends that peak we call Ağrı and they call Masis. I want the tourists to hike through the hills and cloud-laced monasteries between Dilijan and Trabzon and Shusha. I want people to see their similarity, and for that distant Armenian diaspora to realise gently that it does not hold a monopoly on what it means to be Armenian, and a responsibility to use its voice on behalf of today's Armenia.

From the abstract air of history, I see my cycling body labour up the last final lip onto the ledge of the gorge. He comes into view, and I swoop back down and into him. The legs shake with fatigue, though the gradient is not as wearying as to contest history. I climb from the gorge, just as we all must climb out of history and into the future. The wind hits me in the face, and a new horizon presents itself.

There is now only one stop before Kars. In truth I haven't the time but still I must. I turn from my route, towards the ancient ruin of an old city: Ani. The gorge I began to see opening at Çaldıran, and have just pedalled slowly out of, is now vast and cavernous. On one side is a huge Turkish flag. On the other, a huge Armenian one. A little further, Armenian and Russian flags also fly together. The two states share the history of the Soviet period, and the kin of Orthodox Christianity, which has always underpinned a military coordination but one that has frayed since the 2018 revolution in Armenia ushered in democracy. It is Armenia's southern neighbour, Iran, that is now gradually regarded as a more reliable ally in Yerevan. I look at all the flags, pulled on the wind just as history pulls on their countries, giving us new forms and pointing us new directions. In the image I think back to my first border, at Meriç, with the Greek and Turkish banners fluttering across from one another.

Against the flags with their competing claims, I look down on the ridge of ruins and its simple beauty. Some stonework is toppled, some stands proud, some is braced inside wooden scaffolds, stone and wood taking on a new coexistence. Churches and mosques and cathedrals and grand Armenian halls mingle together. A ruined bridge stands far below in the gorge, and I promise that a version of it will be rebuilt. Smoothed cliffs boast houses in the caves, and I promise that one day hot air balloons will fly above all this, just as they do in Cappadocia. The ezan rings out, so clear in the silence, bouncing back from Armenia, vibrating up from the gorge and its blue river, where an eagle swoops, then soars. I look at the beauty of the ruins, the Armenian script on the stonework. All of the buildings are on the Turkish side, but the gorge is so vast and magnificent that – despite so clearly having two of them – it seems to repudiate the idea of sides at all. Again those words, first thought in Thrace: you were ours, we were yours, for here is a sight so perfect it is as if all the world could be held inside its splendour. I consider that if borders had ever been anticipated, then all this would have been built on the Yerevan side of the gorge. But that was a different time, that was a thousand years ago.

Before leaving, I voice another oath, sending it across to Armenia from above the ruins: "These are yours too, and they are magnificent. And we are looking after them for you. Come soon, visit."

For a final time, as I ride away, the words of John Berger hang over everything. "The past grows gradually around one, like a placenta for dying with."

And it is true. But the past, I realise now, is also a placenta for living with.

So much heat and mist escape off me as I breathe that I am one with cloud, we have converged. If, as the man back in Çaldıran said, a wolf will sometimes attack when the cloud is low, then at least now I am safe, for where I end and cloud begins is hard to tell. No wolf would find me. Camouflaged as a tiny cloud, I float slowly up the mountain, able to see barely ten metres in front of me. Frost weighs down the grasses, a dusting of snow blows across road and field.

Darkness is coming. The road climbs up and up. Even where it flattens it still seems to rise. I am desperate for easy kilometres. On the edge of a village children walk home from school. Hoods up, their silhouettes make their way through the mist down the opposite side of the road. I suppose I must look even eerier to them than they do me. On a particularly long, slow stretch, as I feel my shoulders rolling to extract more energy from my body, a driver comes alongside, looks at me, then accelerates before pulling in ahead. As I come alongside him and stop, he looks over his shoulder at the back of his car, without a word, just a small shake of the head at my idiocy. An unmistakable message: *Put it in.* A stray dog walks tentatively over from the edge of the layby beside us, looks up expectantly. We make for an awkward trio as I ask the driver the road ahead. He says it is downhill from here, twenty kilometres. My eyes brighten, I confirm that it's definitely-*definitely* all downhill. Definitely. Then: "No, thank you, but I'm fine." Body is ready to load in the bike. Swings round. You said what?! Brain looks down at body, already half off the bike and set to throw it in.

Sorry, perhaps a coal truck, a tractor and trailer, and we could have considered it, but finishing in – I check the back of the vehicle – a Citroën Berlingo . . . it really doesn't fit the narrative. Body scowls at brain. You fucking prick, a real piece of fucking work, I fucking hate you, you fucking fuck.

The stray stands there beside me and the car. Tail down, but looking up hesitantly, like he'll take the ride if it's going. The driver makes a noise for it to scram, it backs away, returning into the cloud of a short, cursed life.

I pedal on. The road eases, the ascent is gentler, though we are not quite in the pure descent the driver promised. An engine always has the ability to shrink distances, and so I watch my turning legs and try to practise patience. Finally a sign confirms that I have gone over the top of a pass, 2,200 metres altitude. Just a baby out here and yet big enough to keep a French Alp in its back pocket, to find Alpe d'Huez down the side of its sofa, Ventoux just a burp after dinner. This is good news, though, because I know that Kars is at around 1,700 metres, so I'm now 500 in credit, have got 500 to spare, altitude suddenly the most valuable currency in life. The light is almost gone and I need the easy kilometres to start soon.

Quickly I take my gloves from a pocket and pull them onto my hands, I zip everything up to my chin with me shut inside. The road starts to roll down, and then to plummet, and then it winds and plummets at the same time and I see a valley opening with my road and a few headlights on it. And in that cusp of mountains meeting, I see a grid of white lights pierce the dusk. And is this it? I can't believe that this may be the end of the road, and Kars tonight is the City of Light. Tonight it comfortably eclipses Paris in such a title, and is the only place on earth I want to be. My wheels gather more and more speed, and I flatten to the bars so that the chill need not hit my chest, and so that the hole I punch through the air gets smaller and in the fist of my tucked-up body, I travel faster. My wheels accelerate and I bank round high corners of the mountain road. Kilometres fly by from one road sign to the next as the wind blows chill out of the dusk and asks, "Are these easy enough?"

Kars

A Friday night, a line of musicians play in flat caps and black sweaters. A man sings in the middle of the bar. The accordion heaves. Flute and drum keep time with one another and the music seeps out into the street, where I sit, my feet beside the blaze of a well-fed brazier: a metal sphere with cut-outs of bats and leaves and large-antlered stags. The wood pops as embers smoulder into flame around a new log. At my feet sleeps a street dog, its pale white coat warmed by the fire. As it dreams it spasms, paws twitch, and I wonder if it is on its guard, dreaming of a wolf upon a hill, or if it is a happy dream of cyclists to chase. And I look away, because it's over.

All around is Kars, still filling me with the beauty of its first sight. The night is soft, the stars so bright, the promise of every cobbled alley so great. Russian influence was once here, put down alongside Turks and Ukrainians, Tatars and Georgians and Armenians. The cafés are called Pushkin, Dostoevsky. Built in the Russian style, the houses stand short in grey stone, and their stone-walled rooms glow with light, shards of light breaking through the braced gaps in heavy wooden doors. I speak to a graphic designer in a fashionable down jacket as he goes to enter a bar. His English is good, we talk awhile. He is from here, studied in Istanbul, but can now work remotely, so has come back. His town has changed a lot, mostly through tourism and the Doğu Ekspresi. The train I will soon board back west, to Ankara.

Through a window I see a dance break out within. Arms high, hands above heads, legs bending at the knee as feet kick and the men dance like Cossacks. The room claps, shrill whistles fly, the head waiter breaks from behind the bar to dance better than any other, as if this is his moment of pride, of glory, his chance to be a hero for one night every week. His legs kick and move so fast, so perfect. The room delights. After a while he is out of breath, isn't as young as he used to be, but on a Friday night in Kars he will never stop doing this, and, given the delight of the crowd, his manager wouldn't let him even if he so wished.

I go inside to join the warmth, order another glass of wine. A child plays around the table where his mother eats with a friend. He walks over to me, tottering on his feet, and then with a mouth full of bread and crumbs he roars at me like a small, smiling lion.

Inside I eat goose, the restaurant manager stalks the floor, watching over his guests like a general, a general with a sturdy round belly from a lifetime of eating goose. Outside snow is falling, falling softly upon the Bog of Allen and, further eastward, the Valley of Kars. I speak a little with some Istanbulites who are also taking the train. He works in renewable energy, biomass, collects animal dung from farms and turns it into gas. Is disappointed at recent cuts to renewable energy subsidies. She runs social media accounts for companies, because someone's got to. They are new parents, talk about the luxury of a long weekend away. Grandparents stepping in. Back in Istanbul they have a Turkmen nanny; does not speak English but is very warm, a wonderful person. Filipino nannies are also common; their English is often good but they are less warm with the kids. These are the dilemmas of Istanbul parents with the single alpha-child on whom all hopes rest; it is less about money than success. The hours pass, people come and go. I stay and drink. Red wine flows and as the music finishes I move back outside to the fire blazing in its brazier. Nothing will pull me from this. I am overcome by the luxury of not having anywhere to move on to, of being done.

Others gather with drinks around the fire. A Russian boy has driven across the border on another extended road trip away from the draft. We agree that Russia has never kicked its nationalist habit: the country is based on ideas of empire, Christian supremacy and Russian nationalism barely updated since tsarism. The Soviet Union the only significant effort to reform it. Russia lacks any kind of inclusive identity to export or develop internal harmony, it still seems not to have understood anything but hard power, a truth that does not detract from the similar awfulness of the United States. The boy goes on, says that the problem is that there is no Russia: it is an enormous land mass with no cohesion. I check which parts are, in his estimation, Russia: Siberia is Russia, Vladivostok is Russia, Moscow and St Petersburg are of course Russia. Dagestan is not Russia. I remark on the irony of this: that Dagestani men are disproportionately sent to fight for Russia in Ukraine, while men like him, in his own eyes unquestionably Russian, are sitting by a brazier with a glass of wine in Kars, Türkiye. He shrugs.

Standing with us is a middle-aged man with a large nose and a face that listens intently, then bursts into a smile whenever someone says something of significance about the world, as if he is heartened to hear these matters discussed. A tour guide, he smiles most of all at history, and we express our hopes for the reopening of the border with Armenia.

"Armenians already come," he says, "many from Los Angeles, from France. But they only want the Armenian history. They are not interested in the Georgian history, the Turkish, the Russian."

He too shrugs, like it's all money at the end of the day.

"There used to be more international tourists," he laments. "Now mostly Turks. They only want to take photos. They are not here for the history."

He grumbles, as if he's not sure about the coming future. As if there isn't much history in the future. We talk regional integration, he says Turkish companies are building new roads in Georgia, that people are already working together in the Caucasus. Iran is donating the oil for the Georgian asphalt, the bitumen. "They have so much it is easy to give it, to build good relations." The Iranian tankers I have seen passing me on these roads now make more sense, and, as in Istanbul, in Kars you learn about the world in real time. As always in Türkiye, the bar offers the best analysis going.

Celil and I talk after everyone else has left. He points to a street where the Azeri consulate now stands, tells me he grew up on that street. He asks if I've heard of the National Government of the South-West Caucasian Republic, which I have not. It had its short-lived parliament on that hill there in 1918 at the end of World War I, before the British came and established the next year an enlarged Armenia, which was then pushed back over the gorge with the War of Independence.

"Nobody knows about the Caucasian Republic. But when the British came, they killed many of us."

I look at his face: lively, an energy for life, but ageing, so that 1918, on that street there, must be only his father or grandfather's time. In the way he says it, I am reminded of a Palestinian man on a road beyond Ramallah, telling me of the village of his parents, razed by early Zionists. His words are as if I'm just a Westerner, passing through, an outsider in this history who has probably been taught different things. But it was there, it happened, and the loss hurt him too.

For a week I wander around the town, beginning to commit these words to paper, then doing those jobs and menial tasks for which life lived by bicycle leaves little time. After six weeks I finally take a shirt with a frayed elbow to a tailor. The tailor, an old man for whom not much happens, who is rarely in control of anything but his sewing machine, looks at me, keen to assert some control.

"You Afghan?" he asks suspiciously, adding one more nation-ality to Pakistani, Italian, Russian and "white Arab" – the list of ethnicities of which I have been suspected along my way. Maybe it is true. Everyone has their own east. East is a relative concept. The Afghan hopes to drag his way to Anatolia, the Turk from outside Diyarbakır moves to Istanbul, the university graduate from Istanbul goes to Berlin, to New York. In this a wealth and talent moves out of Türkiye and westwards, a flow that must be staunched – staunched by greater opportunities, by environmental protections, by a knowledge economy in its first stage of building. Flaubert said history moves in cycles east to west, west to east. But I don't believe in that. All this happened alongside the rise of Beijing, Shanghai, Seoul, Kuala Lumpur . . . and as Türkiye too grew more influential as a country. Nothing is destiny. We are active in history.

Doğu Ekspresi – 8 December

The engine pulls the carriages from the station, the train hits rewind for me. I feel emotional: like it's all being undone, like what was the purpose of any of it, if it comes to an end so easily? If I don't know where it leads other than back to the start? I stare out the window, as if everything is coming out of me, as if the thoughts will crystallise, if only I can look hard and long enough at that landscape. Or maybe I just need the calm. Beside the rail track I see the enormity of familiar mountains, but now under the power of an engine, I simply sit and look out the window. And I cannot believe how big all that was so recently, where now it feels so quaint, picturesque and perfect, just for me. Before I was its guest: a stay conditional on good behaviour, on preparation and total respect.

The railway line slips under me, rejuvenated by the efforts of the Turkish state to save energy by shifting transport from road to rail. In the mesmerising clatter of the track, I think of the Hejaz Railway, one of the final infrastructure projects of the Ottomans, running from Istanbul through Jordan to Medina, with a nexus station in Damascus. It opened alongside the twentieth century, then was effectively closed by World War I. By that time the Ottomans had learned the ways of the Western creditors, and the railway was financed significantly by contributions from the Ummah, who thanks to the direct route towards Mecca would also benefit from an easier Hajj through the hard desert and mountains of Arabia. The railway would also serve the Ottoman state, helping it integrate the Arabian peninsula both in sending supplies and deploying troops. In lands that a few years later were reconstructed by the British as

Saudi Arabia, camel drivers sabotaged the track and its competition to their caravan livelihood, no different from the US railroad barons who laid railway cars across their land to disrupt the path of the early oil pipelines that threatened their freight monopoly. All the world is only our evolution of history and technology, and how we master the two with our hearts. The Hejaz would in time have reached all the way from Istanbul to Yemen, building Ottoman cohesion against growing European aggression. As we go, I wonder what might have happened if the railways had arrived a half-century earlier? Perhaps we might have made it, but time was not on our side.

On the railway bank children stand and wave at the passing carriages. Christmas nears and one family have decorated their couchette with lights and cotton-wool snow for the children. Their mother attaches fairy lights to the window and waves as she sees me looking in. On the bunk beside mine, my cabin mate laments that in Europe's media there is only bad news about Muslims. "Propaganda," he sighs, and shakes his head with the sadness of someone who feels he has been misunderstood. From the window of the train I see a man walking with his dog, and my eyes instinctively scan the hills for his sheep, but there are none. This is the moment when you realise you've been a long time in Anatolia.

The train stops at Erzurum, the train stops at Sivas. These two cities hosted historic congresses, both in 1919, as leaders from across Thrace, Anatolia and the northern regions of Mesopotamia came together and resolved that they would not, they could not, accept the sultan's peace with the European powers, by which Türkiye would be humiliated before history, ruled by the same plastic sheikhs the West would go on to install across the Arabian Peninsula. Instead the Turks and Kurds and Arabs and all of the peoples of these lands together would fight, would resist and build a country on their own terms. Through these congresses, a deep democracy is embedded in the very foundation of how Türkiye was made. It could not have won through against such odds without these acts of democracy, by which I mean a spirit of democracy, and a democracy that runs deeper than the ballot box. Will you listen to me, will we act together? This, this is all democracy is, and from that imperative democracy of wartime there came not weakness but strength. Through democracy, Türkiye won a war it by rights should have lost. All along, the Turkish Republic was forged from democracy.

As night falls, in the rocking carriage, I cannot sleep. So many thoughts parade inside me, my memories of the road clash with the abstract unit of a century. States, in general, are crimes. The only way a state can atone for its implicit crime is to help upbuild the lives of those who fall under its jurisdiction, in the hope that in return for the freedoms it takes from individuals, the state delivers security and prosperity to them. By this measure, Türkiye, with much still to do, has nonetheless achieved much. It owes more, always, to those inside of it, but as a state it is often more innocent than those who press charges against it. The twentieth century, too, was one of states. It was not simply that outside of a state fate left you to your village: you either built a state or were used as a building block in someone else's. By this measure, too, Türkiye only did what history demanded of it, and in those circumstances it didn't always do it so badly.

As the train moves into the night and then into the dawn and then into a new day, I worry about leaving you. I must trust that you now know a little more of what is here, that you understand a little better. I always thought of the place I ended the journey as a form of geographical editing, where my bicycle was like my pen on a map, and the journey led the writing. Finish in Kars and I write Armenia. Finish in Erbil I write the Arab world. Finish in Diyarbakır I write Kurds. But there can be only one note on which I leave you.

From the window I watch the country grow, feeling fully a passenger at last. Everything accelerates, everything is a blur of snow-kissed forest and dark green pine. The wheels of the train move, the story ends, a new one begins. A flock of sheep moves over hills, rocks crackle down after them. A highway rises up, trucks loom over the crest of the pass where the wind tries to tear the flags from their poles. And I know one day we will need fewer flags. The stone bodies of the statues can rest, can move their tired limbs, for permanence can be a weakness in a world that changes. At a station I watch a blade move down a spit, the coals glow. Ruby-red, the pomegranates are passing, winter is coming, but spring will soon follow and we will drink tea together in the afternoon sun. I watch it all, I breathe it in. I try to exhale, but words fail me. Build beauty, build beauty and never stop. The old castle walls over Gaziantep will be rebuilt. Antakya will rise. Let history be your judge but never stop making it, for history belongs to all who dare claim it, to those who refuse to let their hearts grow dull and who remember how to dream. In every journey I have ever taken, by bicycle or otherwise, I realise anew that this marvellous world is big enough for all of us, and a country is only as strong as its weakest citizen, its most vulnerable. We must get everyone to safety. Let a country build weapons, but know that weapons are for the weak, and the weapons of your foe break best beneath words and good deeds. Learn from mistakes, because such is the duty of those who wish to improve, and the history of all who did. Exist in doubt, hold truths, multiple and competing. If these words and kilometres ridden can help in any of that, then that is enough for me.

Behind me the Anatolian lands and rivers undulate patiently beside the railway track. I close my eyes and think I can see flamingos standing in the Nestos Delta, in Lake Tuzla. Pink wings spread, feet break the surface and are pulled by beating wings out of water and into sky. In Thrace and Anatolia the cotton stands high and is easily picked. A shepherd rests in the fields, for all this is hers. Rain falls, its droplets blurring the windows and lifting the streams in their dykes. Let all be well, let the banks of the Tigris swell and the Gulf of Basra grow green again. It all moves inside me, too much moves inside me. Bereket. Abundance.

Ankara – 9 December

Off the train, I drink in Ankara bars later than I should. In one bar, as I sit with a roll of kokoreç, Freddie Mercury comes over the speakers, asking if love is such an old-fashioned word, reminding me that love dares us to care for the people on the edge of the night, to change our way of thinking about ourselves. I close my eyes and smile and, as always, let the lyrics sink into me. At the next table, students talk politics, people on streets. At another, two women talk about their men. A couple sitting opposite say barely a word, and I've a feeling they won't make it: they are too attractive, too fearful that saying something stupid, or not funny, or not interesting enough, wouldn't go with that scarf, with that nose piercing. In picture-perfect silence they sit together, wanting it to work, but mostly for the photos.

I pull myself away. I walk, could walk all night. Where to end it? An art historian friend said that when she studied Islamic art the teacher began by drawing a circle, only a circle, saying this was the basis of how to understand it. That circle: as with the dome of a mosque, the wheel of my bicycle. Reject endings, embrace partings in the knowledge that in truth there is no such thing. We meet again, we walk together to a place beyond misunderstanding. Read this country like all the others and as best you can, judge it hard in its faults but also recognise its virtues. Countries are how – limited as we are – we make sense of a world of such beautiful variety. One day we will not need them. They are no more than the vessels that hold us humans, and – bir insan – we are all one human.

Dear Türkiye: I do not believe in battlefields or enemies, but I

will give my all for you, all who are in you, and all around you. Across the world, people learn to love what is close. We are encouraged to trust it even if it harms us, and we are encouraged to fear that which is distant, even if it holds no threat and may even offer much good. If the story of a long bike ride can tip the scales of understanding, even a little, then it has been a success. Even if it cannot, then still, I gave it everything, I gave it all I had. If any of it is good, has worked, it is only because I was able to listen faithfully to the road and the people on it. The credit lies with them. Where I have fallen short of what I intended, the blame lies with me.

This last day the morning is so bright and the shadows on the pavement grow so long. In the street in front of me stands a bıçakçı, the man who sharpens knives and cleavers and hatchets for cooks and butchers and the bakers who use a small axe to chop wood for their ovens. He wears the heavy Ottoman-style waistcoat, a leather apron and thick corduroys, protection against the winter cold and the sparks that fly from where steel meets his lathe. I see a spark fall on the heavy felt of his waistcoat and watch as its light fades.

I consider the row of knives on his wooden board, and think of how a blade can either cut usefully and peel away, or be turned on someone and inflict hurt. For a moment, I see the intimacy of this story – all its hopes and thoughts, meetings and confessions – a little like a blade. I hope that it can help cut away the many mis-understandings of this world, but – by its very closeness to my heart – as I prepare to hand it over, I realise that it can also be used to hurt, to furnish stereotypes, distort histories. I watch as the bıçakçı puts another blade to the stone, where another tail of sparks shoots out. And I think instead, more hopefully, that perhaps the story is not the blade, but the sparks flying free, tiny moments of illumination that quickly fade away, to be absorbed back into the light of the universe.

JULIAN SAYARER has cycled a half dozen times across Europe to his second nation of Türkiye, as well as also breaking a world record for a circumnavigation by bicycle. This journey of 18,049 miles in 169 days took him through 20 countries before becoming his debut book, *Life Cycles* (2014). He is the winner of the Stanford Dolman Travel Writing Award for *Interstate* (2016), an account of hitchhiking from New York to San Francisco, and is the author of *Messengers* (2016), *All at Sea* (2017), *Fifty Miles Wide* (2020) and Ondaatje Prize-longlisted *Iberia* (2021). Julian combines a background in political science to create a critically acclaimed travel writing style – politics at roadsides. In this 12mph view of the world in passing, he uses human stories and journeys to document global issues for a broad audience. His writing has appeared in the *London Review of Books*, *Guardian*, *Aeon Magazine*, among others, and in numerous cycling publications.